Reforming Corrections for Juvenile Offenders

Reforming Corrections for Juvenile Offenders

Alternatives and Strategies

Yitzhak Bakal
Northeastern Family Institute, Inc.

Howard W. Polsky
Columbia University

Lexington Books
D.C. Heath and Company
Lexington, Massachusetts
Toronto

Library of Congress Cataloging in Publication Data

Bakal, Yitzhak.
　　Reforming corrections for juvenile offenders.

　　Bibliography: p.
　　Includes index.
　　1. Juvenile corrections—Massachusetts.
2. Community-based corrections—Massachusetts.
I. Polsky, Howard W., joint author. II. Title.
HV9105.M4B34　　　　364.6　　　　73-11680
ISBN 0-669-90209-8

Published simultaneously in Canada

Printed in the United States of America

International Standard Book Number: 0-669-90209-8

Library of Congress Catalog Card Number: 73-11680

Contents

v

12-19

Contents

List of Figures

List of Tables

Foreword

Large training schools, like most bureaucratic structures, grow up and often forget why they began. Institutional preservation and growth become their dominant realities. They have failed in their stated goals: rehabilitation and public protection. As mandated by law, the Massachusetts Department of Youth Services (DYS) is charged with the care and custody of troubled youths. Few of these youths come from stable family situations. Almost all have exhibited severe school problems, although most are of normal intelligence. The majority of these children have been involved in the welfare system, either indirectly as children of AFDC parents or directly as CHINS (status offender) cases; most have been on probation. All have some degree of health problems. Few of these youths feel they are successes; almost all harbor a great sense of failure. They are angry; they run away; they have few skills; they are scared. Most have a great deal of energy, and some—against tremendous odds—show remarkable initiative.

Institutionalization of such youths will add insult to injury. Treating them primarily within the community is not only humane but also extremely necessary.

It is well known that the present Massachusetts DYS community-based system was born in tumult. In spite of the great controversy and a recent history of vexing administrative issues, the DYS is the legatee of three important traditions.

First, Massachusetts is operating on a purchase-of-service system. Over half the DYS budget is free from the constraints of civil service and of institutions. DYS has the flexibility to spend money for services or to create programs. The purchase-of-care account, which permits a diversity of placement options, is the lifeblood of a sensible and responsive youth services system. It means, quite simply, that each regional director (Massachusetts has seven regions) can design programs appropriate to the youth and citizenry of his or her area. It means that if the programs are ineffective, they can be cut off without a cataclysmic revolution. It means creativity, responsiveness, flexibility, and growth.

Second, the closing of youth correctional institutions has released new energy. The existence of the purchase-of-care account creates a climate of innovation and experimentation. Interested groups wanting to attempt experimental programs for troubled youths are constantly challenging the bureaucracy with new ideas. The fervent sense of change permeates this system, keeping it from becoming stultified.

Third, there is a controversial and constructive debate over the issue of security for hard-core violent youths. The paucity of secure-care facilities has threatened the very existence of the community-based movement.

When the Massachusetts training schools were closed in 1972, many people both in and out of the corrections field, whether liberal or conservative, felt that the state ought to create more secure facilities. Remarkably, however, most agreed that the majority of delinquents should be treated in the community.

At any one time, Massachusetts treats roughly 85 to 90 percent of the youths committed to it in its community programs. The closest state to us is South Dakota, with 59 percent—the national average is 17 percent. There are six states that treat none of their youths in the community. The point is simply that the debate about security in Massachusetts is on a different plateau. It is agreed that more secure facilities are needed, yet all have accepted the fact that deinstitutionalization is here to stay.

The dust of the deinstitutionalization revolution has not settled. Much remains to be done. But extraordinary gains have been made. The Massachusetts experiment is being carefully watched by people from other states and other countries. It has been said that this state serves both as a beacon and as a threat. If we are successful, many states may be encouraged in their attempts to deinstitutionalize. If we fail, the institutional bias of some other states will be confirmed.

The major task in the future will be to achieve those objectives toward which we have been working for the last several years. Major dramatic gains have been made, but many objectives remain to be completed. These include:

— A comprehensive, reliable and useful data system.
— A pilot family program.
— A system of effective casework management.
— A comprehensive and standard intake system.
— Better trained caseworkers.
— Expanded relationships with Department of Mental Health, Massachusetts Rehabilitation Center, Office of Education, and Manpower Affairs.
— Comprehensive education and personnel policies and programs.
— A statewide restitution program.
— A technical assistance and research unit.
— Expanded evaluation and planning units.
— A contracting system more closely allied with data collection and monitoring.

The new community-based system has survived many challenges and, even though it is not completely out of danger, it is enjoying more and more

credibility and stability. In this volume Bakal and Polsky bring together
material that spells out why this is so, and also points toward where we must
(and must not) go in the future.

John A. Calhoun
Commissioner
Massachusetts Department of
Youth Services

Preface

Much of this volume was written as a follow-up to a previous book, *Closing Correctional Institutions*, published by Lexington Books in 1974. Material for both books originated in the Massachusetts Department of Youth Services' decision to close its large training schools and replace them with community-based alternatives. The changes caused by this action were unprecedented because it was massive and dramatic in nature and especially unusual for a state bureaucracy.

The present authors both participated actively in the closing action, one as assistant commissioner and the other as a training consultant. We were also involved in the design and planning of the Boston College Conference.

These and other similar conferences and meetings on the subject of deinstitutionalization that followed clearly indicated that people in and out of the youth services field are deeply concerned and need more detailed information about the entire Massachusetts experience in its reform of youth corrections. This book is an attempt to provide a more concrete description of this process.

In this work we attempt to deal with the many facets of the Massachusetts experience both in closing institutions and in developing new alternatives. Part I is an overview of juvenile corrections in general, and the rationale for deinstitutionalization in Massachusetts in particular. It includes a detailed account of the events that led to the decision to close the juvenile corrections institutions in Massachusetts, the strategies utilized, and the conclusions to be drawn from the experience. Part II is devoted to the new community-based alternatives. Massachusetts has unquestionably taken the lead in youth corrections by offering a broad range of community-based programs, both residential and nonresidential. It must be emphasized that while many innovative community-based programs have been tried elsewhere, Massachusetts is the only state that has used these community-based programs on a massive scale as an alternative to institutionalization. Part II provides an overview of these programs, as well as detailed descriptions of an educational and a foster-care model as used in Massachusetts.

Part III deals with the problems of hard-core violent youths who require a secure setting. One attempt to develop such a program in Massachusetts is presented in the form of a case study. The descriptions of Andros I and II give a vivid account of an intensive secure program and the many dilemmas involved in managing young offenders in such a setting. Reading these chapters makes it clear why the care for the "new end-of-the-line youth"—so-called hard-core violent youths—is the Achilles' heel of the deinstitutionalization process.

Part IV presents two areas critical to the success and further growth of the community-based movement. The first involves staff training and the development of new skills needed to work with young offenders in the community. An innovative framework for examining the relationship between the worker and the youth is suggested. The second involves program monitoring and evaluation. The Massachusetts Department of Youth Services' approach and procedures for such a monitoring process is presented.

Part V provides the authors' conclusions and lessons derived from the Massachusetts experience in social change and correctional reform. Cultural, political, and leadership considerations are examined here in the light of Massachusetts' experience, and principles in the change process in the corrections field in general are outlined.

Despite an attempt to be comprehensive, no book can deal with all the relevant issues of youth corrections. Services for the female offender, examples of residential and other nonresidential alternatives, and many other issues must be examined in the light of the Massachusetts experience.

It is hoped that this work will lead to a better understanding of how to bring about comprehensive and radical reform in the field of human services. Further fundamental knowledge of this process could stimulate innovation and more humane solutions to the programs of young people in trouble with the law.

Acknowledgments

The material presented herein could not have been completed in its present form without the help, the support, and the dedication of many people. We would like to mention those who deserve our thanks and gratitude.

First, we are pleased to have Jerry Miller's chapter on the serious juvenile offender become part of this book. His vast experience in the administration of criminal justice makes his observations and insights extremely valuable in the treatment of this subject. Paula Cardeleen deserves thanks for her contributions to chapter 11. Paula served as the director of the monitoring and evaluation unit in DYS from 1974 to 1977, and her observations come from an insider's point of view. Special thanks are also extended to Joseph Nogelo, the director of the nonresidential program at the Northeastern Family Institute. Mr. Nogelo has made tremendous contributions to the development and implementation of the Experiential Learning Program examined in chapter 6. Special thanks also to Ronald Recina for his contributions to chapter 7. John Isaacson, assistant commissioner in the Massachusetts Department of Youth Services, is owed special thanks for allowing us to use his notes on "A Needs Assessment for the Department of Youth Services, 1976." We also want to thank Dorothy Swarts for her editorial help, and Gloria Webster for typing the manuscript and for helpful editing. Frieda Miller and other Northeastern Family Institute staff members were always willing to give their time and energy to the completion of the book.

Finally, we dedicate this book to the young people of the Massachusetts Department of Youth Services, whose experiences have made this book necessary. We hope it will contribute to their care.

ACKNOWLEDGMENTS

Introduction

The program of deinstitutionalization of juvenile corrections now in progress in Massachusetts provided the impetus for this book. From the inception of this radical reform—closing the state's training schools—we have been concerned with documenting, in both practical and theoretical terms, the sources and dynamics of change as well as the aftermath of this significant movement. This book is an effort to provide a descriptive and theoretical treatment of the underlying issues involved in the transformation from a youth corrections system wholly dominated by institutions to a network of decentralized community-based agencies.

In our attempts to describe and explain this phenomenal organizational change, we have tried to avoid dogmatic theoretical assumptions, to infuse our theory with a practical understanding of what happened, and to guide our perceptions by what we felt was pertinent according to different theoretical models. Thus we do not take a position on whether the radical reform could have taken place without the leadership of the commissioner of the Department of Youth Services, Jerome Miller, who initiated the change, although we do specify in detail his signal contribution to that change. In effect, what we have followed is an open-model theory about a relatively closed total institution and its demolition. Our effort in the following pages is directed at blending selective theoretical concepts within an open-system point of view with our knowledge and understanding of the change process and the network of services that replaced the institutions.

Our approach emphasizes the close circular relationship between the institution and the supporting societal environment. Without continued input, institutions run down, and without significant impact on society and a modification of how it reinforces institutions, the latter would never change.

A critical basis for understanding institutions that are being challenged to the point of their destruction is a close examination of their relationship with outside societal sources for their maintenance and survival irrespective of fulfillment of their mission.

The professed goals of all institutional systems of youth corrections is to rehabilitate those in its care. But while the institution meets the security needs of the outside community and various psychological needs of its citizens, when one takes a closer look at the system—zeroing in on the operation—what one sees is the subversion of rehabilitation by an overemphasis on security. It is in this decisive way that the external system enters the institutional setting and reinforces the custodial orientation in theory and practice. Eventually this attitude prevails in total institutions.

Our approach illuminates a framework for examining a social structure in the midst of radical change. In the integration of the macro approach of the political scientist and the micro approach of the social psychologist, we have created our own peculiar blend. Radical change in the Department of Youth Sevices cannot be understood without a detailed analysis of the various forces at work both within and outside the institutions. But we also need specification of the psychological dynamics at work in this process. The macro approach describes the process of the interrelated behaviors of the various interest groups on the scene in Massachusetts. In general, we know how to look for and how to formulate their motivations and positions taken. In order to know in more detail why deinstitutionalization occurred when it did, we have to look at such system aspects as the institution-wide conditions, the utlization of various strategies to expose them, the resulting polarization and dynamics of a number of political, social, and professional groups, and their strategies for serving their own interests as well as those of the community at large.

We want to emphasize not only the necessary dependence of the Department of Youth Services on its environment, but also how key groups in that environment depend on the institutions to further their own self-interest. It is in this interplay that an imaginative and courageous leadership was able eventually to revolutionize a system committed wholly to large institutions, in favor of a decentralized network of community-based services for troubled youths.

Part I
Deinstitutionalization and the Corrections Field

Introduction to Part I

One way of understanding the difficulties confronting the Department of Youth Services in revolutionizing its services is to clarify the distinction between *problem* and *dilemma*. A problem can be solved in the frame of reference in which it is imbedded. Past precedents can be useful, or an adaptation of existing policy. A dilemma is not soluble within the assumptions contained in its context. A dilemma requires reformulation. We have to abandon habitual ways of thinking and the conventional perspectives from which the dilemma stems and by which it is perpetuated. Hence the administrator in fulfilling the organizational mission must be able to distinguish between problems that can be solved within the existing framework and dilemmas that call for more radical surgery.

It is clear that Jerome Miller, the commissioner of DYS, who initiated deinstitutionalization in Massachusetts, reached a point of no return with various ad hoc treatment programs within the basic structure of the large correctional institution. The institutional system worked against itself and thus could not fulfill its mission of "rehabilitation" except by doing away with itself. Hence the strategy adopted by Miller was based on a novel conceptualization of the problem mainly as a dilemma that could not be resolved except through the destruction of the very structure that reinforced its incapability of achieving its own mission.

The political facts of organizational life are so powerful that they prevent administrations even from recognizing their problem as a dilemma. These powerful constraints not only prevent restructuring, but also obscure the recognition of the institution as a dilemma demanding innovative solution. The constraints stem from within the organization and the public upon which it depends.

An organization permits its functionaries to do some things and not to do other things. This is what we mean when we say a system is organized—it binds itself into certain ways of achieving its goals. This is why organizations are the last to recognize the problematic character of their own structures. What they experience are the frustrations within the organization in achieving their goals without considering the possibility of revamping the entire system.

For example, correctional institutions become good at maintaining controls and limiting overt violence, both among inmates and between them and their custodians. What is more difficult is to build upon the controls a more humanized way of life throughout the institutions. Managers and institutional leaders may hope to modify group norms, maximizing repressive controls and manipulations, and to imbue the staff with a new sense of democratic humanitarianism. They try to open new communication channels, hire fresh staff, improve their training and orientation, and even develop special courses in human relations. Nevertheless, the need for maintaining controls in a highly suppressive manner persists, and this conditions the organizational life of an institution. The dominance of repressive constraints brought on by the very nature of the organization of an institution that has selected personnel to maintain it in such a way makes it impossible to fulfill its goals.

What is pioneering about Massachusetts is that it was one of the first to undergo the revolutionary process of deinstitutionalization. It did not have the precedents of other organizations or other institutions with the same type of solution to its dilemmas.

In the absence of thorough research on an institution's own problems, the experience of others is a natural type of resource with which to identify and to utilize. Policymakers, however, can be trapped by unthinking application of the experience of other institutions to their own problems and dilemmas. There are obviously important differences in every situation, and mechanical imitation of any one model would be quite uncalled for.

Part I describes in detail current theory about delinquency and the large correctional institutions' attempts at community protection and rehabilitation, which failed. The developing contradictions within large-scale juvenile institutions are analyzed. Finally the pressures for change in the direction of deinstitutionalization are described, with special focus upon the role of leadership from within the correctional system.

1 Delinquency and Youth: An Overview

The causes of youth crime continue to elude theoreticians, researchers, and policymakers. Over the past decade both the nature and the dimension of the juvenile delinquency problem in the United States and around the world have been changing rapidly. Crime and recidivism rates have been rising alarmingly, especially among juveniles. The growing public concern over this problem resulted in greater expenditures of money and resources both for prevention and for rehabilitation. But this did not achieve the desired effect, and illegal behavior by young people has grown even more extensive. While a large percentage of young offenders continue to be involved in petty theft, truancy, and in some instances vandalism, there have now been added massive drug abuse, planned violence against established institutions, and offenses against property and person.

Recent literature in crime and delinquency is making some headway in explaining delinquency. The first question is: Who are the delinquent youths and what are their characteristics? The President's Commission on Law Enforcement and Administration of Justice reports that "rough estimates by the Children's Bureau, supported by independent studies, indicate that one in every nine youths—one in every six male youths—will be referred to juvenile court in connection with a delinquent act (excluding traffic offenses) before his eighteenth birthday."[1] Marvin Wolfgang, in a recent detailed cohort study covering all boys who were born in Philadelphia in 1945, reports that approximately 35 percent of them had at least one recorded police contact.[2]

In Massachusetts one out of every five children in 1972 brought before the courts was referred for detention;[3] the number of youths was 6,200, and of those detained approximately 1,260 were adjudicated delinquent. Until January 1972, such youths were sent to one of the training schools operated by the Department of Youth Services (DYS). This book is primarily concerned with children who are court-acquainted, especially those who are incarcerated in detention centers or institutions. More than two decades of longitudinal, biographic, and demographic research present a profile of the delinquent youth.

The young offender is likely to be male rather than female. Only 20 to 25 percent of the total juvenile court cases in the United States involve girls.[4]

5

The young offender is likely to be an adolescent. Delinquency is less frequent before the onset of adolescence; it reaches a peak at the age of sixteen, and declines rapidly after the age of seventeen. Criminal acts are proportionately much lower among adults than among adolescents.[5]

The young offender is likely to come from a poor urban slum. The President's Commission on Law Enforcement and Administration of Justice describes the delinquent child as

> a child of the slums, from a neighborhood that is low on the social-economic scale of the community and harsh in many ways for those who live there. He is generally 14 to 16 years old, one of numerous children (perhaps representing several different fathers) who live with their mother in a home that the sociologists call "female centered." It may be broken; he may never have had a resident father; he may have a nominal male head who is often drunk or in jail or in and out of the house.[6]

A survey of over a thousand juvenile court case files discloses that the typical offender referred to the court is the product of a broken home, has done poorly in school, or is a dropout. Most frequently the young offender commits the offense in his or her own neighborhood. Of those children committed to institutions in 1970, 88 percent were from homes with an annual income of less than $5,000, with 75 percent from homes with an annual income of less than $3,000; 66 percent were from broken homes.[7]

Similarly, DYS-detained and DYS-committed children come from broken homes and low-income families. Over half of the parents have been divorced, separated, or deserted; 79 percent of the families live on welfare or welfare-level incomes.[8]

The young offender is likely to be unemployed. A very significant longitudinal study conducted by B. Fleisher examined 74 Chicago communities, 45 suburban Chicago communities, and 101 cities upon which the FBI's *Uniform Crime Reports* are based, together with relevant data on income and unemployment.[9] This analysis was also supported by unemployment and delinquency rates in Boston, Cincinnati, and Chicago, as well as by corresponding national data for the period 1932-1961. Fleisher's analysis discloses that a 1 percent increase in unemployment is associated on the average with an approximately 15 percent increase in the rate of delinquency,[10] and these findings are similar to findings in Great Britain.[11] Thus Fleisher suggests that the high rate of delinquency at the age of sixteen can be attributed to the fact that many youths quit school at this age and, faced with unemployment, are unable to find a legitimate role for themselves in society.[12]

How Does One Become Delinquent?

There is a growing awareness based on increasing evidence in research that the process whereby one youth is called a delinquent while another escapes the label is based not only on the behavior of the youth, but on many circumstances beyond the youth's control. Some research indicates that there is a process of excluding, scapegoating, and forcing of deviant behavior on children by communities, institutions, and especially public school systems. Public schools tolerate little deviant behavior, resulting in many truant youths, who find themselves without any legitimate activity or affiliation.[13] Once a child has failed at school, chances of becoming involved in delinquent behavior are much greater.

A study by Lamar T. Empey supports similar findings:

> Known delinquents do not possess the requisite cognitive or social skills to cope with the school environment. They tend to score lower on intelligence tests when social class is held constant, and their organizational skills are less than nondelinquents. Thus, very early in their lives, they are sidetracked from the major institutional avenues leading from childhood to adulthood. They find themselves without the institutional activities that provide the kinds of support that make conventional activities more highly appealing than deviant ones. They are socially "defrocked," as it were.[14]

The concept of "delinquency" as opposed to "criminality" involves, in many cases, the passing of moral judgment. Actions that are not considered illegal for adults are treated as such for juveniles.[15] For example, truancy, smoking, and disobeying parents are often treated as crimes. PINS (persons in need of supervision),[16] and children without a guardian, usually end up in a detention home.

Moreover, parents, schools, teachers, police, and neighbors can (and do, to a significant degree) contribute to the court's decision to label a child delinquent. Parents may take their child to a court and ask it to commit the youth to an institution for "incorrigibility" and their inability to control the child. As a U.S. district court judge describes it:

> Tired and apathetic [parents] readily abdicate their parental roles. Frequently, when a child runs away from home and is picked up by the police, his parents refuse to take him home, instead filing a "beyond control complaint." In such cases, the child may be held for weeks and months pending hearing on the complaint.[17]

Once a child comes in contact with the law, evidence shows that the criminal justice system not only is unable to provide justice for the youngster, but all too often is stigmatizing, destructive, and discriminatory in its treatment of lower-class youths as opposed to middle- or upper-class youths.

Police treatment of youths seems to vary according to the socioeconomic level of the community. Goldman, in his study of Pennsylvania communities, reports that the community with the highest socioeconomic level also had the highest arrest rate, but the lowest rate of court referrals,[18] while the community with the lowest arrest rate, which had a low socioeconomic level, had the highest rate of court referrals.[19] Thus, a poor youth, once arrested, is more likely to be sent to court.

Once referred to court, a lower-class youth is also more likely to be incarcerated in a detention center because of inability to post bail. "It clearly appears that one of the factors least taken into account is the defendant's financial ability to make bail in the amount contemplated. For those who can make bond only in a small amount, bail becomes a vehicle, not to permit release, but to insure detention."[20] Furthermore, "since no determined effort has been made to make systematic use of alternatives to bail, it is not surprising to find that many defendants are denied release because they are too poor to buy their freedom."[21] The child who is poor is also shortchanged because he or she does not possess "alternative child care systems which largely eliminate the need for intervention of the juvenile justice system. By definition, the poor and the minorities have no such assets, or if they do, are seldom in a position to have them accepted by officials as suitable alternatives to official care."[22]

Patricia Wald offers an excellent case study that illustrates this process:

Defendant D, a 17-year-old Negro male, unemployed and a school dropout, is stopped by a Youth Division Officer at 12:30 a.m. on a street corner while loitering with a noisy gang. There is a 10 p.m. curfew in effect for juveniles. The officer tells the gang to disperse and go home; D retorts that he doesn't have to and "no . . . cop can make me." The officer takes him in custody, frisks him for weapons, marches him to the precinct station, and calls his home. A man answers the phone, but is either intoxicated or unable to understand what the officer says. D is taken to the juvenile detention center for the night. . . .

The morning following defendant D's apprehension, the arresting officer finds he has a record of prior juvenile offenses, minor thefts, truancy, gang activity. Several years ago he was put on juvenile probation, and completed the period without further incident. The officer goes to see his parents and finds the mother, unmarried with several younger children, working a 3:00 to 12:00 shift in a bar. The home consists of two rooms in a dilapidated, overcrowded tenement. The mother reacts to the news by bitterly complaining of the boy, the company he keeps, the troubles he has already caused her, and the miseries yet to come. Based on the interview and D's past record, the officer decides to petition to juvenile court. . . .

As soon as the petition involving defendant D is filed in juvenile court, the court's intake worker decides whether to proceed with the case. If she thinks the family can control the boy and he is likely to avoid trouble again, she can dismiss the case or place him on informal probation for a few months. To make the decision she has to assess the child himself, his home situation, his school, and police record.

In D's case, the lack of home supervision, his mother's self-admitted defeat in holding him in line, and his record of one previous probation rule out dismissal. The decision is made to charge him with violation of the curfew and disorderly conduct and bring him before the juvenile court that afternoon. (Had the offense been more serious, he might have been waived to an adult court for a full-scale criminal trial.) In a few jurisdictions, the child and parent will be asked if they want a lawyer when a decision to petition the case is made; if they have no money, counsel will be assigned. In most jurisdictions, however, there is no procedure for assignment of counsel before hearing.[23]

At his first hearing, defendant D waived counsel because of lack of funds, admitted to his offense, and was sent to a detention center to await disposition of his case while a social study was done on him by the court. The outcome was that defendant D was later adjudicated delinquent and sent to a training school for an indeterminate period, not to exceed his twenty-first year of age.

The case demonstates clearly how policies and procedures established to help or protect people actually discriminate against the poor. This case could have been closed at almost any point along the way if the boy had an adequate home to return to. Either the police, the court intake worker, or the judge could have exercised discretion to dismiss the case. Throughout the process, either advocacy or community resources could have prevented the young man from being sent to the institution. Instead, as a result of his poverty, he received the maximum sentence.

Causes of Delinquency

Theories and research explaining delinquency cover a wide spectrum of issues. Some emphasize individual responsibility, others focus on the period of adolescence, while still others look at society's structure and norms as the primary reason behind this phenomenon.

The function of deviance or criminal behavior in society. George H. Mead suggests that criminals basically do not challenge the cohesiveness of society. On the contrary, they contribute to society's unity by uniting its members against them.[24] Chapman, a British sociologist, arrives at the same conclusion with a different explanation:

The designation and social isolation of a relatively small group of victims permit the guilt of others to be symbolically discharged; identification of the criminal class and its social ostracism permit the reduction of social-class hostility by deflecting aggression that could otherwise be directed towards those with status, power, reward, and property. A special part of the ideology functions to prevent the designated criminal from escaping from his sacrificial role, and institutional record-keeping maintains his identity.[25]

Legal norms. Legal norms are important in the explanation of delinquency. Becker argues that "social groups create deviance by making the rules whose infractions constitute deviance, and by applying those rules to particular people and labeling them as outsiders.[26] Platt supports Becker and uses the court as an example of a conservative, middle-class institution that rejects lower-class values and tends to scapegoat the poor.[27]

Adolescence. The high rate of delinquency among adolescents demands explanation. Erikson explains this phenomenon as being the result of a loss of identity suffered by adolescents, "where historical and technological developments severely encroach upon deeply rooted or strongly emerging identities."[28] Most writers who discuss the adolescent period point out that youth delinquency stems mainly from the adolescent's exclusion from full social participation.[29]

Failure of Socializing Institutions

Research dealing with socializing institutions exposes the community's failure to provide adequate legitimate opportunities for lower-class children, thus reinforcing delinquent behavior.[30] Also, in a lower-class community there is pressure on youngsters to achieve according to middle-class standards. This pressure needs an outlet, and sometimes this outlet is found through gang activity.[31]

Other institutions related to delinquency, such as the family, receive elaborate treatment in the literature. Many studies show strong correlations between delinquency and broken homes.[32] Other researchers, such as Jackson Toby, found that broken homes have a differential effect on the children, with girls and young children more affected than older boys.[33]

Research also suggests that being a member of the lower class limits the family's ability to maintain external controls over the children.[34] Frequent family tensions, disharmony, and lack of affection due to pressure imposed by deprived circumstances prevent families from using child-rearing techniques that involve the children rather than alienating them.[35]

Lamar Empey focuses on the school as the institution most clearly related to the causes of delinquency. The following two paragraphs summarize statements he made at a conference in 1972:

> Dr. Empey began by explaining the connection between delinquency and failure in school. Failure in school leads to strain and alienation. Juveniles who are doing badly in school acquire a peer and official identification as delinquents, which in turn causes stigma. This leads to feedback that reinforces the strain and alienation they are feeling, and continues on. If this labeling theory is correct, the problems lead to further identification as delinquents, and this forces the juveniles to live up to certain roles to keep the image—a circular process.
>
> In any neighborhood in one of our urban centers, or even in some of our rural areas, there are five major structures that affect juvenile behavior: (1) the system of formal norms—the rules that define who is delinquent and who is not; (2) the policies and practices of the police and the courts; (3) socializing institutions—family, church, school, and the neighborhood itself; (4) illegitimate institutions—violent gangs, for instance and, finally, (5) social control—the police. The socializing institutions in the ghetto tend to be intimately related with illegitimate institutions.
>
> There is only one institution that cuts across all neighborhood differences: the school system. Thus, problems in the school are the prime contributors to delinquency, rather than the larger stratification system—social classes and so on—which are imposed upon the school. This is important because youth on the college track are rarely involved. Those who begin to fail, start to identify with people who are not in the system, and yet they still look with admiration on those who succeed. Schools are where the action is; even dropouts congregate around schools. there is no acceptable social role for a youth not in school or at least in a school atmosphere.[36]

Several recent studies on children out of school indicate that this is a problem of a very high and disturbing magnitude. A recent report sponsored by the Children's Defense Fund provides detailed documentation of children who are either enrolled or suspended from school, truants, or not reported by parents. The number of these children exceeds two million. Seventy-five percent are between the ages of seven and thirteen, with a slightly higher percentage found in rural areas and the South. This report is also very detailed in its documentation of the reasons for school suspension, which were found to be mostly unilateral, with juvenile or parents' rights seldom considered.[37] Nonenrolled children were disproportionately from poor, minority, and innercity families. Among other reasons for nonattendance were misbehavior, poor language skills, pregnancy, and so forth.

Another study of school suspensions revealed that in New Orleans in 1969, 1,075 students, out of a total enrollment of 88,317, were suspended. Those who were suspended, it was noted, were already alienated from school, and their parents had negative attitudes toward education and the school system. The report further revealed that insubordinate behavior in the second half of the year produced fewer suspensions than at the beginning of the year.[38] Thus, nonenrollment, exclusion, and suspension are substantial problems in the schools today, and no doubt affect the level and the range of delinquent behavior among young people in the United States.

Summary

Evidence shows that what the law defines as a delinquent child is usually an adolescent who comes from the slums where opportunities to provide for oneself through legitimate means are limited. There is also a process of exclusion, stereotyping, stigmatizing, and labeling carried out to the greatest degree by those very social institutions that are supposed to help the young person in the school, the court, and the training school.

Theories explaining delinquency, although they disagree on the causes, arrive at the same conclusions: (1) there is a need to involve youths in accepted and legitimate social roles that provide "a sense of competence, a sense of usefulness, a sense of belongingness and a sense of power or potency";[39] (2) there is a need to increase opportunities for lower-class youths; (3) there is a need to combat the negative stigma attached to the "delinquent" youth at the school level; and (4) there is a need to divert most youths from criminality and the presently inadequate system of juvenile justice.

Notes

1. President's Commission on Law Enforcement and Administration of Justice, *The Challenge of Crime in a Free Society* (Washington, D.C.: Government Printing office, 1967), p. 55.

2. Marvin E. Wolfgang, Robert Figlio, and Thorsten Sellin, *Delinquency in a Birth Cohort* (Chicago: University of Chicago Press, 1972), p. 243.

3. This information was furnished on February 1, 1973, by William Madaus, assistant commissioner in charge of clinical services, Department of Youth Services, Massachusetts.

4. President's Commission on Law Enforcement and Administration of Justice, *Challenge of Crime*, p. 56.

5. Barbara Wootton, *Social Science and Social Pathology* (New York: Humanities Press, 1959), pp. 152-72; Wolfgang, Figlio, and Sellin, *Delinquency in a Birth Cohort*, p. 252. This study confirms previous findings.

6. President's Commission on Law Enforcement and Administration of Justice, *Challenge of Crime*, p. 60.

7. Patricia M. Wald, "Poverty and Criminal Justice," in Norman Johnston, Leonard Savitz, and Marvin E. Wolfgang, eds., *The Sociology of Crime and Punishment* (2nd ed.; New York: Wiley, 1970), p. 291.

8. "Background Information on the [Massachusetts] Department of Youth Services," unpublished document prepared by the Planning Department, 1972.

9. B. Fleisher, *The Economics of Delinquency* (New York: Quadrangle Books, 1966).

10. Ibid, p. 68.

11. Ibid, p. 84.

12. Ibid, p. 83.

13. Larry L. Dye, "Juvenile Junkyards: A Descriptive Case Study of the Organization and Philosophy of the County Training Schools in Massachusetts" (Ed. D. Dissertation, University of Massachusetts, 1971), pp. 2-6.

14. Lamar Empey, Steven G. Lubeck, and Ronald LaPorte, *Explaining Delinquency* (Lexington, Mass.: Lexington Books, D.C. Heath and Co., 1971), p. 164.

15. The dividing line between juvenile and adult is age 21, 18, or 17, depending on the state.

16. New York's classification of such children.

17. David L. Brazelton, *Beyond Control of the Juvenile Court* (Washington, D.C.: Youth Development and Delinquency Prevention Administration, Department of Health, Education and Welfare, 1971), p. 2.

18. Nathan Goldman, "The Differential Selection of Juvenile Offenders for Court Appearance," in William J. Chambliss, ed., *Crime and the Legal Process* (New York: McGraw-Hill, 1969), pp. 264-90.

19. Ibid.

20. Charles E. Ares, Anne Rankin, and Herbert Sturz, "The Manhattan Bail Project," in Johnston, Savitz, and Wolfgang, *Sociology of Crime and Punishment*, p. 160.

21. Ibid.

22. John M. Martin, "The Creation of a New Network of Services for Troublesome Youth," in Yitzhak Bakal, ed., *Closing Correctional Institutions: New Strategies for Youth Services* (Lexington, Mass.: Lexington Books, D.C. Heath and Co., 1973), p. 11.

23. Wald, "Poverty and Criminal Justice," pp. 272-82, 291.

24. George H. Mead, "The Psychology of Punitive Justice," *American Journal of Sociology* 23 (1918), 577.

25. Dennis Chapman, *Sociology and the Stereotype of the Criminal* (London: Tavistock, 1968), p. 4.

26. Howard S. Becker, *Outsiders: Studies in the Sociology of Deviates* (New York: Free Press, 1963), p. 9.

27. Anthony Platt, "The Rise of the Child-Saving Movement," *Annals of the American Academy of Policy and Social Science* 381 (1969): 21-38.

28. Erik H. Erikson, *Insight and Responsibility* (New York: Norton, 1964), p. 93.

29. See R.D. Hess and I. Goldblatt, "The Status of Adolescents in American Society: A Problem in Social Identity," *Child Development* 28 (1957):459-68.

30. Richard A. Cloward and Lloyd E. Ohlin, *Delinquency and Opportunity*; (New York: Free Press, 1960); Robert K. Merton, *Social Theory and Social Structure* (Glencoe: Free Press, 1957).

31. Albert K. Cohen, *Delinquent Boys* (New York: Free Press, 1955).

32. Clifford R. Shaw and Henry D. McKay, "Are Broken Homes a Causative Factor in Juvenile Delinquency?" *Social Forces* 10 (1963):514-24; Eleanor and Sheldon Glueck, *Family Environment and Delinquency* (Boston, Mass.: Houghton Mifflin, 1962); Walter Slocum and Carol L. Stone, "Family Culture Patterns and Delinquent-Type Behavior," *Marriage and Family Living* 25 (1963):202-8.

33. Jackson Toby, "The Differential Impact of Family Disorganization," *American Sociological Review* 11 (1957), 505-12.

34. Martin Gold, *Status Forces in Delinquent Boys* (Ann Arbor: University of Michigan Press, 1963).

35. Ivan F. Nye, *Family Relationships and Delinquent Behavior* (New York: Wiley, 1958).

36. Summary (paraphrased) of Lamar T. Empey, "The Group Home and the Local School System" unpublished paper presented at a conference entitled "The Closing Down of Institutions: New Strategies in Youth Services," under the auspices of DYS and Fordham University, at Boston College, 1972.

37. Rosemary C. Sarri "Juvenile Delinquency and School Psychology: Issues and Opportunities," paper presented at APA Convention, Chicago, August 30, 1975, p. 2.

38. J.J. Stretch and P.E. Crunk, "School Suspension: Help or Hindrance?" R.C. Sarri and F.F. Maple, eds., *The School in the Community* (Washington, D.C.: NASW, 1972), pp. 161-95.

39. U.S. Department of Health, Education and Welfare, Youth Development and Delinquency Prevention Administration, *Delinquency Prevention Through Youth Development* (Washington, D.C.: Government Printing Office, 1971).

2 Juvenile Corrections: The Archaic Institutional System

The Institutional System

The U.S. Department of Justice, in its October 1977 publication "Children in Custody," has reported that 46,980 juveniles were living in public juvenile detention and correctional facilities. This represents a 5 percent increase over the 1975 census, but showed a downward trend from an alarming 54,729 peak reached in June 1971.[1] Every year, according to the National Council on Crime and Delinquency (NCCD), "over 100,000 children from seven to seventeen inclusive are held in jails or jail-like places of detention."[2]

These training schools and detention centers are large. Of the 325 institutions reporting to the National Center for Social Statistics in 1970, over half held more than a hundred children, and 55 had three hundred or more. And "because of indiscriminate use, detention homes are often dangerously overcrowded to the degree that an adequate program is impossible to achieve."[3]

Few institutions or detention centers provide counseling, psychiatric, or health services. Most training schools have part-time psychiatrists who can do little more than diagnose new admissions or respond to emergency situations.[4] High-quality educational or vocational programs are almost nonexistent in these institutions.[5]

Children are confined for an average of 8.4 months in a training school.[6] Many of these children do not need to be either in detention or in a training school—NCCD has suggested that only 10 percent of the total number of children who are picked up by the police for juvenile offenses actually require detention.[7] The federal Youth Development and Delinquency Prevention Administration has stated that "mildly delinquent youth or neglected children are being detained unnecessarily and harmfully in close association with sophisticated delinquents."[8]

Strict discipline and even brutality prevail in these training schools. Joseph Rowan, executive director of the John Howard Association in Illinois, stated in a public hearing before a subcommittee of the Illinois Senate that he had seen more brutality in juvenile correctional facilities than in adult correctional facilities.

In one training school most of the teachers and group supervisors were using brutality in the form of hitting boys, banging their heads against lockers

15

and taking boys off to "side rooms" to work them over. Sitting at attention for several hours, holding shoes out until their hands dropped, standing for up to five hours looking at the wall (in other institutions) have been less brutalizing but very damaging practices.[9]

Similarly, Howard James found five boys in training schools who had punctured eardrums resulting from beatings by guards.[10] Such brutality occurs mainly because of the frustrations of the untrained and underpaid staff people who often do not come from the same ethnic, cultural, and racial groups as the juveniles.

Training schools are expensive. The cost per capita in public institutions for delinquents in 1975 was $11,471 per year.[11] Furthermore, only a fraction of these funds are spent directly on programs serving youths. Patronage jobs, kickbacks, and all-out corruption often characterize these operations.[12]

Institutional confinement inflicts a process of degradation and results in a loss of self-respect. In detention, "the juvenile is photographed, fingerprinted, weighed, searched thoroughly, given a shower and a new set of clothes."[13] He has "to adjust to the low status accorded him and to accept the attitudes of others toward him."[14]

Treatment through institutional confinement has proved to be ineffective and destructive. Recidivism rates are high. The institutional environment tends to increase alienation and criminalization of the young offender and to foster the development of a criminal self-concept. Correctional facilities thus crystallize the criminal identity by further stigmatizing and labeling the child.

The literature dealing with the socialization of inmates offers poignant descriptions of this process. A report by a Massachusetts DYS field worker before the training schools were closed, details a typical institutional situation at a training school for girls. So-called "secure rooms" (solitary confinement rooms) were used both to prevent "contemplated runaways" and as punishment for poor behavior. Meals were served erratically, sometimes consisting only of sandwiches, and toilet times were minimal. No reading material was allowed. There were no observation windows on the steel-reinforced doors. The report concludes that "the impressions of [DYS] methods that would be gained by an investigator who found naked girls of 13 and 14 lying on bare bunks [not provided with mattresses] in unheated locked rooms" would not be positive.

Perhaps the strongest indictment against training schools are those numerous studies showing that early commitment to a juvenile training school is a key forerunner to an adult career of crime. McKay's findings in a follow-up study of boys committed to the Illinois Training School for Boys are convincing. His data show that 76.1 percent were subsequently arrested, and 60.5 percent were later convicted of a crime.[15]

Research studies consistently show extremely high rates of recidivism among those who have been committed to juvenile training schools. McKay concludes that "behavior of significant numbers of boys who become involved in criminal activity is not redirected toward conventional activity by the institutions created for that purpose."[16] A major conclusion of these studies, as well as one by Wolfgang, is that offenders who start at a young age continue into adult life and account for a major part of the crime problem. Lack of early prevention undoubtedly costs society large sums of money each year.[17]

The reasons for the failure of these large training schools and detention centers are multiple. David Street, Robert D. Vinter, and Charles Perrow, in their comparative studies of institutions for the delinquent, describe the organizational conflicts that develop in these institutions because of their multiple goals—that is, custodial objectives versus therapeutic objectives. Even in institutions where treatment goals are dominant, the conflicts between these opposing objectives can lead to inconsistent treatment. In this way, therapeutic gains become insignificant.[18]

There is no doubt that these conflicts stem from society's confused and ambivalent attitude toward the lawbreaker. The paradox of attempted justice was well articulated by sociologist George M. Mead not long after the turn of the century:

> It is quite impossible psychologically to hate the sin and love the sinner. We are very much given to cheating ourselves in this regard. We assume we can detect, pursue, indict, prosecute and punish the criminal and still retain toward him the attitude of reinstating him in the community as soon as he indicates a change of social attitude in himself, that we can at the same time overwhelm the offender and comprehend the situation out of which the offense grows. But the two attitudes, that of control of crime by the hostile procedure of law and that of control through comprehension of social and psychological conditions, cannot be combined.[19]

Another significant problem that contributes to the failure of correctional institutions is their overpopulation. Overpopulation leads to organizational problems, and the custody and control of the institution become more important than rehabilitation and programming. The custodial staff members bargain with the inmates and delegate power to the deviant, thus reinforcing the criminal subculture. Inmate role models are antisocial, and the institutional environment reinforces these roles. Such a system increases the dependency of the inmate, making the youngster more vulnerable to reinstitutionalization after release. In extreme cases former inmates have been known to commit crimes in order to be caught and returned to the more familiar institutional surroundings.

Review of the research and literature dealing with correctional pro-grams involving institutional confinement raises important questions: Why are these institutions and training schools still operating? Why is the process of change so slow? There is little in the literature that deals with this ques-tion, but several factors are emerging. It appears that knowledge of organizational change both in theory and practice as it pertains to correc-tional reform is very scarce.

Several theoreticians, especially Chapman, Miller, and R.D. Laing, sug-gest that the criminologist and social-science worker help maintain the system by providing the scientific rationale for it.[20] Chapman has said that "the social sciences attempt to provide rational, scientific explanations in competition with magical and quasimagical explanations of the priesthood of some parts of the medical profession."[21] Also, there is resistance to change on the part of those groups with a vested interest in the institutional system—that is, staff at the institutions, the criminal justice system, and the local officials and social agencies that have a stake in keeping the delinquent outside the community setting.

Public bureaucracies work within the context of interest groups, which exert a variety of pressures, some of them in support of and some of them contrary to change. Interest groups include the media, the public, the con-sumer, as well as the legislature and various other arms of the government. Lloyd Ohlin, in analyzing interest groups, suggests that they constitute the basic institutional structure that gives form and content to correctional ac-tivities.[22] He further explains that there is a dynamic interplay between these interest groups and the internal shifts and changes within the institutional setting. Interest groups can thus become concerned with what happens within a department when changes occur. Incidents such as mass runaways or staff conflicts over issues of control versus treatment may gain public at-tention: "When there is much at stake and the power of conflicting interests is relatively balanced, an issue may become public."[23] Once this occurs, there is a crisis, and a new equilibrium is achieved.

Rosemary C. Sarri, in a review of selected findings from the National Association of Juvenile Corrections, concludes:

Evidence from across the nation can be read, at worst, as suggesting collu-sion among influential community elements to send more and more youths into the justice system; at best, the evidence can be read as revealing a slow drift toward more formal handling and processing of youth rather than *serving* them based on social institutions. . . . These persons and agencies know well why such youths have not and will not be served adequately through conventional agencies, including the schools, and the real nature and origins of their problems. They should also know, although many may not, what is and what is not happening *within* the justice system. Failure to proclaim that it does not and cannot remedy the problems assigned to it has the effect of authenticating both its rationale and its operations. The acquiescence of these persons and agencies has been part of a "noble lie" and constitutes negligence if not culpability.[24]

Reforming Versus Closing Large Institutions

A basic issue in the correction field revolves around either reforming or dismantling the large institutions. It is possible to gain new insights about the forces that resist radical change by attempting to change an institution. Retrospective lessons have been learned in Massachusetts about the forces resisting institutional change. They tell us about the *how* of getting out of a system that has been perpetuated far beyond its usefulness.

It is becoming clearer that the raison d'être for these institutions is not community protection or rehabilitation. This is the commonly held misconception. In actuality, vested interests accumulate around the perpetuation of these institutions, and it is they—the various professional and nonprofessional groups that "feed off" institutions—that are the most resistant to change.

The Massachusetts experience made clear that reform in juvenile corrections would not fail because of any great community uprising or because of any hard-hat, right-wing backlash. The remarkable aspect about resistance to deinstitutionalization in Massachusetts was the strange role played by liberal and professional groups and interests.

In Massachusetts it was easy to deal with the traditional-conservative vocal opposition to deinstitutionalization, which was basically uninformed but honest. It was much more difficult to deal with liberal and professional associations. Actually, there are many options for placement of youngsters in trouble in addition to correctional institutions, argues the basic rationale for institutional isolation, partly in terms of continuing self-interest and partly because those options incur very little risk and avoid pressure upon the community.

Professional associations and liberals provide the rhetoric for the continuation of institutionalization. Institutions require little risk. It is much easier to persuade the state government of the need to change, or even to create a public awareness and back-up for change. In Massachusetts the League of Women Voters was an important source of support for deinstitutionalization. The changeover in Massachusetts would have been much more difficult without the support of the League. The members did their homework, talked about reform, lobbied (without being identified as a radical group), and were convinced on the face of it that what the DYS was doing made good sense. The DYS could depend upon an impartial and influential citizens group that did not have a vested interest in maintaining the old system.

There was little pressure for change and pressure upon the DYS from youths, their relatives, and friends, whom the DYS basically serves. In fact, concern has to be created. The main resistance to change stems from staff, the legislature, and professional groups.

The pressure for or against change is highlighted during budget time. Legislators become concerned about the cost of institutional care. Staffs have to be taken care of. Staff members want jobs guaranteed. The career administrator learns quickly that to keep legislature and staff content and secure, he must stay within the budget; he is regarded as a top administrator despite institutional dysfunctioning.

Today, more than ever, the rhetoric calls for "community-based treatment programs." But a sagacious commissioner of corrections will also campaign for back-up systems for the very disturbed, disordered, and dangerous. He will also campaign for more trained staff, more diagnostic centers, better education for the youngsters, and so forth, for "no good deed is unrecognized."

Several important lessons about institutional change came out of Massachusetts. One was the need for clarity concerning the issues of administration and policy. Bad administration can harm good social policy, but good administration can never make up for bad policy. What we hear about mostly is the importance of good administration. What is becoming clearer is that bad social policy cannot be saved by superior administration. It is essential to turn these concepts around in the public's mind when effecting basic change in institutions in the correctional field.

An important obstacle to correctional change is the institutionalized staff. During deinstitutionalization in Massachusetts, for two and a half years, the names of 300-700 staff members were submitted to the state government as candidates for retraining or reassignment to other state agencies. These were never followed up, and the institutional staff remained long after deinstitutionalization, at a cost to the state of several million dollars. More and more people, in recognizing that large institutional concepts will no longer work, are also compassionate about what to do with all the superfluous staff.

The second lesson gained from the radical reform in Massachusetts was the need for dedicated change agents, primarily administrators high in the system's echelons, to go beyond the legislature, beyond the state government, beyond the staff and professional groups, to the people. Public hearings can be helpful. Naive but honest citizens ask: Why perpetuate a system that neither rehabilitates nor provides security for the community? More people are less willing to settle for the lesser of two evils. They would rather do away with the evil altogether.

Thus the problem of deinstitutionalization is political and has to be approached by nontraditional political avenues. Present administrators and procedures in corrections are designed to sustain present programs. Here and there minor rearrangements crop up—a community outreach program; a therapeutic community; a fusion of paraprofessional, demonstration, and experimental programs—all within a purview for which the administrative structure allows. But in no way do these pilot programs replace the present system. When federal and special funds for the maintenance of reform programs run out, the programs go under. But the system goes on.

Another lesson learned in Massachusetts was that no significant change can occur through the regular administrative routine. It is important to expose the institution, including the staff, and bring in the public and present the truth. If the administrator stoutly defends his system, nothing can happen. The only way to bring about change is to expose the institution from within, even though this risks demoralization of the staff.

It is a question of priority. Those deepest within the system are of course the inmates, and they are most hurt by it and therefore will gain the most by dismantling the institution.

To work for the poor, the disenfranchised, and the disadvantaged within bureaucratic human services is a great responsibility. When this system is an institutional one, that responsibility is heavier because the clientele has no power. Any "settlement" serves first the providers and then the provided. The provided are always at a disadvantage, and this is why institutional change is political. Institutions keep the clientele powerless. This is true for many systems, but much more arbitrarily and cruelly so in institutions.

The greatest advantage of the smaller community-based treatment programs that are replacing the large correctional institutions is that when they do not work, it is much easier to close them down.

Perhaps at one time one could justify the large instituion located somewhere in a meadowland far away from the hustle and bustle of the large city. But the institutions have become archaic, and that fact must be dealt with.

Notes

1. U.S. Department of Justice, LEAA, *Children in Custody* (Washington, D.C.: Government Printing Office, October 1977), pp. 1-6.

2. National Council of Crime and Delinquency (hereafter cited as NCCD), *Standards and Guides for Detention of Children and Youth* (New York: NCCD, 1961), p. xxi.

3. HEW, Youth Development and Delinquency Administration, *State Responsibility for Juvenile Detention Care* (Washington, D.C.: Government Printing Office, 1970), pp. 1-2. It must be noted that the LEAA

October 1977 *Children in Custody* report indicates that the number of public juvenile facilities numbered 874 on June 30, 1975. However, this figure includes ranches, forestry camps, and group homes, while the number of large facilities remains approximately the same as the HEW 1970 report (above).

4. Chief Justice Warren Burger, "No Man Is an Island," speech given in February 1970, quoted in *Journal of the American Bar Association*, April 1970, p. 58.

5. Frederick Thacher. "Effecting Change in a Training School for Girls," in Yitzhak Bakal, ed., *Closing Correctional Institutions: New Strategies for Youth Services* (Lexington, Mass.: Lexington Books, D.C. Heath and Co., 1973), p. 82.

6. HEW, *Statistics on Public Institutions*, p. 6.

7. NCCD, *Standards and Guides for Detention*, p. 18.

8. HEW, *State Responsibility for Juvenile Detention Care*, pp. 1-2.

9. U.S. Senate, Subcommittee to Investigate Juvenile Delinquency, *Hearings* (86th Cong., 3d sess., 1969), p. 5142.

10. Howard James, *Children in Trouble* (New York: David McKay, 1969), pp. 105-7.

11. U.S. Department of Justice, LEAA, *Children in Custody*, p. 12.

12. Kenneth Wooden, *Weeping in the Playtime of Others* (New York: McGraw-Hill, 1976), pp. 163-95.

13. HEW, Office of Juvenile Delinquency and Development, *The Handling of Juveniles from Offense to Disposition* (Washington, D.C.: Government Printing Office, 1970), p. 198.

14. Ibid.

15. Henry McKay, *Report on the Criminal Careers of Male Delinquents in Chicago* (Chicago: University of Chicago Press, 1938).

16. Ibid., pp. 107-13.

17. Ibid.

18. Marvin Wolfgang, Robert M. Figlio, and Thorsten Sellin, *Delinquency in a Birth Cohort* (Chicago: University of Chicago Press, 1972), pp. 243-55.

19. See Mayer N. Zald, "Power Balance and Staff Conflict in Correctional Institutions," pp. 22-49; David Street, Robert D. Vinter, and Charles B. Perrow, *Organization for Treatment: A Comparative Study for Delinquents* (New York: Free Press, 1966).

20. For a thorough treatment of this subject, see Dennis Chapman *Sociology and the Stereotype of the Criminal* (London: Tavistock, 1968); Jerome G. Miller, "The Latent Social Function of Psychiatric Diagnosis," *International Journal of Offender Therapy* 14 (1969):254-58; and R.D. Laing, *The Politics of the Family* (New York: Random House, 1969).

21. Chapman, *Sociology and the Stereotype of the Criminal*, p. 15.

22. Lloyd E. Ohlin, "Conflicting Interests in Correctional Objectives," *Theoretical Studies in Social Organizations of the Prison* (New York: Social Science Research Council, 1960), p. 59.

23. Ibid., p. 60.

24. Rosemary C. Sarri, "Juvenile Delinquency and School Psychology: Issues and Opportunities" (paper presented at 1975 APA Conference, Chicago, August 30, 1975), p. 4.

3 Closing the Massachusetts Training Schools

The Massachusetts Youth Service Board (YSB) was created in 1948, by a legislative act, as a quasijudicial tribunal with the responsibilities of classifying, placing, training, and supervising adjudicated delinquents committed to the board by the courts.[1] This act removed the authority for sentencing a youth from the presiding judge and placed the case in the hands of YSB.[2] In 1952 another legislative act changed YSB into the Division of Youth Services, under the direction of the State Department of Education but not subject to its control. The director of the division, John Coughlin, was responsible for making all decisions pertaining to the treatment, custody, and parole of youthful offenders.

While these legislative acts provided a mandate for change, no reform followed. Instead, the various studies and investigative commissions that reviewed the division's operation described the agency as stultified by the rigid enforcement of outmoded practices, and as one that lagged far behind agencies in other states in establishing progressive programs for the youths in its care.

Three important studies were conducted during 1965-1967 that gave a detailed analysis of the division's operation.[3] These studies criticized the administrative structure of the division for investing too much authority and responsibility in one man. The previous director had failed to delegate responsibility to his staff in the central office, yet at the same time had allowed the various institutions and detention centers to become relatively autonomous. They were free to do their own hiring and firing, and to develop their own programs without the direct supervision of the central administration. Even budget appropriations were made on an institution-by-institution basis.

In 1969 the division operated five large training schools: the Lyman School for Boys (ages 12-15), the Shirley Industrial School for Boys (ages 15-17), the Oakdale Residential Treatment Unit for Boys (ages 9-11), the Lancaster Industrial School for Girls (all ages), and the Bridgewater Juvenile Guidance Institute, a maximum-security unit. The division also operated four regional detention centers: two in the Boston area—one for girls at South Huntington Avenue and one for boys in Greenhaven; one in Worcester—a coeducational center; and one in Westfield, which served the western part of the state.

The facilities, with the exception of the Worcester and Westfield detention centers, operated on a custodial, training-school model for the treatment of the children in their custody. They were mostly outmoded, uncoordinated, with idiosyncratic management and only sporadic links to other social services.[4] Their communication with the division at large was almost nonexistent. The institutions themselves were located either in suburban or rural areas, isolated from outsiders, and very often were subject to the influences of local patronage.

Programs in the institutions were poor.[5] There were no certified academic or educational activities, and the limited vocational training taught outmoded skills that would be of little assistance to the youths in securing future employment.[6] Clinical services were also nearly nonexistent because of the lack of professional staff.[7] Those who were hired as clinicians spent their time producing reports at the reception centers, although these reports were seldom used for classification or treatment since the children were assigned to the institutions according to age rather than individual needs. In addition, staff members were untrained, unskilled, and unlikely to change their roles because they ranged in age from forty to sixty.

The treatment of youths inside the institutions was at best custodial and at worst punitive and repressive. Marching, shaved heads, and enforced periods of long silence were regular occurrences. Punitive staff used force; they made recalcitrant children drink water from toilets, or scrub floors on their hands and knees for hours on end. Solitary confinement was used extensively and rationalized as a mode of treatment for those who needed it. It must, however, be noted that the children who happened to be sent to the Worcester or Westfield detention centers were treated more humanely and were involved in much richer programs.

The communication between the various offices of the division was almost nil. The offices of parole, aftercare, clinical services, educational services, and so on operated autonomously, with no coordination and with little knowledge of what was going on elsewhere in the system. The most disjointed and incoherent part was the parole system, which lacked accountability and supervision, and by and large operated as a police model rather than as an advocate for the youths.

This system, with its retributive and custodial orientation, produced many angry youngsters whose attempts to strike back at the system by stealing cars, other thefts, or running away brought them further trouble with the law. A high percentage of the division's children started their careers as truants, runaways, or on "stubborn child" charges, and a few years later were diagnosed and labeled as "habitual runners," "assaultive," "violent," or "hard-core." They thus became the victims of a vicious spiral, ending up in adult correctional institutions.

Pressure for Change

From the mid-1960s on, the Division of Youth Services was subjected to increasing pressure for change by the legislature, the public, the media, and professional and civic associations, all of whom associated the division with repression and punishment. This external pressure led directly to the legislative reorganization of the division and to Jerome Miller's appointment as commissioner, and contributed in no small measure to the accomplishments of his administration. Since widespread support for reform—and Miller's skillful use of that support—played so important a role in the change process, this chapter will examine its sources, forms, and influence.

In Massachusetts as elsewhere, the training schools have been a deservedly popular target for the reform-minded since the mid-nineteenth century. But they have also demonstrated the bureaucracy's renowned ability to close ranks and weather passing storms of criticism. What seems to have made the difference in Massachusetts was that by the 1960s, conditions in the system had deteriorated to an almost pathological state. Once a leader in youth services, Massachusetts had evolved one of the worst systems in the country.

Recidivism, the most telling measure of effectiveness, was estimated to have reached 86 percent,[8] corruption was widely suspected and frequently proved. In the state's three largest training schools and other facilities, which had no academic, vocational, or even recreation programs, discipline became the watchword. Punishment for offenses against discipline ranged from denial of privileges, to solitary confinement in the lockup, to brutal beatings by guards. The ratio of custodial to professional staff in the division was 22 to 1, most of whom were protected from review, promotion, or demotion by civil service or political cronyism.[9] The institutions had almost universally hostile relations with surrounding communities, in part because they were obvious warehouses for the children of the poor.[10]

These and other weaknesses of the system were documented by a series of reports, investigations, and exposes, coming with increasing frequency and effectiveness. The most comprehensive report was done in 1965 by the Children's Bureau of HEW for the governor's office at Governor John Volpe's request.[11]

The scathing findings and recommendations of the HEW study were withheld for almost a year until they were discovered and exposed by the Boston *Globe* in 1967.[12] The disclosure of the report prompted a new wave of studies both by public bodies, such as the Massachusetts Committee on Crime and Youth, and by private groups, such as the Friends of Youth

Association and the Parent-Teachers Association. The Massachusetts legislature conducted hearings to review the policies of the division and to consider new legislation; the governor appointed a blue-ribbon panel to review all aspects of the HEW report and to conduct a definitive investigation of the division.

During this period the press also contributed to the campaign for change through numerous editorials and reports, including several undercover stories written by reporters who had gained positions in various institutions. The keynote of the media case for reform was the simple and dramatic issue of humane treatment. "Simply 'caging children,' as Governor Francis Sargent so aptly put it, 'is not the way of an enlightened society.' "[13] Less visible but certainly present in the popularization of the reform movement were the various other charges of the division's critics, such as civil service formalization and protection of political appointees; centralized and undelegated power in the hands of the director; poor coordination among institutions and a developing autonomy and lack of control within institutions; lack of effective therapeutic and educational programs at the institutions and very few qualified professionals to staff them.[14]

Naturally the division's senior staff defended the system against the growing pressure for change, but its critics were apparently correct in citing a breakdown in leadership as a serious problem. While it is difficult to single out a particular event as the one that catalyzed the reform movement into legislative action, ceratinly the most likely candidate was an internal dispute. Institutional superintendents enjoyed considerable authority over their own staff, and autonomy from other institutions and the central office. Each institution had its own state-appropriated budget and personnel, and did its own hiring and purchasing. Few institutional decisions were beyond the personal control of a superintendent. At the Bridgewater Juvenile Guidance Institute, for example, a conflict developed between the superintendent and the assistant superintendent, which involved the reform of the installation's maximum-security practices. Supported by the director of the division, John Coughlin, the superintendent brought charges against the assistant, who appealed to the Civil Service Board. In a much-publicized hearing, the assistant successfully defended his case and was reinstated. Responding to the public outcry against the division's leadership, Governor Sargent pressured Coughlin to resign; Coughlin submitted his resignation in March 1969, effective in May.

While the political battle over reorganization did not end with Coughlin's resignation, the Bridgewater incident and its aftermath did seem to mark a turning point for the reform cause. In May a panel established by the Massachusetts Conference on Social Welfare called for still more resignations of senior staff members and the closing of several facilities. Governor Sargent appointed a former professor of the Boston University

School of Social Work, Frank Maloney, as acting director of the division, and lent his support to a reorganization bill pending in the legislature. While reorganization had been debated in the legislature since the 1967 HEW report and a succeeding senate committee investigation, the bill now moved easily through the Senate and House.[15]

Opposition was based principally on the argument that "decision-making powers" would be taken "away from a trained and experienced board and given to 'clinicians.' "[16] A preliminary House vote of 211 to 5 in early July, however, demonstrated the weakness of the opposition. Throughout July, Boston newspapers maintained the momentum of the reform movement. For example, the *Globe* described the institutions as a "mess," "antiquated," "old," and "dreary," all under the headline, "There's No Lobby for the Outcasts."[17] When the governor signed the Reorganization Act in August, it was in much the same form as presented by the Massachusetts Committee on Crime and Youth several months before.

The Reorganization Act had several impacts, some of them subtle and not foreseen at the time of its enactment. First of all, the bill's very passage increased the credibility and visibility of the reform movement. Second, the act elevated the division to the full status of a department, and moved it from the Department of Education to a superagency, consisting of the departments of Welfare, Health, Mental Health, and Corrections. The new department (DYS) was to be headed by a commissioner and four assistant commissioners of his choosing. Third, the act set up a new professional tone for the agency, using key words and phrases such as "therapy," "prevention," "community services," "purchase of services," and "research." Finally, the act broadly empowered the new department to establish necessary facilities for detention, diagnosis, treatment, and training of its charges, including post-release care. While these powers in themselves did not mark a major new thrust, the language of the act later proved sufficient grounds for Commissioner Miller and his assistants to implement a noninstitutional system.

The intent of the act was clearly reflected in the search for a director. The search panel consisted chiefly of professionals, such as Lloyd Ohlin, head of the Harvard Center for Criminal Justice. They, in turn, looked for a fellow professional capable of upgrading the department. While the panel officially did not rule out the possibility of choosing a new director from within the department, it was expected that an outsider would be selected. Three months after the reorganization bill had passed, Jerome Miller was the leading candidate. His training at the Ohio State University School of Social Work and his experience in the military, developing a youth services agency for Air Force dependents, met both academic and pragmatic criteria. Governor Sargent confirmed Miller as the first commissioner of the Department of Youth Services on October 28, 1969.

To sum up, the movement for reform of the Massachusetts Department of Youth Services was prompted by outrage at the high human and financial costs of operating an almost pathologically ineffective system. The movement was external; it had little support among DYS staff, and next to none among the leadership, who did not succeed in defending the system against change. In fact, a leadership breakdown was catalyst for legislative reorganization of DYS and a search for a new director.

The thrust of the campaign for change was for more humane treatment for children, not for a set of specific reforms. This thrust was sustained in the Reorganization Act, which broadly charged the department with improving services to youth, and in the composition and activities of the search panel, which sought a commissioner qualified to upgrade the department. The role of the commissioner, then, was all but explicitly defined as that of an outside change agent who would reform the department from the top down. The mandate of the new commissioner and his assistants, however, was not necessarily to close institutions and to develop radically new systems for the prevention and treatment of delinquency, but simply to better the quality of services to youth committed to the department.

Trial Changes

When Miller came to DYS in 1969, he found an agency in turmoil, divided internally by critical reports and external political conflicts. He found massive public support from reform groups and professional organizations, and encountered high expectations from the press and the legislature for a professional upgrading of the system. Miller, however, found no funds for experimentation, training, or research, and political appointees were still in command of the institutions.

During his first year in office, Miller attempted to prepare the system for change by hiring consultants to provide staff training and to introduce new concepts. His efforts were supported by many of the younger staff in the department. His aim was to introduce therapeutic community concepts within the institutions. He invited Dr. Maxwell Jones, a British expert on the therapeutic model, to start a pilot training program at the Shirley Industrial School for Boys.

Jones's therapeutic community concepts are intended to alter the traditional passive role of the "inmate" or "client" throgh a process of active resocialization, in which roles are broken down and relationships become more equalized among staff and between staff and residents. The therapeutic community approach also intends to promote a close and trusting relationship between staff and the youths in order to promote growth and a process of self-actualization in both residents and staff.[18]

Introducing these concepts in the Shirley structure brought immediate polarization, created staff tensions, and resulted in mass escapes. The older staff, who were by and large unskilled, saw these new concepts as a threat and a challenge to their authority. The new staff had difficulty integrating the concepts into the daily operations of the institutions without further training and support. This resulted in a number of legislative investigations and further staff entrenchment.[19] Hence, Miller's initial effort was unsuccessful. He would later become aware that he had to change the system "without blowing it."[20] In mid-1971 he decided to slowly phase out the Shirley facility. This decision was made with the support of his assistant commissioners and was accomplished by moving several cottage residents to other institutions and by using staff housing to operate group homes.

The Maxwell Jones training sessions provoked further resistance. They symbolized the beginning of a strong and visible staff alienation, which created additional pressures on the system. Some of this resistance became overt, as in the organized correspondence to state legislators and the press, as well as covert sabotage, such as inducing runaways, work stoppages, misuse of sick leave, and early retirements. However, these staff confrontations had a limited negative impact on the department because they were skillfully used by Miller to justify setbacks and program failures. Thus, they elicited sympathetic support from the press and from reform groups.

Lacking resources and middle-management personnel, Miller's first year, despite its chaos, was effective in three different ways.

1. He provided the rhetoric and the tone for later reform through his public appearances, press releases, and lectures around the state. During his lectures, Miller was very often accompanied by youngsters from the institutions, who described their experiences and attacked the system of which they had been a part.

2. He used his administrative power to change and to rotate top administrators in the different institutions. Shirley's administrators were changed several times, as were those at Bridgewater and Lyman. These changes broke staff opposition and kept the process of change on the move.

3. He introduced humanizing effects into the system through administrative orders. He prohibited staff from striking children, from the excessive use of lockups, haircuts, marching, and imposing silences.[21] Despite staff resentment, these measures had a certain degree of success, especially in those institutions where changes in administration had taken place. Lastly, Miller closed down the maximum-security unit at Bridgewater in the late spring of 1970.

Even though this was expected, this last action was extremely significant in several ways. There was no institution available to take its place, and Miller began actively to advocate that there was no need for one to take its place. Bridgewater had been the "end of the line" for juvenile offenders and had always been used as the ultimate threat by the other facilities in DYS. Without this threat, institutions were forced to find better solutions and to operate more effectively and independently. Most important, this decision provided a direction for the new department. Miller discovered the strategy he was to use in the future; he also found that closing down an institution does not necessarily cause insurmountable problems.

On the program level Miller had few community-based innovative successes to show for his first year in office. The Mary Knoll facility at Topsfield, which was to be used as a teach-in center, faced so much community opposition that it did not get off the ground. Therapeutic community concepts had also created staff turmoil, and funding for parole volunteers and other community-based programs did not materialize.

Incremental Changes and Innovations

With the appointment of four professionally trained assistant commissioners, each in charge of his respective bureau, DYS moved into the second year, which was to see major innovations and program changes. The highlights were as follows:

1. On the institutional level, several structural changes were introduced, all geared to create a decentralized cottage-based system and to promote staff and youth involvement in the decisionmaking process.[22]

2. The Oakdale Residential Treatment Unit for Boys, a custodial-oriented institution for the youngest youths (ages 9 to 11) was closed in March 1971. After half the children had been placed in private residences, the remainder were transferred to the Lancaster Industrial School for Girls, where they became involved in a unique program designed by the staff and girls at the school. The presence of young boys at the school created a number of program alternatives for the school, and mutual involvement of the girls in working with the boys' program.

3. With the availability of a federal grant, a staff training program began. Several teams, which included both the old and the young staff, received training in counseling and operating a group home. The training sessions also prepared the staff to work with the hard-core youngsters in the care of the department.

4. Extensive group home experimentation began in early 1971. Hyde Park House, a self-help center, opened in Roslindale, housing nine youngsters. Six group homes were opened on institutional grounds using available staff housing. Group homes such as "Mary Lamb" and "I Belong" were extremely successful in producing good programs, and served as examples for additional programs in the department.

5. A parole volunteer program was funded, giving the parole operation a much-needed boost.

6. Western Massachusetts received a strong impetus toward the creation of program alternatives from the involvement of the University of Massachusetts, which provided the Westfield detention center with ongoing consultation, student volunteers, and increased staff training.[23]

7. Regionalization began to take hold. Nine regional directors were hired, and a reorganizing staff was hired for the regional offices.

Closing Down the Institutions

Despite these changes, Miller and the department were under increasing pressure from different directions. The hiring of new and young staff at the institutions increased polarization, with the "old guard" building up more and more opposition. Institutional staff opposed to the new approach became demoralized, restive, and fearful about losing their jobs. Most important, the youngsters themselves were caught in the middle between dying institutions and alternatives yet unborn. Services suffered accordingly. Staff continued to be underpaid, and most lost hope for advancement when DYS decided to secure purchase-of-care services from outside private groups. Changes at the institutional level increased runaways, bringing more opposition from the local communities and pressure from the legislature. In addition, there was a growing bureaucratic force exerted on the department from the state Administration and Finance Office because it regarded the changes in youth services as chaotic and administratively lax.

The decision to close the institutions was made amid all these pressures, and despite the havoc it initially created, the shutdown was extremely successful in defusing the bigger threats—those of staff unrest, of political opposition, and of local community resistance.

DYS abandoned gradualism, for it only provided causes for political opposition and more time for it to form in the legislature. During the January 1972 legislative recess, Miller used his commissioner's discretionary powers to officially close the institutions. Youngsters who could not be immediately paroled, placed, or referred to community programs were housed temporarily on the campus of the University of Massachusetts.

This operation was called the JOE II conference, and was essentially planned and executed by a core group of the university's volunteers and regional DYS staff. The operation, in spite of many administrative problems, was successful in that it made the closing of the largest and oldest institution, the Lyman School for Boys, relatively painless for the 100 youngsters involved, since this method eliminated staff opposition and sabotage. The youths, who lived for about a month on the university campus, were matched with youth advocates while arrangements were made to place them in community-based programs, preferably in their home regions.[24]

The closing of the institutions overshadowed all other accomplishments and incremental changes. It had important psychological impacts. First, it set the tone and clearly defined the task for the year 1972. After initial staff bewilderment and surprise, energies were released toward the creation of alternatives. Groups began to develop proposals, resources were found, and children filled these placements at an accelerated rate. There were new goals, new tasks, and new hope. Second, it gave Miller and the department national recognition. Numerous newspaper articles and several television networks covered the series of events, and DYS was described as a bold, action-oriented agency willing to take risks to ameliorate the deplorable conditions of training schools for young offenders. In professional circles, this action was described as a new breakthrough in providing services for youths in trouble. Third, the drama involved in closing Lyman, the oldest training school in the country, effectively attracted public attention and brought about much public debate and edification. Finally, the closing of Lyman symbolized the end of punitive and repressive institutions even though other facilities in the state remained open, waiting to be phased out in the near future. It was as if all the institutions had been closed.

In retrospect, this move succeeded for these reasons:

1. The University of Massachusetts and the western region of DYS provided a good cushion to absorb youngsters, and moreover proved to be a rich resource for program alternatives.[25]
2. Forestry camps and programs of the Outward Bound type were very effective in handling and providing programs for DYS youths.[26]
3. Detention centers were still available to accommodate youngsters who were awaiting placements.[27]
4. An intensive-care unit, Fairview, was immediately opened at Greenhaven. This unit, which later was staffed primarily by ex-offenders, was able to work effectively with hard-core youngsters, and thus gave the court the assurance that the dangerous youngsters were not on the streets.
5. The publicity generated by closing the institutions caught the attention of many groups who proved to be resources for the department and developers of its alternatives.

The closing of institutions, however, did not lack critics from inside and outside the department. Opponents of reform talked about an increase in the crime rate and the loss of community protection. The old guard was concerned with job security and other vested interests. Supporters of reform were afraid of a possible backlash over critical incidents that might set back reform. And there were others within the agency who doubted the department's administrative capabilities to withstand such a change and feared further bureaucratic entanglements.

But the change process had begun in earnest, for by closing down the physical plant of an institution, alternatives of some kind would have to be used to care for the child in trouble. These alternatives will be discussed in Part II.

Notes

1. This is an updated, revised version of Yitzhak Bakal, "Closing Massachusetts Institutions: A Case Study," in Bakal, ed., *Closing Correctional Institutions* (Lexington Books, 1974). It is included here to give continuity to the description and analysis of deinstitutionalization in Massachusetts.

2. This historical review is based primarily on Edwin Powers, *The Basic Structure of the Administration of Criminal Justice in Massachusetts* (Boston: Massachusetts Correctional Association, 1968); U.S. Department of Health, Education and Welfare (hereafter cited as HEW), *A Study of the Division of Youth Services and Youth Service Board* (Washington, D.C.: HEW, 1966); and, of course, the author's personal observations of the events.

3. HEW, *A Study of the Division of Youth Services*; Massachusetts Committee on Children and Youth, *Report and Recommendations of the Massachusetts Committee on Children and Youth*; Commonwealth of Massachusetts, "Report of the Special Committee of the Senate Investigation and Study of the Division of Youth Services," Senate . . . No. 1310, June 1967.

4. HEW, *A Study of the Division of Youth Services*, Part 1, p. 5.

5. Ibid., Part IV, pp. 46-52.

6. Ibid., p. 47.

7. Ibid., pp. 34-38.

8. There are no exact official estimates.

9. HEW, *A Study of the Division of Youth Services*, Part VI, p. 18.

10. DYS Planning Unit, *Programs and Policies of the Department of Youth Services*, pp. 5-6.

11. HEW, *A Study of the Division of Youth Services*.

12. Boston *Globe*, July 15, 1967.

13. Ibid., March 27, 1969.

14. HEW, *A Study of the Division of Youth Services*.

15. *Massachusetts General Laws*, Vol. 2A, Chaps. 13-28; DYS, chap. 18A, as amended by Chap. 838 of the acts of 1969.

16. Boston *Herald-Traveler*, June 4, 1969.

17. Boston *Globe*, July 14, 1969.

18. Maxwell Jones, *Social Psychiatry: A Study of Therapeutic Communities* (London: Tavistock, 1952); Maxwell Jones, *Beyond the*

Therapeutic Community: Social Learning and Social Psychiatry (New Haven, Conn.: Yale University Press, 1968).

19. Commonwealth of Massachusetts, *Report of the Special House Committee to Investigate and Study the Number, Causes and Prevention of Runaways from the Industrial School for Boys at Shirley*, House . . . No. 6152, August 1970.

20. Boston *Globe*, March 8, 1970.

21. Barry C. Feld, "Variations of Inmate Subcultures in Juvenile Correctional Institutions," unpublished paper, Center for Criminal Justice, Harvard Law School, 1972.

22. Barry C. Feld, "Subcultures of Selected Boys' Cottages in Massachusetts Department of Youth Services Institutions in 1971," unpublished paper, Center for Criminal Justice, Harvard Law School, 1972.

23. For a detailed description of programs originated at the University of Massachusetts in collaboration with DYS, see Larry L. Dye, "The University's Role in Public Service to the Department of Youth Services," in Yitzhak Bakal, ed., *Closing Correctional Institutions: New Strategies for Youth Services* (Lexington, Mass.: Lexington Books, D.C. Heath and Co., 1973), pp. 117-25.

24. Robert B. Coates, Alden D. Miller, and Lloyd E. Ohlin, "A Strategic Innovation in the Process of Deinstitutionalization," in Bakal, ed., *Closing Correctional Institutions*, pp. 127-48.

25. Dye, "The University's Role in Public Service."

26. These programs expanded after Miller became the DYS Commissioner. For a report see Jerome G. Miller, "Report to the Governor and General Court, for the period November, 1969 to November, 1970" (Boston: DYS, 1970).

27. The Roslindale, Worcester, and Westfield detention centers were open and overpopulated. An assistant commissioner for clinical services estimates that detention centers' population more than doubled with the closing of the institutions.

4 Leadership and Change in Massachusetts

A Philosophy of Change

The reform leadership of Jerome Miller stemmed primarily from his unique vision of the correctional dilemma (by comparison with virtually any other correctional administrator in the country), and from his willingness to stand alone during the inevitable period of turmoil once the institutions were closed.

Miller based his reform stance on four basic perceptions of the correctional establishment and societal needs:

1. He described society's relationship to the correctional problem as being essentially a double standard—a claimed rehabilitation objective based on positive motives, when in fact the effect was destructive, punitive, and based on hostility.
2. Miller rejected the premise that a consensus should come before change, and instead held that administrators must force alternatives to break the existing cycle. A consensus, he felt, could form *ex post facto.*
3. Miller saw institutions as instruments of isolation that allow society to feel no longer responsible for the care or condition of proclaimed "deviants."
4. Miller challenged the stereotyped idea of delinquency and demanded that blame for delinquent acts be placed on social conditions; delinquents, he held, served the social desire to scapegoat part of the population, and as a common "enemy" further served to unify "straight society."

Using the words of George H. Mead, the American social scientist, Miller outlined what he believed to be the dilemma of society vis-à-vis the correctional issue:

> But the two attitudes, that of control of crime by the hostile procedure of law and that of control through comprehension of social and psychological conditions, cannot be combined. To understand is to forgive, and the social procedure seems to deny the very responsibility which the law affirms, and on the other hand the pursuit by criminal justice inevitably awakens the hostile attitude in the offender and renders the attitude of mutual comprehension practically impossible.[1]

37

Having acknowledged this societal dilemma, Miller held that the present system does not, in fact, achieve its avowed goals of rehabilitation but rather serves its own ends. The system, he said, is "only remotely engaged in its stated purpose (correction or rehabilitation) and is primarily fulfilling other social or moralistic functions for the society."[2] Among these functions is the aim of holding society together "by hostile procedures directed at those who break the norms of that society."[3] Further, Miller held, the punitive impulse among average citizens is a force to be reckoned with:

> The term "delinquent," and that term is applied equally to a boy who is stubborn or truant or steals or has engaged in assault, calls forth a host of negative responses. It is no happenstance that if one wants to find an expert on delinquency, he need merely ask the next person he meets. The fact that so many have such strongly held views tells us that this phenomenon must be of great importance to the majority of citizens.[4]

Miller's belief that society was caught in this punishment-rehabilitation dilemma that was in need of resolution contributed to his stance as an agent of change.

The central method for bringing about reform, as Miller came to perceive it, was to eliminate institutions and substitute community programs. Community programs, he said, "have the potential to reeducate the public as to who and what 'criminals' and 'delinquents' are in a variety of social roles," and can "provide a new ideological backdrop against which diagnoses must take the initiative." Moreover, "institutions must be closed as rapidly as possible." The administrators have to "force the alternatives" and "anticipate turmoil in reform." "It cannot happen by consensus," he said, "although once done and sustained, a consensus will begin to form."[5]

Miller, however, did not believe that simple program changes would bring ultimate reform. The problem is one of "ideology and utimately of politics," he said, and any reformer would need a "sense of process and a capacity for informed loneliness" to survive the delay between changes and the growth of public awareness and the consensus which he felt would form.

In terms of social organization, Miller felt this could only come by breaking the cycle of accepted definitions:

> The question of correctional reform is . . . whether we can (1) effectively break the vicious circle of definitions calling for institutional arrangement, which in turn re-validate the definitions; and (2) build in new definitions (since they will come) and categories that show the social and psychological strengths and developmental life space of those defined as "delinquent" or "criminal."[6]

Miller's rejection of institutions as instruments of constructive or rehabilitative significance expressed itself in his relentless drive to close all reform schools in Massachusetts. "Crucial to any basic and lasting reforms in corrections must be the demise of the institution which isolates the individual from the community in a 'society of captives.' "[7] Miller denied that institutions exist for worthy purposes. "Institutions exist not to be effective, but to provide reassurance, albeit a false reassurance," he said. Further, Miller held that by isolating delinquents, "institutional settings encourage ignorance of the correlates of crime," and therefore encourage public ignorance of unhealthy social conditions. Miller's determination to rid the system of institutions was based on a simple premise, namely, that "if institutions are there, they will be used."[8] A key factor in assuring that reforms would last, he felt, would be to eliminate institutions altogether as an alternative.

Finally, Miller relied heavily on the premise that "to understand is to forgive"[9] to bring the concept of delinquents into a just perspective. A new method of helping troubled youth he felt was inevitable in light of the fact that "those involved are poor and their families are nonexistent, fragmented, or powerless." Further he saw that past experience not only proved past incompetence but guaranteed a threat for the future:

> Our best efforts to treat the delinquent for the most part have begun in incompetence and have built to a climax of punishment and physical or psychological violence toward the offender—a process which assures for the most part the intensity of his bitterness and the escalation of his crimes.[10]

This damaging treatment, he held, persisted despite superficial attempts to change definitions—for the definers continued to operate from the same punitive stance. "The problem is whether society has evolved to a point where it will tolerate defining delinquents and criminals in terms other than those which demand exclusion and isolation from society as the primary embodiment of public safety and the basic tool of rehabilitation."[11]

> Until the ideology underlying the definitions is questioned, it matters little to the slave who runs away whether he is called spiteful or suffering from "drapetomania" (a nineteenth-century medical diagnosis of runaway slaves). "It matters little to the person locked alone in a stripped cell whether it is called the 'hole' or the 'adjustment center' or whether he is classified as a sinner, a constitutional psychopathic inferior, a defective delinquent, or a sociopath."[12]

Miller concluded from these premises that "we must recognize that although we have preached rehabilitation, we have been involved in producing scapegoats who present ever greater dangers to all of us." "All of this," he allowed, "is not to condone the behavior or delinquencies of young persons who come under our care. It is simply to say there must be better ways of handling the problem."

In addition, Miller saw himself as an example of "informed loneliness" and an administrator able to step partially away from the correctional system. To escape the dilemma proposed by administering a system only "remotely engaged in its stated purpose," Miller said, one wished to step "aside or away," but "to do so is to lose touch." Conversely, "to be of it is to claim it and that is self-destructive. How does one claim a Bridgewater or an Attica?" Miller's defense against what he saw as the co-opting influence of the system was to remain naive, in a sense. "To fight naively is perhaps the best after all—if one can survive," he said. This acknowledgment of his own dilemma—a man in the system seeking to destroy it—set him apart.

Philosophy into Action

Miller's ideas about correctional reform and youth fit within a broad philosophy of humanism. He denied so-called "expertise" and defied research and isolated methods of treatment that manipulate the minds or actions of people. He wanted things to happen spontaneously, to grow out of people's interactions as human beings with one another without manipulation. Although he remained a humanist in philosophy and practice, many of his ideas about correctional reform changed radically between the time that he came to Boston and when he left. In the beginning he believed in the therapeutic community concept; he had hoped for humanitarian institutions.

After seeing at first hand the realities of the existing institutions, his ideas changed radically. Miller became convinced that all institutions per se are bad, that the bureaucratic structure, and the fact that people put other people away, creates a totally complex and destructive situation that no method of treatment, no staff, and no honorable intentions can rectify.

At the core of Miller's philosophy is the constant theme that one cannot rehabilitate youths by violence. There is no way to curse and at the same time to help. Youths are suppressed and need the right to their own ideas and feelings, and to treatment—humanitarian treatment. In the guise of help, many destructive, manipulative things are done to young inmates. Miller disagreed vehemently with all methods of manipulation and behavior modification, and all varieties of "scientific" or pseudo-scientific approaches to youth.

One important strategy used by Miller was his constant exposing of society's double standard—its double message, to society on the one hand and to its youth on the other. By exposing this double standard, he returned the responsibility to the society from which youth come and to which they must ultimately return. By directly communicating his ideas to large numbers of people throughout the state, he hoped to make people aware that they were not really achieving true reform.

Jerome Miller thus denied the validity of dogmas geared to isolating inmates and looking at them as the source of the problem. He saw delinquency, criminality, and corrections within the context of the social, economic, and political institutions of society, and he saw correctional reform as social reform.

A Case History of Radical Leadership From Within An Establishment Institution

Opening the System

Miller's first year in office was noted for his effort to loosen up the rigid system in order to make it more amenable to change. In approaching this task, Miller had several liabilities and obstacles: (1) he was an outsider and lacked support within DYS; (2) he was limited by a lack of funds; and (3) years of institutional autonomy almost precluded any central authority's intervention via the public.

Altering communication patterns. An important strategy used in opening the system was to increase public involvement through the use of the mass media. During the early period of his administration, Miller made many local television and radio broadcasts and was interviewed often by the press. He continually cast himself in the role of the outside change agent. He explicitly exposed and criticized the wrongs of the system: "We must eliminate the little totalitarian societies which dominated the juvenile institutions in the past. Most of the units were set up so that their successful kids could only function in a dictatorship."[13]

At the same time, he was vague about the changes he was planning to implement. In this way, he gathered support while depriving his opponents of a focus for opposition, keeping himself on the offensive. He also exposed the internal conflicts and the staff sabotage. He made the inner workings of the department visible to the press and the public and let them know that he was as concerned as they were about the problems.

This continuing dialog brought about greater understanding and support of Miller and his philosophy. It helped to make the public more aware of DYS and its functions, and improved immensely the public's image of the department.

Public exposure of the Department of Corrections began *to change the image of a juvenile delinquent from a criminal to a victim.* More people became aware of the institutions; more people were made aware that children were being victimized, not rehabilitated. He made the public feel responsible for allowing such treatment to exist:

> You can control runaways, you can produce model institutional kids by brute force and fear if that's what you want, to reassure legislators, the police or the communities. Lock doors, handcuff kids to their beds and you'll have no runs. But they will react when they get out; they have learned to con the adults.[14]

Thus, a new voice was heard at DYS, the voice of the concerned public. Once Miller exposed the injustices of the system, he was obligated to correct them. He had the support of the public in doing this.

Whereas the institutions had previously been autonomous, now they were becoming accountable to the central administration. Miller began to ask for written reports of cases involving force or brutality.[15] In the Boston *Sunday Globe,* March 8, 1970, he complained that "a staff member alone was often judge, jury, and prosecutor in regard to particular incidents, with facts often grossly distorted to protect the staff."[16] Using his authority, more intermediaries became involved in the transactions between the staff and the youth. The system was no longer closed and arbitrary.

Youth involvement. Another useful strategy was the involvement of the youths in decisions that affected their lives. Miller frequently toured the institutions, often appearing unexpectedly. He went directly to the inmates and listened to their grievances. Through them he found out what was going on rather than what the staff wanted him to know. And he gave youngsters the feeling that they had an important advocate, encouraging them to call him or come to his office. Institutionalized youngsters became an important source of information to him and his staff. By making himself accessible to the residents he was in fact breaking down the institutional hierarchy. The youngsters began to realize they had some recourse if they were mistreated, while the staff realized that they were accountable for their own actions. One of the costs of this change was the insecurity it wrought among the staff. They were robbed of their former means of discipline, leaving them without any feeling of support from the administration. This at times caused conflicts, resistance, even sabotage. It also presented problems to middle-management personnel, who had to deal with the disgruntled staff at the institutions and whose responsibility it was to implement the new policies. In terms of increased staff unrest, the cost of this change was great.

However, all these strategies—the use of public relations, divesting the institutions of their autonomy, the breakdown of the hierarchy, and listening to the grievances of the young people—had the result of opening up the system. The institutional staff people were now accountable to many segments of the population—the young people, the public, and the central adminstration.

Introduction of new concepts of treatment. Miller's attempts to introduce innovative therapeutic methods were less successful. The training sessions administered by Dr. Maxwell Jones on therapeutic milieu concepts created staff polarization and resulted in mass runaways of the juveniles. It is important to note that these concepts proved to have many limitations for application in antiquated institutions that lacked programs, resources, and progressive young staff members.

A few months later, in mid-1970, another attempt to change was made at Shirley Industrial School for Boys. The "guided group interaction" approach was introduced by staff members.[17] This is a modified version of the Maxwell Jones approach, but more structured and geared to institutional settings. This method was adopted by a group of staff from Shirley and used in running an intensive security unit at the Oakdale Residential Treatment Unit for Boys.

Another approach that was tried, in collaboration with Dr. Matthew Dumont from the Massachusetts Department of Mental Health, was the self-help groups.[18] DYS explored these programs as alternatives that would provide massive changes inside the institutions. The idea was to turn several institutions over to self-help groups that needed space for their own operations. They, in turn, would accept DYS youngsters in their programs.

For a number of reasons, these groups held high promise for radically altering service delivery practices in the department: (1) they have a high degree of success in terms of their acceptance by the community, the public, and the legislature because they are "clean" and well-structured; (2) they provide a therapeutic environment for residents interested in introspection and change; and (3) they maintain themselves on a minimal budget with strong demands exerted on the residents.

Despite high hopes, however, the outcome proved to be very limited for two reasons. First, the groups were able to work with only a limited number of DYS youngsters. These therapeutic modalities have high expectations and exert tremendous pressure on the residents. In order to continue, the groups had to work with motivated children, and thus the attrition rate was very high. Second, these programs have an authoritarian approach that proved to be at odds with the department's emerging philosophy of humanism, permissiveness, and equalitarianism.

Because of the high visibility of DYS and its many opponents, it was difficult to support new programs before they proved themselves. Although all the programs had only limited practical success, they were useful inasmuch as they challenged the old system and demonstrated that there are many possibilities for the treatment of youth.

Introduction of new roles. Another means that Miller employed was the introduction of new roles into the system. As mentioned earlier, the young inmates began to play a new, more vocal role. DYS began to consult with youngsters before placing them in a program. Joint decisions appeared between youth and DYS acting as an "agent." These young people now clearly affected the conduct of the department, and thus their own lives. Miller believed that "the ideology of correction will not change until those labeled by it have some say in that defining process."[19] He further maintained that "if we can stay in community settings for a generation, then the beginning of a democratic proces within corrections may guarantee some elements of enduring reform because the clientele, the residents, will be part of the body politic."[20]

To some extent the youths began to operate as a source of support. Many of them began attending lectures and spoke of their experiences in the institutions. They attended community meetings of all kinds. Their stories of brutality presented a very convincing case against the old system.

Introduction of new staff. New people were introduced into the department through a tremendous turnover of staff. The records reveal that when Miller left, 60 percent of the DYS staff had been hired since he took over.[21] Many of the older employees left DYS because the old machinery of opposition had no influence and no power to resist the changes. The new staff members generally were attracted to DYS because they were interested in its liberal outlook; thus they tended to agree with the central administration. The process of change attracted more progressive people who tended to reinforce this process. Thus the new staff was both a result of—and eventually a continuing source of—change, rather than resisting it as the old staff had done.

Miller's first year in office was used mainly to "loosen up" the system by introducing new concepts, practices, and people. Therapeutic community concepts had limited impact because of staff polarization. More impressive were the results of introducing and involving new people with DYS, which seeded more intensive program collaboration for the future.

Miller used the press very effectively in exposing the old system, legitimizing the role of children in the new system and breaking down institutional isolation and autonomy. Other strategies, such as undermining the hierarchy by going directly to the youths, the creative use of his role as an outsider to the system, and the show of humane authority by introducing changes in "form" (no haircuts, no lockup, and so on), rather than "content," proved to be effective tools and could be replicated elsewhere.

Changing the System

The changes that have been introduced in DYS have been massive and dramatic, and especially unusual for a state bureaucracy, even considering the many elements that made such change possible, including the mandate for change as expressed in the state's Reorganization Act,[22] support of local groups, and the definite commitment of a governor who expressed his support frequently. A department of youth services is controlled by many groups, which exert strong pressures to resist change. First, within the state government are the legislature, which controls the budget, and the governor's executive office, which exerts bureaucratic controls. There are also other agencies of the criminal justice system: the police, the courts, and probation. Internally, the department is comprised of staff who can exert controls through their unions or political groups. And finally there is the general public, the communities, and the press.

All these pressures manifest themselves as drawbacks; they can, however, become assets if properly informed and stimulated. It is these alignments and realignments that determine the degree of flexibility and support available to the commissioner in his efforts toward change.[23] These forces, when they are exerted to maintain the system, work to deprive the commissioner of his authority, thus making any action for reform extremely difficult. This was not allowed to happen at DYS under Miller. Opponents of reform were put into a defensive position, forced to explain unjustifiable situations. On the other hand, the department continually broadened its base of support, thus moving into a more powerful offensive position. This power was gained by depriving staff and institutions of their autonomy, cutting into the power of the bureaucracy and patronage systems of government, and building upon the growing relationships with outside forces. Similar strategies were also used with the police, the courts, and the communities. This realignment meant involvement of youngsters, staff, new groups, and private groups from whom DYS was purchasing care.

The question that needs to be answered here is how this happened. The following is an analysis of the strategies and approaches employed by Miller and his associates in order to effect change.

Flexible agenda. It is more accurate to describe the change process in the department during these years as *emergent* rather than *planned*. These changes were often determined by chance, imagination, opportunity, and personal strategy, primarily in the commissioner's style. The strategies depended largely upon options and solutions that arose spontaneously, and which the department was flexible enough to exploit. These options increased with the opening of the system and the introduction of new roles and actors into it.

Frequently, DYS would adopt a new approach as soon as it proved useful or successful. In the same way, if a program proved infeasible, it was immediately abandoned or modified. Two examples illustrate this process.

1. There was an early policy decision to open group homes, which would be run by DYS. However, in the process of establishing these homes,

it became evident that the department's flexibility would be enhanced by contracting for these services, rather than operating them directly, and thus the policy was changed. This shift from the traditional role of providing services exempted DYS from bureaucratic entanglement and the intricacies of staff training and retraining. Although the policy change created some staff alienation, it insured quick and efficient movement toward meaningful alternatives.

2. Another example is the Community Action Program (CAP), a private, nonresidential aftercare program. CAP began as a small operation when the institutions were closed, and proved to be extremely successful in working with groups of youngsters in storefront operations, both by providing jobs and counseling and opening recreational activities. The success of the program encouraged DYS to increase the number of referrals from 20 to 175 in only one year.

Shotgun approach. Miller invited a variety of programs and ideas in the hope that some projects would be successful. Such a shotgun approach gave DYS the flexibility to try out a number of options in many different directions and to experiment with limited resources. This approach was also consistent with Miller's oft-stated belief that the old system was destructive and "insane" and that any new alternative would be better than what the training schools had to offer.

Thus, the department's lack of a concrete plan proved to be helpful in that it made it flexible enough to find opportunities and to use them. Different approaches were tried, each with limited success. When the therapeutic community concept failed, "guided group interaction" was tried. When this method had limited success, the department introduced the "self-help group" concept into the institutions.

Cottages were closed when the occasion arose and staff members were constantly rotated, some for the purpose of training and others for the purpose of starting new programs or assuming new responsibilities. Programs that proved themselves were claimed as new and innovative; those that failed were terminated.[24] In this manner there were always a few good programs that met the criteria of being humane and effective, and to these the department could point as successful.

This shotgun method also explains to a great extent the diversity of the new alternatives. The programs covered a broad scope and were developed by a wide range of agencies, traditional and nontraditional, as well as by educational institutions and even recreational organizations, such as the YMCA. The approach posed difficulties for the opposition because the changes in DYS were so constant that it was impossible for them to focus an attack on any particular program. However, it also posed difficulties for the department. Many of the older staff members were alienated because they felt unsupported and could not understand the department's changing direction. There was also a considerable amount of confusion and wasted effort in the central office because many of the changes were made without enough staff involvement, especially those decisions that were made unilaterally by Miller.[25]

Some of the younger staff saw this movement strictly as opportunism, lacking any real commitment to programs for youth. Changing directions sometimes meant abandoning programs run by new staff who supported Miller. The most striking example occurred when the decision was made to close the institutions. Several good programs operated by DYS within the institutions had to be disbanded in favor of contracting with outside groups, which resulted in some antagonism and anxiety among new staff. Yet, despite the turmoil and resentment, the shotgun method was effective and necessary, given the limitations of a public bureaucracy.

Avoidance of conflict. By espousing a direction rather than a program, Miller was able to avoid confrontations on specific issues with staff, communities, and the legislature. Thus he could find followers and maintain the department's visibility to the press, the rest of the bureaucracy, and the public, without directly confronting the most rigid and intractable forces in the system. By denouncing the institutional failures in general terms, Miller was never forced to explain specifically his plans to ameliorate these conditions; neither was he compelled to specify the cost of the changes to staff and other vested interest groups.

In effect, Miller's ability to articulate institutional failures forced the defenders of the old system into an impotent position. Who could argue, for example, with a call to "open up" institutions and "make them responsive to new ideas?"[26] Who could attack Miller's practice of visiting institutions spontaneously and talking with youngsters? How could anyone counter the following argument: "If you continue to turn out more criminals after treatment, something is obviously wrong."[27] By placing himself on the side of justice and humaneness, he made it difficult for detractors to criticize him publicly for fear of placing themselves on the side of injustice and inhumanity.[28]

Within the department, at the institutions, similar strategies were used. Staff people were promised a place in the system without being told specifically what that place would be. After isolating several key personnel who were resistant to change, Miller promoted a few staff members who showed by their commitment or rhetoric that they were willing to support him. These promotions created a feeling among the staff that the system was open to them and that promotions were possible. This new sense of security among some of the older staff made it possible to make certain alliances that were necessary in order to work out compromises, and thus achieve specific objectives. Also, several of the newly promoted staff members proved helpful in dealing with local community conflicts. They were able to present and defend new programs to communities and legislators in a manner that made them more acceptable. All of these personnel maneuvers had the temporary effect of dispelling conflict.

Conflict could not, however, be postponed indefinitely. Staff members became increasingly resentful because promotions did not materialize, constant changes were occurring, and there was a lack of communication and support from the central office. Despite all of Miller's strategies to avoid conflict, the personnel in the field were becoming increasingly alienated. This set the stage for increased opposition and discord, which could have erupted eventually.

But the cataclysmic step of closing the institutions scattered the opposition and irrevocably committed DYS to a new approach that was more than experimental; it was definite, permanent, and all-encompassing. Thus the staff people were forced to come to terms with it or leave; they could not fight it, and they could not escape it and still remain within the department. Their brewing battles over promotions or changes in policy were suddenly rendered meaningless in light of this new change. This is how Miller was able to avoid conflict over relatively minor issues long enough to effect a change that was so revolutionary and extensive that it practically defied opposition.

Stabilizing Deinstitutionalization

Support from outside. The lobby for change was present even before Miller came to DYS. It consisted of the media, professional associations, the legislature, and other interest groups. Lacking control over these institutions, Miller's first efforts were to broaden the base of decisionmaking by bringing the public and the press into the debate. An example was Miller's policy decision to eliminate lockups.

Miller recognized that a memo to this effect would not make the change, so he publicized the decision at a series of press conferences. Shortly thereafter, in surprise visits to the institutions, he discovered that lockups were still used. A series of discussions and negotiations with individual superintendents produced a modified policy statement: lockup would be used only in extreme cases, and then only with the expressed permission of the commissioner. Thus the policy was clarified, modified, centralized, and adjusted, but became clearly the responsibility of the central office.

The press was also used to document the failures of the institutions and to dramatize the changes introduced in DYS. For example, long after Bridgewater was closed, the physical facility was used as a showplace for the media, to dramatize the plight of the youngsters who had been incarcerated there.

When Shirley had already ceased to be used as an incarcerating institution, the press and the public were invited to a ceremony to destroy the "tombs," or solitary confinement cells, which were a symbol of the old, punitive system. But most dramatic was the closing of Lyman. Attention was drawn to the fact that Lyman was the first training school in the country to open and the first to close.[29] The impressive scene of moving out all the youngsters in one day hid the fact that several programs continued on the grounds for many more months, that Lancaster was still in operation six months later, and that other institutions had been phased out prior to Lyman. (Oakdale was closed in March 1971, and Shirley was almost completely phased out by January 1972.)

Introduction of temporary transitional structures. The practice of dramatizing the changes served several purposes. It maintained the momentum for internal changes, and it attracted outside resources to make the changes possible. But foremost, the drama kept the press interested and thus the public informed. These dramatic actions created in the public mind the image of an aggressive, active, forward-moving public agency, and showed the closing of institutions to be consistent with success and progress.

Outside groups, such as ex-offenders, universities, and child welfare agencies, proved indispensable in the development of new alternatives, because they had no stake in maintaining the old system. These groups were willing and able to make decisions and take actions that DYS staff were unable and unwilling to make because of their vested interests. A perfect example is the involvement of the University of Massachusetts through the JOE II program, which made possible the closing of the Lyman School.[30] DYS staff, and especially workers from Lyman, were incapable of making a commitment to close the institutions in which they were working. They were preoccupied with developing a rationale for keeping the school open, holding on to their jobs, and thus maintaining the status quo.

It is important to note that the University of Massachusetts and other agencies provided the temporary structures necessary for the changeover from institutions to community-based programs. On the regional front, many groups, some new and private as well as public agencies, became a vital resource for the department's new community-based operations. Most of these agencies needed this new venture partly because of their dwindling resources and partly because of their desire to become involved in a new field. DYS ultimately signed contracts with only a small portion of the agencies that submitted proposals. However, the interaction with these agencies served to orient them to the functions and needs of the department, and to increase significantly the consideration given to the problems of youths in trouble throughout the state.

Change for change's sake. The philosophy of change espoused and acted upon by Miller was that change is an end in itself, and chaos and turmoil are unavoidable by-products of social change.[31] He believed that a firmly entrenched bureaucracy "can chew up reform much faster than reformers can dream up new ones."[32] This is why constant change itself is as relevant as the direct consequences of that change. The idea is that significant change can only occur within a system after the destruction of the foundation of that system. Thus destroying a system *before* creating alternatives was a characteristic mode of action for the department. Miller undertook immediately the destruction of the internal control system of the institutions, leaving the system vulnerable, confused, and searching for new controls.

The most dramatic example of the effect of this change was when the decision was made to close the institutions. Despite the confusion that this decision wrought within the bureaucracy, it did force the staff, the regional offices, and the communities to develop immediate alternatives. Thus this action shifted the responsibility from DYS to the community.

This strategy of change for change's sake allowed DYS to accomplish rapid and massive alterations, but the costs were high. Many committed and experienced staff people were unable to cope with the changes. Some left, and the turnover was costly. The quality of new services was adversely affected. Some of the programs appeared overnight without time for careful planning. Some existing programs, with no prior experience in dealing with DYS youth, suddenly had to accommodate themselves to these youngsters. The lack of management, administrative, and technical expertise within the department, furthermore, left many programs to improvise and find their own solutions.

The shift involved in moving away from institutional, fiscal management to a flexible purchase-of-care arrangement caused the administration to lag behind the services. As a consequence, newly founded programs with limited financial resources often did not receive funds for weeks. This impaired their functioning and the delivery of services.[33] Yet based on its overall effectiveness and its innovativeness, this planned-unplanned approach warrants merit and further study despite the problems it created. This is especially true since the planned change approach has long proved ineffective in dealing with entrenched bureaucracies.

Institutionalizing institutional change. Miller's main fear always was that a series of critical incidents, a major change in the political climate, or a temporary loss of public support could negate the changes that DYS had accomplished. To insure that a succeeding administration could not retreat into the old institutional pattern, several steps were taken. Some institutional properties were made available to the departments of Correction and Mental Health and to private groups. Most of them, however, were still under the administrative control of DYS. Miller also attempted to organize the private sector that is now providing care for DYS youths into an aggressive advocacy lobby for children. The danger exists, however, that this lobby can also become self-serving and too involved in maintaining its status quo.

The closing down of institutions and the gradual improvement of community alternatives proved too decisive for the forces of reaction to turn back the clock. Exercising the courage to capitalize on a fuzzy reorganization act and to set in motion and sustain the closing down of an outmoded institutional system was the most significant event in this century in the youth corrections field.

Notes

1. Jerome G. Miller, "Corrections: Reform or Retrenchment?" unpublished paper, Massachusetts Department of Youth Services, 1972, quoting from George H. Mead, " The Psychology of Punitive Justice," *American Journal of Sociology* 23 (1918):577.

2. Jerome G. Miller, "Troubled Youth in a Troubled Society," unpublished paper, Massachusetts Department of Youth Services, n.d.

3. Ibid.

4. Ibid.

5. Ibid.

6. Ibid.

7. *Recorder Gazette*, December 4, 1972; Boston *Globe*, February 4, 1970.

8. Lowell *Sun*, June 7, 1970.

9. Miller, "Troubled Youth in a Troubled Society."

10. Ibid.

11. Jerome G. Miller, "The Latent Social Function of Psychiatric Diagnosis," *International Journal of Offender Therapy* 14 (1969):148-56.

12. Jerome G. Miller, "The Politics of Change: Correctional Reform," in *Closing Correctional Institutions: New Strategies for Youth Services*, ed. Yitzhak Bakal (Lexington, Mass.: Lexington Books, D.C. Heath and Company, 1973), pp. 3-8.

13. Boston *Globe*, March 8, 1970.

14. Lowell *Sun*, June 7, 1970.

15. Barry C. Feld, "Variations of Inmate Subcultures in Juvenile Correctional Institutions" (unpublished report, Center for Criminal Justice, Harvard Law School, 1972) p. 10.

16. Boston *Sunday Globe*, March 8, 1970.

17. Harry H. Vorrath, "Positive Peer Culture: Content, Structure, and Process" (Redwing, Minn.: Minnesota State Training School for Boys, 1968).

18. For a detailed description of the self-help programs, their underlying assumptions, successes, and limitations, see David Sternberg, "Synanon House," in Norman Johnson, Leonard Savitz, and Marvin E. Wolfgang, eds., *The Sociology of Punishment and Correction* (2nd ed.: New York: Wiley, 1970).

19. Miller, "The Politics of Change: Correctional Reform," p. 6.

20. Miller, "Corrections: Reform or Retrenchment," p. 7.

21. These statistics were furnished by Harold Kramer, DYS Planning Department, January 1973.

22. *Massachusetts General Laws*, Vol. 2A, chaps. 13-23; DYS, chap. 18A, as amended by chap. 838 of the acts of 1969.

23. For a conceptual framework explaining this process, see Lloyd E. Ohlin, "Reform of Correctional Services for Youth: A Research Proposal" (unpublished paper, Center for Criminal Justice, Harvard Law School, 1970).

24. For example, out of the three group homes introduced on the grounds of Shirley School in mid-1971, two were closed a few months later ("We Care" and "Green Acres") because they had operational difficulties, such as staff conflicts, runaways, and lack of leadership. On the other hand, "I Belong" house, which proved to be successful, continued operation and moved to Lancaster Industrial School for Girls even after the institutions were closed.

25. In a statement to a senate subcommittee investigating corrections, Miller said on October 4, 1972, that correctional reform cannot happen by consensus, "although once done and sustained a consensus will begin to form."

26. *Christian Science Monitor*, February 2, 1970.

27. Boston *Globe*, May 14, 1970.

28. Most newspaper accounts described Miller as a reformer fighting an important cause.

29. This fact has been repeated in almost every report issued by DYS since the closing of institutions and is used as a public relations device.

30. Larry L. Dye, "The University's Role in Public Service to the Department of Youth Services," in Bakal, *Closing Correctional Institutions,* pp. 117-26.

31. Jerome G. Miller, "Corrections: Reform or Retrenchment," p. 15.

32. *New York Times*, January 20, 1972.

33. Boston *Sunday Herald-Traveler*, March 18, 1973, p. 46.

Part II
New Programs, New Providers, New Services

Introduction to Part II

Socialization and resocialization systems, like the school, the church, the recreation center, and the correction systems, are designed not only to impart special skills and knowledge to youngsters but also to teach the values and norms of our society. One of their major functions is to preserve the stability of the social structure by tying people into its essential normative system. The social institutions above all emphasize obedience and obeying the rules.

But in another sense, institutions project an abnormal set of values rather than a description of existing practices in society or a realistic prescription of what these youngsters are expected to face or become upon leaving the institutions. Hence there was always the paradox that the resocialization institution, by its emphasis upon maximizing certain norms in an extreme way, created additional pressures for these young people under their control. The youthful offenders are there because they cannot control themselves, yet they are placed in a pressure-cooker situation that places even more stress upon them. When they are "broken," it is often more a mechanical response to authority than internalized control. It is through these kinds of paradoxes that repressive institutions by their extreme emphasis upon conformity furnish a prototype for perpetuating deviance.

The key distinctive characteristic of the total institution is the absolute control exercised by staff over inmates. Total institutions are organizations in which there is comprehensive control over all aspects of the inmates' lives by the supervising staff. This culture is mirrored by the inmates' cells, which reproduce in microcosm among the captives the unilateral control that staff members have over them.

The correctional system was a device created to protect society, to deter potential deviants, and to reform offenders. It is now clear that the correctional institution's mandate was to perform two contradictory functions. It would isolate the deviants, retrain them, run an efficient custodial organization, control them with scarcity of resources, regard inmates as basically expendable, and at the same time rehabilitate them.

One of the fuzziest concepts of all was that of rehabilitation. Does it mean inculcating new knowledge, skills, values, character habits? These delicate changes obviously cannot be brought about by a staff primarily committed to keeping inmates in line. This role contradiction between being a guard and a "helping person" has never been resolved.

The conflict between custody and rehabilitation can never be solved in a total institution. It can only be resolved by doing away with a contradictory organization in which these two goals can only be contradictory. And here must come the realization that a more effective way to protect society is through rehabilitation and deinstitutionalization.

The training of new staff can now be done outside the rigid requirements of playing a role in an institutionalized system. There are many accounts of the effects of role on personality that have to do with dysfunctional effects of sustained work in a bureaucratic organization. Veblen referred to this process as "trained incapacity"; Dewey described it as "occupational psychosis"; and Warnotte referred to it as "professional deformation."

By removing the walls of the institution, personnel are liberated from these institutional restraints and enabled to create a role that does not depend on rigid rules and regulations. Hence staff need new kinds of knowledge, skills, and values to create a culture in which the youngsters themselves can internalize constructive roles and values.

Large organizations create specialized maintenance subsystems to keep them going. A set of supervisory roles is created whose function is to see to it that the requirements of the basic organizational roles are fulfilled both by the institutionalizers and the institutionalized. The elaboration of this sequence produces a conventional pyramid of authority in organizations, and most of the business in total institutions dealing with health and welfare is centered on problems of control. This is another reason why these organizations become increasingly inefficient and costly.

The decentralization and the small size of the child-caring agencies require much more attention to the creation of a humanistic culture, which becomes the functional equivalent of the walls and rigid rules of the large institution. The model carriers of this culture are the staff and the leaders among the staff who have created this kind of agency. Out of the disciplined interaction of staff members with each other and with the residents in the daily life of the child-caring agency, a new culture is precipitated for youngsters within which more humane values and behavior can be internalized.

This section is about the network of decentralized community-based agencies that filled the vacuum when the institutional training schools were closed in Massachusetts. This new network is obviously in transition. The primary mission of many of the agencies as perceived by their leaders furnishes only clues to their actual organizational functioning and impact upon young people.

There is a serious problem in equating the purposes and goals of organizations, programs, and services with the purposes of their leaders and workers. It is manifest that the organization as a system has an output or outcome that is not identical with the stated purposes of its functionaries. It has been our intention to by-pass that rhetoric by using direct observations of insiders of what is going on within these diverse agency settings.

It is our belief that it is important to be generous at this point concerning what these struggling organizations are accomplishing. They do not have a long history and they were created in an emergency with not the most impressive support from the Department of Youth Services. An organization is a device for accomplishing its purposes, but it is only a blueprint and must not be confused with the actual outcome of the organization.

Instead of adopting at face value the functioning and purpose as stated in official proclamations by the organization, we identify the inputs, outputs, and functioning of the organization as a system, and describe the weaknesses and strengths on a cross-system comparative basis.

The present diversity of agencies in Massachusetts working with troubled youths emphasizes "equifinality," a principle suggested by L. Von Bertalanffy, (as presented in the 1956 *Yearbook of the Society for the Advancement of General System Theory*). According to this principle a system can attain its objectives from differing initial conditions and by a variety of routes. If the goal is to help youths who are in trouble, the system—now a network of diverse services to youths—can reach this goal through a variety of modalities and services. This suggests not only that these youngsters, as well as the people working with them, differ one from another, but also that the agency structures and community-agency relationships differ.

This is not to say that there may not be underlying common characteristics. As these much more open systems and decentralized agencies move toward a more coherent and stabilized structure, and as the regulatory mechanisms to monitor their operations are refined by DYS, *the amount of diversity may indeed be drastically reduced.*

5 An Alternative Network of Services for Young Offenders: The Massachusetts Case

Strategies

Since the closing of the youth correctional institutions in the winter of 1971/72, a new system of service delivery has been emerging in Massachusetts. In this chapter we will look at six years of the Massachusetts alternative network, analyze its characteristics, describe the new alternatives, and assess the new role and future direction of DYS in caring for its detained and committed youths.

The new approach initiated three major strategies: (1) regionalization; (2) purchase of service from private agencies; and (3) community-based programming. Each approach will be discussed separately below.

Regionalization

Even before the institutions were closed, DYS officials realized there was a need for a new structure to replace the service delivery system. This structure was formed by developing seven regional offices that conform to distinct geographic areas of the state. The main task of each of these administrative units is the development of new community-based alternatives. As soon as the institutions were closed, the regional offices assumed the responsibility for contracting services and coordinating programs with other agencies and the courts. Later they became the focus of fiscal control for their regions.

Gradually the regions became more autonomous. Their proximity to, and familiarity with, local communities makes them better able to secure the best services for their youths. They are able to provide advocacy for youngsters, with their families as well as with the courts, the school system, and other state and local authorities. Most important, by their presence in the region and their visibility in the local communities and other agencies, they have proved to be an extremely important asset for advocating the community-based approach. Advocacy was accomplished by developing ties with other agencies, programs, and officials in the local communities. Initially their primary task was the development of new programs; it quickly became clear that their presence in the community was extremely helpful in diffusing apprehension about new programs.

There have been some problems with the regional system. For one thing, because the regions were set up very quickly, they lack uniformity of operation. Certain regions were able to move very rapidly in assuming control over contracting, in addition to maintaining ties with the community. Others are still trailing behind in these functions. There is a lack of uniformity in staff recruitment, training, and service contracting. Some of these differences reflect the department's interest in maintaining diversity and allowing freedom and autonomy so that each region can offer the best programs possible for its youths. Other differentiating factors include the personalities of officials, the degree of competence of those who staff various regions, the special social-political make-up of the local communities, and the resources available.

Service delivery for youths has improved measurably. The quality of services differs, however, from one region to another, and with it the impact of these programs upon the youths they are servicing. Regions with rich resources have been able to develop a diversified service delivery system. It is significant that the Harvard Center for Criminal Justice found, in its six-year study, that regions with elaborate systems of community-based services had less recidivism than those that relied more heavily on traditional programs. The seven regions also differed in the way they monitored programs. Some monitor very extensively, while others move the task completely into the hands of the providers.

Despite regional autonomy, the central DYS office can coordinate service to bring to par those regions that are lagging behind.

Purchase of Service from Private Agencies

The move from state-operated programs to the purchase-of-service model is an extremely important characteristic of the new community-based programs in Massachusetts. The purchase-of-service model is not new; it has been used extensively by the Department of Public Welfare and even DYS in the past on a very minimal basis. What is unique now is that DYS is currently using this model to service almost all the youths in its care.

In 1973, when purchase-of-service was first used in an extensive way, many programs suffered financial hardship, primarily because the department had not established the financial mechanisms necessary to transact such business on a large scale. Furthermore, many of these private agencies were not adequately prepared for the complexity of such a system. Programs with limited resources were particularly vulnerable because of the delay in payments. Many organizations lacked understanding of bureaucracy, and closed after the initial period of service delivery. Others, discouraged by the financial problems, left in disgust. Still others survived to become the cornerstones of many of the present community-based systems.

An important phenomenon of this purchase-of-service mechanism, unanticipated even by the planners of deinstitutionalization, was the availability of people with new programs willing and interested in delivery services to youths in trouble. Currently, DYS is purchasing services from more than three hundred programs, residential as well as nonresidential alternatives, educational institutions, and foster parents. All are run by private, nonprofit organizations or grassroots organizations.

Much of the fiscal crisis that DYS struggled with in the early stages of the deinstitutionalization process is over. The purchase-of-service mechanisms have been regionalized, and the procedures are working extremely well. Hardship to private vendors has lessened tremendously.

The purchase-of-service model has many advantages. First and perhaps most important is the fact that it provides advocacy. In the institutional model, youngsters in trouble had few or no advocates. The private agencies certainly can provide much better advocacy. They also have the ability to lobby, both through staff and the board of directors, for these include men and women who are generally well connected and influential in the community.

At the present time, a private group is supporting DYS in its request for increased funding from the commonwealth and other sources. Providers themselves are organizing to provide leadership for improvement in the quality of services, stressing a new ordering of priorities with regard to the commonwealth's commitment to youths in trouble. The future of the Massachusetts experience will in large measure depend upon the success of these groups in avoiding self-interest and in maintaining as their paramount goal flexible service to youths in their care. At the present time, DYS can contract out either for total programs or for individual youths. In contrast to the large institutions, which prescribe the same remedy for all youngsters, these individualized programs generally are tailored to the specific needs of each child, reflecting a varied degree of structure and different intensive-care relationships. Flexibility allows DYS to purchase services for its charges from practically any program, and to terminate programs that are found to be ineffective.

However, flexibility is not without its own problems. Improperly used, it can degenerate into a weapon that politicians and bureaucrats could use against the private vendor, destroying quality services. A case in point is the complaint by some private agencies that youths are sometimes withdrawn from programs prematurely to make space for other youngsters. Given the reality that payments are on a per-youth basis, the programs have no choice but to conform to DYS decisions or go out of business.

Keeping a good mix of programs from various agencies, while constantly cultivating new ones, is an important skill for regional DYS administrators. With fiscal control of regional spending, these administrators are planning more and more programming in coordination with the agencies and resources in their communities. At the same time they are able constantly to assess the needs of the youngsters under their care, monitor programs, and develop new resources. A useful tool to aid them in placement of funding is the range of costs per youth per week for various types of purchase-of-service care. These costs are outlined in table 5-1.

Community-Based Programming

Deinstitutionalization required the development of alternatives based in the communities from which the children came. At first the community-based alternatives envisioned were small group homes, foster homes, and other nonresidential support systems for the children and their families. It was also believed that the organizations running such programs should be grass roots in concept, and well connected in the community, in order to provide support and advocacy for the youths in its care. Today, while many programs fit that profile, others do not.

Not all programs are well connected to the local community. Some do not even know the community prior to the establishment of their programs. Certain programs are run by large, private vendors who operate in more than one region or community. Yet many DYS officials believe that these large agencies have valuable experience, resources, and technical knowledge for dealing with youths. Grass-roots organizations generally do not have this extensive knowledge. Traditional social service agencies based in the community generally lack the know-how or interest to work with acting-out, delinquent youths. Grass-roots organizations tend to be composed of young, idealistic people who have few background resources available to them; they do not have the stamina necessary to set up such programs and stick with them during the early stages of trial and error.

But community-based programs do need ties in the community, since the youths they service generally return to their own homes and original

Table 5-1
Comparative Costs of Alternatives, 1977

Type of Facility	$/Week	Type of Facility	$/Week
Psychiatric hospital	$500-$600	Intensive care	$350-$450
Boarding school	$150-$170	Foster care	$80-$100
Vocational education	$60-$80	Family counseling	$25-$35
Nonresidential	$85-$115	Group care	$160-$250

areas of residence. Programs that fail to develop ties tend to become isolated, fostering the youths' dependency on the program, slowing the process of termination, and failing to integrate the youth back into the community. Residential programs, which generally served youths from more than one region, have focused on changing attitudes and behavior. Reintegration into the community was a lesser priority. Generally, the programs have failed to become truly community-based. On the other hand, nonresidential programs have generally succeeded in becoming community-based, and have helped their youths in many areas important to their survival in the communities.

Successful community-based programs generate strong advocacy for youths in their care. And in spite of the tension such advocacy generates with courts, local schools, and social agencies, they produce many benefits for DYS-committed youths.

How the Alternatives Work

Despite the enormous variations among programs and regions, there are certain general characteristics common to all:

1. They are small and individualized rather than large and impersonal.
2. They are humane and therapeutic rather than punitive and custodial.
3. The placement process involves the youth and the family, rather than imposing a decision upon them.
4. The alternatives tend to depend upon and use resources from the community, rather than becoming self-sufficient.

Alternatives fall into the following general categories: services for the detained; residential alternatives; nonresidential alternatives; and secure units. The relative numbers of youngsters in various alternatives has changed in the past three years, as shown in table 5-2.

Table 5-2
Number of Youths in Alternative Programs, 1974 and 1977

	1974	1977
Secure detention	84	90
Foster care and shelter care detention	102	170
Group care	360	173
Foster care	227	290
Nonresidential	732	580

Detention

Services to the detained in Massachusetts improved so radically that in 1977 DYS has an array of alternative care programs completely superior to the old ones. In 1970 the quality of care in detention facilities in Massachusetts did not differ much from that in the traditional training schools. At that time DYS was operating three secure detention facilities for boys, and one for girls. These facilities held, on the average, three hundred youths. Detention was merely a holding action for the court, providing strict security. Of the approximately 6,500 youths per year who went through the detention facilities, 80 percent returned to their own communities within fifteen days. Those who returned were usually found to be on "light charges," or their cases were filed, or they were found innocent or placed on probation. Very few needed security, yet all were exposed to the maltreatment of over-crowded units, brutality, and the criminogenic and inhumane environment of detention centers.

In contrast, DYS now has seven shelter-care detention settings, which house approximately fifteen youngsters in each; foster-care detention for approximately one hundred youths, including one-to-one detention care such as the "proctor" program; and other specialized foster care emphasizing various intensities of supervision and advocacy. At the present time, secure detention does not exceed ninety youths, who are housed in four separate, small facilities. Even though they are still custodial in nature, these centers are nevertheless more humane and generally less destructive to the children than were those in the past.

The first detention alternative started on a very small scale at a YMCA serving one of the regions. It provided facilities, room and board, and a liaison staff to tie in with its programs and resources. DYS provided the clinical, professional, and line staff. Fewer youths ran away from this shelter-care facility, which was essentially an open setting, than from secure facilities like Roslindale.

To a large extent this was due to the changing manner in which DYS conceptualized the detention process. Instead of serving as strictly a holding action, detention assumed an advocacy role for the youngster who was anticipating the trauma of court appearance. This advocacy produced a great many benefits for both line staff and the youths they served. For example, at one of the facilities no youngster went to court unless accompanied by a representative from DYS who had already worked out collaborative treatment plans with the probation staff, to be effected at the time of disposition. Consequently the youth was aware that someone cared and was working with him and his family to determine the form of care most appropriate to his needs. Since line staff were utilized in this process, their role was redefined from that of a strictly custodial nature to advocacy and casework. Morale among the detention staff members rose dramatically.

As the success of the shelter-care concept was demonstrated, the idea was adopted in other regions by YMCA organizations. A cottage on the grounds of Lancaster School for Girls followed suit. Changes were, however, not without problems. One arose as the alternatives emerged and the number of youths referred to detention by the courts increased. For example, a child with a difficult family situation coming before the court would previously have been sent directly home. Now, however, the judge who wanted to create a cooling-off period had a humane option in the detention center, where the child would be treated well on a temporary basis. But the resulting involvement of more children in the juvenile justice system, with all its possibilities for negative labeling, was alarming. Increased referrals also meant spiraling costs, an unwelcome development for DYS during a period of fiscal austerity. Eventually the number of detained and referred youths stabilized as DYS's court liaison personnel were able to take advantage of the increase in court diversion programs.

Detention practices both in Massachusetts and in other states are increasingly being questioned by civil libertarians, who argue that instituting treatment programs at the detention level is more likely to deepen the children's involvement in a system that will eventually fail them. Libertarians also question the input to the courts from DYS and other social agencies. Such people believe that the court should base its decision on guilt or innocence, and not on the service needs of the child. Thus, by assuming an advocacy treatment role, DYS now finds itself on a collision course with legal and civil libertarian groups.

In addition to the use of shelter care for detention, another strategy used by DYS has been foster homes. Early experience in placing youngsters on detained status for short periods in traditional foster homes, however, revealed the complexities inherent in such placements. Since the average stay is only two weeks, detention placements admit the possibility of placing as many as fifteen youths in one foster home within the space of a single year. Then, too, traditional foster homes have difficulty relating to detained youths, who are generally restless, anxious, and even hostile. They find themselves out of their own homes without adequate preparation necessary for placement. But even when a youngster responds well to detention in a traditional foster home, a new problem arises. Since there are no built-in safeguards against the formation of an attachment between the youth and his or her foster parents, separating from that home when the detention period is over may be difficult. Finally, foster homes that are not well prepared do not work out very well.

Experience directed DYS's thinking toward a new definition of detention foster homes. New models emphasize the transitory nature of placement, and define the foster parents' role as one of youth advocate, calling them "proctors" or "mentors." The first program of this sort, called the Detained Youth's Advocates, designated the foster parents as advocates for the child. They worked with the Probation Department and school staff to assess information, and also participated in treatment decisions that affected the child's life. This program ran relatively well, especially with girls. Another innovation, the Proctor program, is run by the New Bedford Child and Family Services. This short-term, one-to-one model for detained youths calls for the constant supervision by an adult who lives and works with the youth on a twenty-four-hour basis. This and the Mentor program provide intensive supervision by adults hired to assume a role on a full-time but short-term basis, usually not more than ten weeks. Their role is different from the traditional foster parent, in that they help the child find his or her way back to school; they advocate with probation officers, assist in the search for a job, and lend support at court appearances. Advocacy for the children and their removal from the criminal justice system is the primary goal of such programs.

All these detention alternatives use shelter-care or group-care facilities as back-ups. They have a high success rate in retaining youngsters and have demonstrated, especially in the area of girls' services, that secure detention is needed only for a very few cases. It is important to point out that most shelter care for girls has failed, primarily because of the need girls have for privacy and for individual relationships. And since most girls are status offenders, a foster-home environment that is well supervised and individualized has proved to be superior to shelter care for them.

Residential Alternatives

Group care. The department's first venture into group homes started on the grounds of training schools. Several secluded cottages and housing formerly reserved for staff were used to create homelike environments. Newly hired counselors worked in combination with institutional personnel to staff these homes. Besides the training and experimentation these homes provided DYS, they dramatized to the media and the public the striking difference between institutional programs and group homes. They helped to gather support and momentum for the community-based movement. These homes and others were moved into the community through LEAA funding. Later on, the cost of running them was assumed by DYS.

With the closing of institutions, DYS began to contract with the private sector to set up alternative forms of care. Since there was little knowledge of the impact of community-based programs on the youngsters served, a course emphasizing diversity of programming and treatment modalities was pursued. Consequently DYS funded a large number of grassroots organizations. Many young, idealistic people with committed, progressive, and innovative ideas were hired.

Yet the people hired frequently lacked experience in program development and the handling of delinquent youths. DYS had no technical development capacity and was reluctant to pursue a course it feared would lower creativity and the initiative to produce new treatment alternatives. As a result, a great many of the group homes were set up with staffs that, although they could empathize well with young people, were unable to confront or to set limits. Programs that started in an extremely permissive and democratic format ended up closing or becoming authoritarian and rigid. It then became difficult to loosen rigid structures and limit-setting procedures.

As a result of these kinds of problems, DYS's romance with the group home movement cooled off considerably after the first eighteen months of experience. Tension developed between DYS and the line personnel over the length of time youngsters should stay in group homes. Originally DYS set three to four months as the period within which the child should be reintegrated into the community. In addition to the obvious budgetary considerations, DYS believed that longer stays would create dependency, which would interfere with reintegration. On the other hand, the group home personnel, mostly inexperienced in dealing with delinquent youths, tended to avoid taking the risk of bringing in new children who might destroy the balance and rapport established within the group homes. Consequently, they tended to hold on to the children placed with them for an average of about ten months.

Many group homes became disillusioned with the purchase-of-care mechanism. There were essentially no start-up funds. Payments were slow, and on a per-capita basis. Such funding procedures squeezed the vendors between the need to establish programs and culture slowly within the home on the one hand, and the need to take on enough youngsters to survive fiscally.

Finally, most group homes are community-based only inasmuch as the facility is within a community. They are frequently isolated and insulated. Programs looked very much in on themselves and failed to look outside at the resources of the community. This attribute fostered a great deal of dependency by the youths, and contributed to their difficulties with the termination process and reintegration into their communities. Stiff community opposition through zoning ordinances has sometimes shut group homes out altogether. Those that have been able to establish themselves have kept a low profile, avoiding critical incidents through an intake policy that eliminated high-risk youths. The group homes gradually became not only isolated from the community, but unresponsive to the department's needs, as well.

Despite these problems, residential programs are still being used by DYS, accounting for approximately one-quarter of all placements. Furthermore, there are several highly skilled vendors now providing a good quality of service. They vary in form, but can generally be grouped in four categories, as detailed below.

1. *Traditional group homes* provide services for youths who are in need of a structured environment. Housing between ten and fifteen youngsters each, these homes provide individual counseling and some group counseling. They rely heavily on community resources. The young people placed in traditional group homes either go to local schools or hold regular jobs. Although a large percentage of DYS-committed youths were placed in these homes immediately after the closing of institutions in Massachusetts, currently only a very small number of youngsters are in group settings.

Group homes are especially valuable for youths who are stabilized and can respond to group living. One such program is housed in a family-type structure north of Boston. The staff for the ten youngsters consists of a live-in couple, a set of relief parents and another relief person for weekends, two additional counselors, a tutor, and two practicum students. Group counseling focuses on the problems of daily living. Family visits are encouraged, but there is no family counseling component. The program seems to be successful in stabilizing youngsters who cannot function effectively in their own homes, in spite of the fact that there is no individual counseling.

2. *Therapeutically oriented homes* provide individual, family, and group treatment. They tend to have in-house programming for education, art, and other types of training, which they provide in a therapeutic milieu. Such programming puts a great deal of emphasis on group techniques. It uses a staff composed of former clients, plus a resident hierarchy structure with professional supervision. The group and community meetings stress reality therapy, with a very limited use of drugs and psychiatric back-up. Participation is generally of one- to two-years' duration. The level system is used to reinforce attitudinal change and encourage new patterns of behavior. This program has had difficulty retaining unmotivated youngsters, and generally does not accept those who run away.

3. *Modified concept houses* are designed for youths who have a pattern of drug or alcohol use requiring strong confrontation. These houses are effective with certain youngsters, but their confrontation style of therapy causes many to run away. Because certain concept houses were accused of brutality, some were closed by DYS. Again, a restrictive intake policy tends to limit the number of clients they admit.

4. *Residential schools* are basically boarding schools set up in a cottage-style facility. Since they are well structured, they are geared to meet the needs of the acting-out youth. DYS placements generally comprise only a very small percentage of the students in these facilities, but the DYS youngsters fit in well. Counseling in such schools is minimal, and most youngsters need continued support and counseling from DYS. A major advantage to placement in residential schools is that there is little or no stigma attached to attendance.

Foster care. In the early stages of deinstitutionalization, DYS attempted to run its own foster-care programs. Since individual regions lacked expertise in home-finding and the screening and training of foster parents, foster-home programs proved inadequate, or quickly deteriorated for lack of support. Gradually DYS drew upon established social agencies that had experience with foster care. These agencies modified their approach for DYS youths as they learned to serve this special population.

First, it became evident that foster parent recruitment must attract people who can tolerate adolescent rebellion. Further, there is a need to provide support, training, and continuous supervision for foster parents. Finally, day programs must be provided for youths from foster homes, who should not be left to the twenty-four-hour responsibility of their foster parents.

Despite the high rate of attrition, foster care has become an important alternative for youths who need to leave their home environment. It permits an individualized approach, free of stigma. Since it does not face all the bureaucratic entanglements, health requirements, and zoning regulations that confront group care, foster home programs are easy to implement. The number of youths in such placements has been increasing steadily. Today in some regions, such care accounts for one-third of all youth placements.

Nonresidential Care

Initially, nonresidential care—working with youths while they live at home—was used as a form of aftercare rather than as an alternative to residential care. Ater it became evident that this form of care was effective in working with children as an alternative to residential placement, a more structured program began. The nonresidential program has many advantages. It supports the ideal of working with a child in his own community, rather than separating him from home. It emphasizes survival skills, rather than therapy and custody. It manipulates the environment for the benefit of the youngster, and generally provides structure, supervision, and sanctions for the child's behavior within his own community setting. Nonresidential programming emphasizes job placement, remedial educational skills, family counseling, and advocacy. Bureaucratic difficulties, including rate-setting, zoning, public health, and public safety issues that plague residential programs, do not apply to nonresidential programs. It is relatively low in cost, stigma free, and in many ways is more effective than other forms of care for children who have viable home situations.

It was simple to regionalize nonresidential care. Unlike residential alternatives, it is easy to monitor and control by the regions, who develop alternatives tailored to their needs. The number of youths in nonresidential alternatives has been consistently high (see table 5-1).

In spite of its success, nonresidential care proved to be the most controversial for two reasons. First, placing the child in his own community directly after a court decision to commit him brings a public outcry. Unlike institutions, which at least separate the youth from his community even if they fail to treat him, nonresidential care puts the child back into the community immediately after his commitment to DYS. Any new offense, particularly within the first month of treatment, angers the courts and police, and leads to charges that DYS is in fact failing to provide treatment for youths committed to their care. If it has no immediate impact upon the youth's behavior, nonresidential care essentially renders court and police action ineffective. To this segment of the criminal justice system, nonresidential programs imply that law and order are breaking down, and that juvenile delinquency is allowed to ravage uncontrolled.

Second, advocacy for the youth in the community places new demands on institutions such as the schools and social and health agencies, which also generally prefer to have such disruptive young people removed from their purview. Since many traditional agencies in local communities do not even accept the concept of community care, they become another source of criticism of nonresidential care.

From the department's point of view, nonresidential care is being used effectively by the various regions in diversified programming. Traditional counseling programs emphasize weekly contact with the youths and their families. They provide advocacy for the youths in the courts, local school systems, and other institutions within the community. Alternative education programs provide a setting for many DYS youths who cannot function in regular school systems. A variety of programs fit into this category, emphasizing environmental education, field trips, one-to-one tutoring, and small-group counseling. An example of such programs is the Experiential Learning Program (see chapter 6).

Federally funded programs such as CETA and neighborhood youth corporations are available to some DYS-committed youths. Other programs funded by DYS provide job training, counseling, job placement, and stipends. These programs, which are flexible enough to change placements in mid-stream when they have proved unworkable for a youth, have proved to be quite successful in introducing youths to the job market. Other programs designed to provide intense supervision for those youths who need more structure than a regular counseling program can provide are commonly designated as "tracking" programs. The "tracker" spends approximately three days a week with each youngster in his or her charge. For chronic runaways and children who lack impulse control, such supervision can be quite successful.

Secure units. Services for hard-core youths who need locked-up facilities were the most controversial aspect of the Massachusetts experience. The priorities of Jerome Miller and the planners of reform were deinstitutionalization and the development of community-based programs. Services for the hard-core violent youths who require security were ignored. No well-thought-out strategy or plan had been developed, even after the institutions were closed. This lack of action was defended on the basis that locked-up settings easily deteriorated into institutions that could be misused by the department and the courts.

There was disagreement in the department as to who the hard-core youths were, and what kinds of treatment and programming they required. Those who criticized the reforms felt very strongly that a high percentage of DYS youths needed secure settings. On the other hand, Miller and his associates felt equally strongly that the number of youths in this category did not exceed 5 percent of the total DYS population. And there was disagreement as to whether such programs should be run by the department or contracted out.

Once the institutions were closed, it became evident very quickly that a certain number of boys—about thirty—needed immediate secure confinement. These youngsters had long records of previous institutionalization or long histories of violent crimes, or both. To answer their needs, a program was hastily put together and contracted out to a local psychiatric institution. This program, called Andros, pointed up DYS's lack of knowledge about hard-core elements, and the contractor's naivete and inexperience in working with such children resulted in problems.

Besides Andros, two other detention facilities, each accommodating approximately twenty-five youngsters, were developed as secure treatment programs. Although Andros operated for a certain period of its existence with some effectiveness, it and the two other programs eventually failed. Among other things, no adequate intake process was established to determine which children really needed secure treatment, so there was constant pressure on the facilities to accept more youths than the programs were planned for.

All of the programs used the therapeutic community concept, emphasizing the level system and the gradual increase of freedom with responsibility. In some cases, because of the lack of skill of the staff, this system was easily manipulated by the children, who demoralized and eventually destroyed the program. Also, the programs suffered from numerous runs, which challenged their credibility with the courts and other agents of the criminal justice system.

Lack of credible secure facilities invited strong criticism from law enforcement officials and jeopardized the entire process of reform. A good portion of the criticism was diffused by the newly appointed commissioner, John A. Calhoun, when, in April 1976, he convened a task force composed of both conservatives and liberals, and charged this committee with the development of recommendations and guidelines for secure facilities. The task force conducted a study which concluded that DYS requires secure settings for about a hundred and fifty youngsters, or approximately 11 percent of the total population in the charge of the department. Ninety of these youngsters need detention; the remaining sixty are in need of treatment. In addition, the task force called for the recognition of intensive secure settings as part of, rather than separate from, the spectrum of commmunity-based programs. It stressed the need to keep these hard-core facilities small in size and heavily programmed.

Currently, DYS has contracted out several secure programs. These are generally small (up to fifteen beds), and while they have more programs than the institutions ever had, they are still custodial in nature.

DYS has also developed an elaborate intake system that insures that youths will not be haphazardly placed in secure facilities. Such placements require agreement by several people on a special board. In addition, youths must have had prior placement experience and an up-to-date clinical study before they can be turned over to an intensive-secure program.

Most of the programming lacks coherent treatment philosophies; none has an aftercare component. The relationship with the community-based program system is not defined, and in most cases they are isolated from the community. Several more units are planned, with increased attention to the idea of aftercare for the youths sent to such a program.

Despite the lack of progress in this area, the department's credibility in holding on to the young people who need secure custody has improved tremendously. Under the leadership of Calhoun, there have been few (if any) runs, while the number of youths in these programs has been kept to a minimum. Table 5-3 presents a breakdown of slots utilized by one of the regions, which has approximately three hundred youths in its care.

Conclusions

The new community-based programs in Massachusetts are clearly superior to the old institutional system. They are diversified, individualized, easier to monitor, and more responsive to the needs of the children in the charge of DYS. One of the most important, yet unanticipated, results of this system is the increased input and control the youth and his or her family can exercise within the system. Most placement decisions in the community-based programs involve the youth and the family. Unless a young person is being held on a severe charge, or has been a chronic repeater of serious offenses, his or

Table 5-3
One Region's Use of Alternatives, 1977
(number of youths)

Residential		Nonresidential	
Forestry and outward bound	6	Jobs	30
Group homes	30	Educational/vocational	30
Detention shelter care	50	Tracking	40
Boarding school	10	Outreach counseling	30
Foster care	70		
Secure settings	20		

her prior consent to the placement is sought. Programs that fail to meet the needs of the youths placed in them cannot stay in business. The purchase-of-service model allows parents and youths to have an impact on programs for the first time in the history of juvenile corrections. Those programs that suffer frequent runs are generally closed. Consumerism is becoming a factor in an area that traditionally has been dominated by an authoritarian approach.

The Massachusetts experience in community-based programming indicates that no single set of alternatives is the answer. The move from institutions to groups homes, to foster homes, and thence to nonresidential settings demonstrates the need for flexibility and responsive programming. The new regional system emphasizes the need for alternatives to meet different requirements and different stages. Most of the community programs are currently being stabilized and professionalized, setting higher standards of operation and service delivery. The question is whether these structures will become as rigid in the future as was the old institutional system in the past. Stronger community involvement can be a good buffer against this eventuality.

Appendix 5-A presents data for the operation of the various programs run by DYS from 1974 to 1978.

Appendix 5A
Massachusetts Data

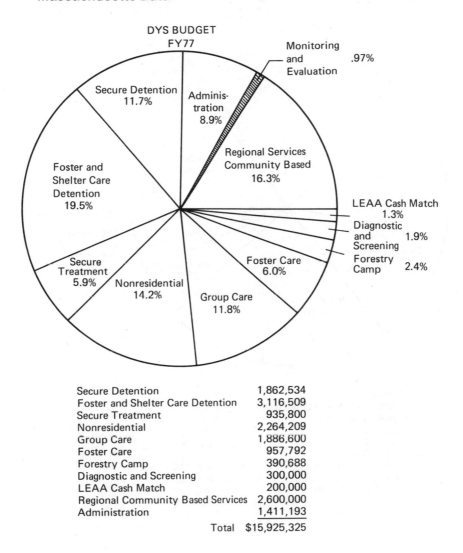

Figure 5A-1. DYS Budget, 1977 and 1978.

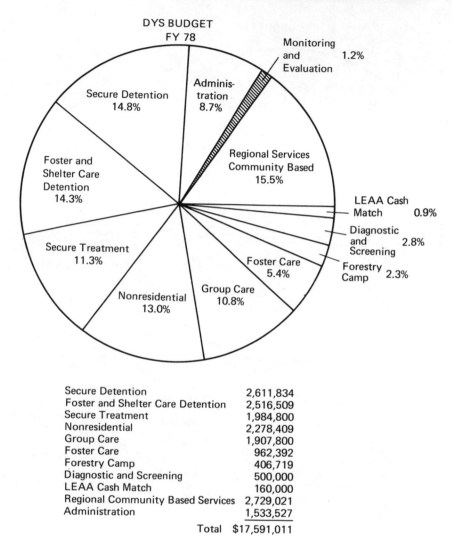

DYS BUDGET
FY 78

Secure Detention	2,611,834
Foster and Shelter Care Detention	2,516,509
Secure Treatment	1,984,800
Nonresidential	2,278,409
Group Care	1,907,800
Foster Care	962,392
Forestry Camp	406,719
Diagnostic and Screening	500,000
LEAA Cash Match	160,000
Regional Community Based Services	2,729,021
Administration	1,533,527
Total	$17,591,011

Fig. 5A-1. *(Cont.)*

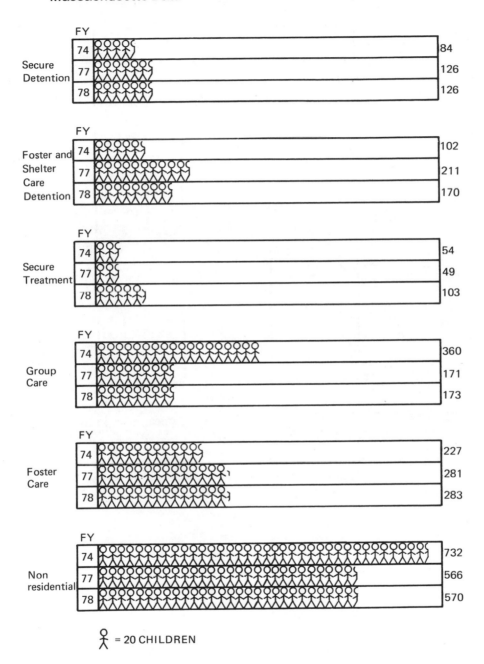

Figure 5A-2. Number of DYS Children Served in an Average Day in Six Categories of Care.

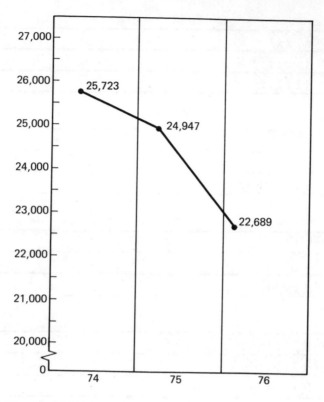

Figure 5A-3. Total Number of Juvenile Court Appearances in Massachusetts, 1974-1976.

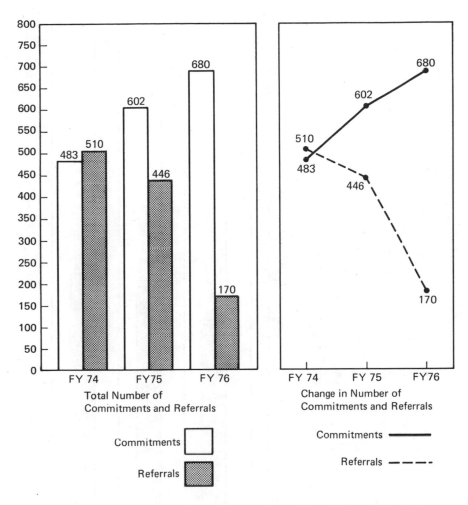

Figure 5A-4. Commitments and Referrals by DYS, 1974-1976.

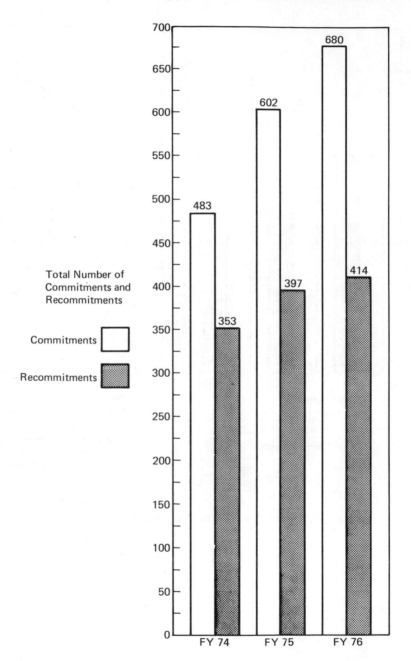

Figure 5A-5. Total Number of Commitments and Recommitments by DYS, 1974-1976.

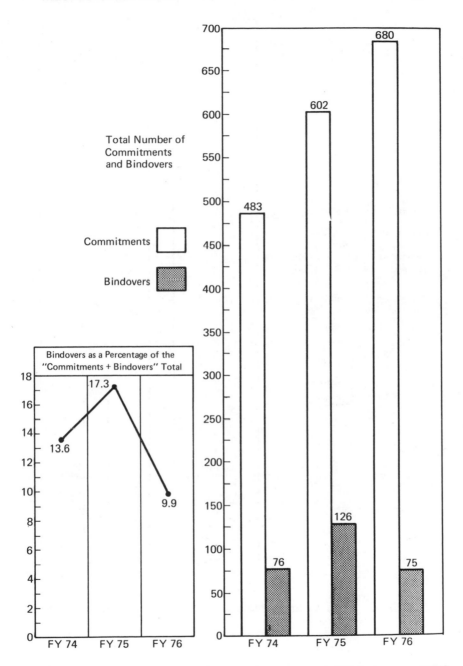

Figure 5A-6. Total Number of Commitments and Bindovers to DYS, 1974-1976.

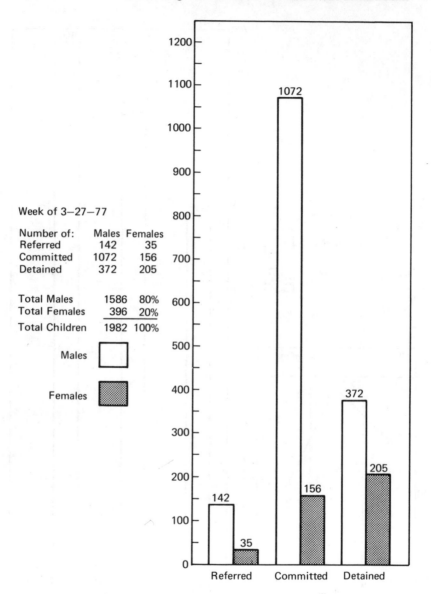

Figure 5A-7. Commitments to DYS during Typical Week, 1977.

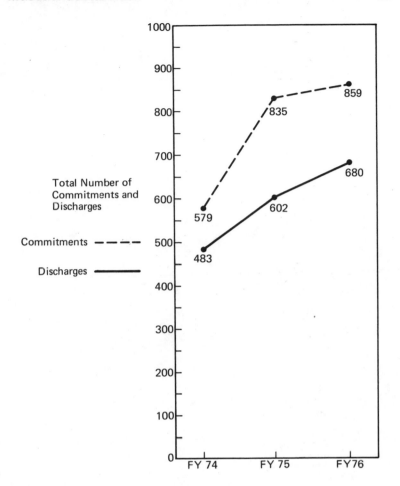

Figure 5A-8. Total Number of Commitments and Discharges by DYS, 1974-1976.

6 An Innovative Education Model for Troubled Youths: The Experiential Learning Program

Traditional educational and job-training programs have been ineffective in their efforts to work with youthful offenders to the point that a negative school experience has been observed to be an important factor contributing to delinquent behavior. Frustration and failure lead to bitterness and anger, and the youthful offender's first antisocial behavior typically is directed toward school.

Even progressive special-education programs within the traditional system, set up in recognition of the widespread existence of special needs in the school population, usually exclude at least one category of student—the delinquent who exhibits violent, destructive, and disruptive behavior in and out of the classroom. As the school rejects the delinquent, the delinquent in turn rejects the school and is left without the basic educational tools so necessary for success in our society.

Traditional job-training programs have had similar experiences in dealing with delinquent youths. Unable to cope with the demands of the program, such a young person reacts with negative behavior or poor attendance. The program then labels the student as a failure, and the mutual rejection process is started. The potential for learning is lost in the struggle.

The failure of traditional programs is to a large extent due to their inability to individualize the program of each student in order to address the individual's specific needs. Without individualized programs, students who have needs beyond those addressed by a limited educational program are often unable to succeed. The problem is complicated by scapegoating, labeling, and rejection by the traditional institutions, which in turn compounds the student's failure. Frustrated in attempts to succeed in socially acceptable channels, such students are likely to intensify their acting-out behavior as a means to achieve status and recognition within the negative identity that is imposed upon them.

Traditional programs generally fail to be comprehensive enough in scope, focusing instead on limited performance goals, either academic or vocational. A strong case could be made for the fact that all students need programs to meet their emotional, psychological, and everyday living needs, but for delinquents this is particularly true because of environmental factors, and especially true for children from families that do not provide the basic feelings of security necessary for growth in these areas. Programs that do not take a comprehensive approach are therefore destined to fail,

87

and delinquents fall short not only in meeting performance criteria of the educational institutions but in the larger society as well.

Successful alternative programs for youthful offenders therefore must be both individualized and comprehensive. Individualization requires that intensive evaluation of each student takes place, and the process must involve the student as much as possible in assessing his or her own needs. Rather than establishing a program into which each student is required to fit, programs must be willing to deal with each person as a separate entity and tailor each program accordingly. By taking this approach, not only is the program able to develop goals and means to attain them that are reality-based, but each student is put into a situation where success is measured in terms of individual achievement rather than in relation to the performance of others. In this way a student who must contend with major environmental handicaps can succeed on realistic terms. The problem of failure generating a negative self-image and loss of esteem can thus be for the most part eliminated.

Flexibility is another important characteristic for a successful alternative education program. This includes the necessity of individualization and then of being open to revision of the student's particularized program. Programs must avoid the trap of establishing an approach, setting goals, and then sticking with them even though they are not working. By being both individualized and flexible, a program can work continually with the student as he or she really is, instead of as that person was hypothesized to be. This will ensure that effort and motivation, not handicaps or liabilities, are determining factors for success.

Students in this situation are able to have real control over whether or not they succeed, regardless of their background. Being able to experience success is the primary means for one to establish a positive self-image as an achieving person, which is a prerequisite for constructive and responsible life decisions.

Individualization and flexibility in a comprehensive program are essential, but other factors are necessary, as well, to ensure that a program has direction and focus. Delinquent youths typically lead lives devoid of the structure necessary for educational development. Disorganized or scattered families, lack of appropriate adult role models, and school situations in which the youngster cannot find a place except in a negative sense, combine to produce a confused individual who is unable to postpone gratification, lacks self-direction, and views authority as arbitrary and threatening. It is thus imperative that alternative education for these youths include both firmly set limits that can be readily understood, as well as intensive supervision. Participation by the student, not only in establishing his or her program, but also in monitoring progress, is an important ingredient if the young offender is to make sense of experiences and start to develop a sense of internal structure and control over life.

Staff people working with youthful offenders must be willing to become honestly involved with them in order to instill trust as people the students can rely upon. The staff must not be afraid to set limits and firmly abide by them. They must have a sense of solidarity among themselves so that students cannot manipulate and play one off against the other as a means of avoiding the necessary acceptance of responsibility for their own actions and growth.

Staff people in traditional settings tend to fear delinquents, and to reject them on the basis of their unacceptable behavior. In a successful program the staff must be composed of people who are not afraid of the students and who will not be coerced by them. They must accept the students as worthwhile human beings even while refusing to condone the negative aspects of their behavior. Those who work with delinquents have to avoid a trap here: the possible tendency to become concerned exclusively with the overt portions of the student's behavior, acting out or not acting out. The worker must be aware that the students are complex human beings and that delinquent youths are basically a lot more like "normal" youths than they are unlike them. Staff members who are genuinely involved with the students will not fail to attend to the full range of their needs, interests, and behaviors.

Supervision. Intensive supervision is necessary to maintain a high degree of accountability on the part of the student, for this is an important motivational tool. Workers who provide the supervision must be willing to confront students on their shortcomings in the areas of cooperation and effort, and this must be done in such a way that consistently reinforces the concept that each student as an individual will succeed by trying his best. Close supervision also ensures that improvements and achievements will be noticed and reinforced. Delinquent students generally have difficulty giving themselves credit for their accomplishments until they have experienced positive feedback on numerous occasions. In fact, their criminal or disruptive behavior is for the most part a means for them to get attention instead of being ignored, and this pattern can best be broken by a focus on the positive.

Communication. For an education program to be comprehensive, covering a broad range of goals, and still be effective and focused, it must be clearly thought-out and well rounded. Staff members must work closely together and plan carefully. Communication among staff members is as important as between staff and students. Goals must be established for the program and for the individuals involved, and each component of the program needs to be developed and planned with those goals in mind.

Alternative teaching methods. The needs of the students are diverse, complex, and interrelated. A narrow, isolated approach will not succeed because of the interrelation of numerous areas of development, many of which are likely to be impaired in members of a delinquent population. Since traditional classroom methods have produced failure and unhappiness for these youths, and their life styles tend to be action-oriented rather than passive or verbal, they generally have active learning styles as well. Hence an alternative program for them should encompass an active, experiential approach.

Adolescents in general tend to identify closely with their peers, adopting their subgroup's values and style of behavior, often to the consternation of parents and other adults. For delinquent youths, whose rejection of adult authority is much more complete, the identification with the peer subgroup tends to be even stronger and to have much more seriously negative consequences, since criminal exploits are held in high regard. A successful program cannot ignore or minimize peer pressure, but instead must attempt to neutralize or turn it in a positive direction.

Group methods. Use of the group process can effectively take advantage of peer pressure if intensively regulated by staff to see that it is being applied toward appropriate ends. Development of a sense of belonging, as well as group investment in and responsibility for the success of the program and individuals within it, should be cultivated. At the same time, any formalized hierarchy within the group must be avoided, since this has been shown to produce brutality and failure among weaker members. Equality and shared responsibility should be encouraged at every turn, but it must be clear that the staff is running the program.

The Experiential Learning Program (ELP) of the Northeastern Family Institute, headquartered in Danvers, Massachusetts, is an alternative program based on these principles. The ELP presently works with sixteen youths, male and female, placed by the Massachusetts Department of Youth Services after commitment by the courts. Almost all the students live in foster homes in the Salem area. All failed in public school and either dropped out or were expelled and never returned. The students range from fifteen to seventeen years of age and all have somewhat lengthy court records, mostly for stealing cars, breaking and entering, larceny, and assaults. For the most part students who enter the ELP are severely lacking in basic educational skills and motivation to learn, and are likely to be still active in delinquent activities when placed.

The ELP has not yet been in existence long enough to accumulate solid data about its success. It is certain, however, that this program has been able to keep its students and that education is taking place, neither of which happened with these youths in their previous traditional setting. Beyond this there are individual success stories about those who have been able to make substantial changes in their behavior, with the ELP as at least one of the major factors. Some of these students have gone on to succeed in jobs or in the United States armed forces, while others who have done very well continue in the program as workers.

The ELP provides vocational training at job-training sites, and also has a broad educational program. Education is viewed as a process of helping youngsters to make decisions about their lives in a constructive and responsible manner. Self-sufficiency through the exercise of control over their lives and their environment is the basic goal for all ELP students. The program includes job training, weekly field trips, individual tutoring, small-group learning experiences in various subject areas, group meetings, and individual counseling. Intensive supervision is provided by counselors, and weekly individual evaluation sessions are held for each student. Students may earn up to $40 per week as a stipend for participation in all required components, half for working and the other half for the balance of the program.

After being referred and placed in the ELP, an extremely important planning period takes place for each new student. Staff members work with the youth to determine what interests he or she has, and they then jointly formulate an individual plan. The student is helped to make a commitment to the plan, and the need to assume responsibility for making decisions is stressed. Once the plan is formulated, the student is held responsible for either meeting its conditions or participating in the process of making changes in it. Because the planning process is complicated and dynamic, the student typically attempts to leave decisions and responsibility in the hands of the staff. This, of course, is resisted.

The individualized program that is developed is geared toward building the student's self-esteem and self-confidence by providing educational and vocational tasks at which the individual can succeed. Positive aspects of behavior are emphasized in order to begin the development of a new, positive identity. A curriculum consisting mainly of basic life skills is also drawn up at this time.

Because each student's program plan is developed on an individual basis through a process in which the student directly participates, and the possibility of revising the learning contract is always present, the ELP provides the flexibility necessary to tailor each program to meet the individual youngster's needs. The youth's achievements are judged in light of individual capacities, using self-evaluation devices whenever possible. These factors are intended to help the student form a sense of personal responsibility and to avoid competition between individuals of disparate achievement levels, which could perpetuate the stigma of failure for those on the lower levels of ability.

Recognizing the need for an educational program to be comprehensive in scope, particularly when dealing with a population that requires intervention to help correct problems in a number of developmental areas, the ELP curriculum is aimed at meeting six categories of individual learning needs: (1) cognitive; (2) affective; (3) life or survival skills; (4) volitional; (5) moral; and (6) aesthetic. There is considerable overlapping among the six areas, which further necessitates considering all of them in establishing educational plans.

In the area of cognitive development, the ELP not only is concerned with the need for learning basic skills in reading, mathematics, and language arts, but also emphasizes the relationship of these skills to the student's own environment, survival in that environment, and potential for achieving future goals. Other work in the cognitive area includes efforts to enlarge the capacity to think, analyze, and understand various phenomena that are important in the student's life. Reading newpapers and help-wanted listings, budgeting, going shopping, and using road maps to plan automobile trips are examples of techniques used to bring cognitive learning into the practical realm.

Individual tutoring is the basic method used in cognitive educational work. This provides for a maximum degree of individualization in an area where differences among students are great and where resultant self-consciousness in a group setting could present serious barriers to participation. Small learning groups are also employed in appropriate subjects and with students who are functioning at a somewhat higher level in that particular area. Some examples include creative writing, current events, and intermediate mathematics, all conducted in groups of five or less and selected by students who have some degree of competence in reading or mathematics. Materials of high interest are used whenever possible, and some innovative variations have been utilized. For example, products of creative writing classes have been typed and then used as reading material for those who are working to improve their basic skills in reading.

Most delinquent youths have had deficient or negative affective or emotional training, mainly due to inadequate parenting. Shortcomings here can block progress and learning of any sort. Thus, affective development is a central aspect of the ELP program. The ELP helps students learn to relate, to give and take, and to handle their feelings effectively, as well as the feelings of others toward them. This component is carefully designed to help the youths in the following essential areas:

1. Fostering a more positive self-image through experiencing certain successes in learning.
2. Learning to identify personal assets and potentials.
3. Learning to interact with others with an awareness of one's impact on others as well as the impact on oneself.
4. Learning about family dynamics and the impact of family members on each other.
5. Developing the capacity for intimacy and sharing.

A variety of program components is designed to assist students achieve gains in the affective area. Regular small-group meetings deal with person-to-person relationships, and supplementary, spontaneous group meetings are held when deemed necessary and appropriate. Expression of emotions in nonviolent and nondestructive ways is encouraged. Groups are used for teaching and using transactional analysis to examine how people can act and react to one another in varying ways with different results. Value-clarification exercises to demonstrate that individuals' values and beliefs differ, and to analyze group reactions to those differences, are also used. Role-playing, drama, and psychodrama are used in these groups and in other learning groups to encourage self-expression and to teach a better understanding of the feelings of others. The ELP regularly uses videotaped sessions to preserve role-playing and drama exercises, and to allow students to observe themselves as others see them.

Individual counseling plays an important part in the affective area of the ELP as students experience continual contact with an assigned counselor as well as with other staff members. A personal relationship is established through exposure to a great variety of situations: educational and vocational field trips; group meetings; program planning; evaluation sessions; learning sessions; visits to job sites; preparation for and advocacy in court; meetings with foster and natural families; and informal activities—all in addition to individual counseling sessions and crisis intervention.

Students know their counselors as real people, and trust can be developed, often a new feeling for this group of youths in their experiences with adults. The counselor becomes a powerful role model, and the counselor's affective skills influence the behavior of students with whom the counselor works. Youths also can feel confident in verbalizing their feelings, and know that staff members are available at all times if they need someone with whom to discuss any concern whenever it arises.

Survival or life skills are the sum total of all the skills one needs to understand cognitively and relate on an affective basis to one's environment. One must set personal goals and carry them out within accepted roles in society. Job sites for the practice of vocational skills are a major tool in the development of a most important survival skill—the ability to earn a living—ideally while doing work that is satisfying.

The ELP curriculum also helps students to identify and understand the workings of all institutions that are important to them in their immediate environment, such as banks, courts, jails, social service agencies, schools, and government. Survival skills that are even more basic and routine in nature are also considered to be very important. Students are taught to use public transportation; to maintain acceptable standards of personal hygiene, grooming, and dental care; consumer skills; cooking and nutrition; and the dangers of alcohol and drugs. In essence, survival skills involve the mechanics of survival in the immediate environment and in society. Adequately equipped with these skills, one can make one's way in the world; without them, one is unable to gain control over one's own life.

The methodologies utilized in achieving success in the survival skills include every component of the ELP. Skills in personal habits are an ongoing subject and are monitored continually by each counselor. Field trips include visits to, and learning about, various institutions. On the job sites the youths learn not only important vocational skills, but also work habits, such as punctuality, following directions, relating to supervisors and fellow employees, and cultivating self-motivation. Special group learning experiences are conducted with specific survival-skill goals. An example of this was a series done for all ELP students on the legal system, which included discussions with a probation officer, a film and discussion on juvenile corrections, and some mock trials in which students played a number of different roles—judge, witness, prosecutor, defense attorney, arresting officer, defendant, and counselor/advocate.

In the volitional skill training, the intent is to help the student plan something and initiate action to carry it out. This capacity requires the ability to have a sense of an attractive personal future. It is also based on experiencing a certain amount of success, as well as learning how to endure hardship, to postpone immediate gratification, and to tolerate frustration. Through a well-designed, individualized approach to learning, students in the ELP experience certain amounts of frustration and pressure without going beyond their limits. The emphasis, again, is on helping people experience success by establishing individual goals rather than subjecting them to anxiety-producing competitiveness. A specific example of volitional education is helping students establish and maintain a savings account.

Moral education is directed toward helping the student to understand rules, the need for them, and that they are shared by the group and society to which the student belongs. Developing a system of ethics and an understanding of one's personal values is also encouraged in the ELP. This is carried out by the establishment and enforcement of easily understood rules of conduct within the program and through value-clarification exercises. Students who commit illegal acts, whether they are arrested or not, face sanctions within the program, which involve extra work, temporary loss of good standing and their stipend payments, plus discussions and written assignments in which they must examine moral and ethical aspects of their actions.

The final area of education the ELP stresses is aesthetic. Here the program provides exposure to and training in art, music, photography, drama, and athletics. The goals include developing interests in positive leisure-time pursuits and providing further avenues for self-expression.

Examples from the ELP program. Each youth's program provides a degree of balance. Students generally work at their jobs for approximately 15 hours per week. An educational or vocational field trip is scheduled every week to support achievement in as wide a variety of goals as possible. Group meetings and individual evaluation sessions are held weekly, as are individual tutoring and various group learning sessions, such as photography, creative writing, current events, mathematics, and a newsletter project. Classes at a local karate school, where self-discipline and physical fitness are emphasized in addition to self-defense, are offered twice a week. An art program and videotape studio session are usually held on alternating weeks. In order to achieve real individualization, an array of combinations is used and a great amount of variation established within some of the components, particularly at the job sites and in individual tutoring.

One female student we will call Ruth has been in the program for three months and is involved in a typical schedule, but one that is tailored to her particular needs. On Mondays she has her weekly evaluation session for about half an hour in the morning. In the afternoon she has a two-hour creative writing class with three other students, then attends a karate class for two hours in a group of nine. Tuesdays she goes on the weekly field trip, which ranges from three hours to all day. She works at a clothing store Wednesday through Thursday from 9:30 a.m. to 1:30 p.m. (Friday she stays until 3:30). After work on Wednesday she attends her hour-and-a-half weekly group meeting with six others, followed by an individual tutoring session of similar length, where she works mostly on basic math, her weakest subject. Thursday afternoons she is involved in either two hours of art or a videotape session with six other students, followed by karate, this time a one-hour class. Ruth keeps a simple journal and has started a savings account. She sees her counselor several times a week, mostly in an informal setting, such as riding home with him at the end of the day. She participates in periodic family meetings at her foster home. Ruth has some motivation for academics and would like to take the GED test for a high school diploma when she is eighteen.

A male student we will call Maurice has been in the program for almost a year, and his schedule has evolved to a somewhat different balance. He is primarily interested in learning a trade, and has had four job placements. His current job is with a plumber, and he has held it for three months. Maurice is very much delayed in cognitive development and is self-conscious about it. He tried karate for five weeks, off and on, and decided that he did not like it. On Monday he has his evaluation session in midmorning, then works from 11 to 4. Tuesday he goes on a field trip, and Wednesday he works from 8 to 1:30 and on Fridays from 8 to 5. After work on Wednesday he attends his weekly group meeting, and after a break he has individual tutoring in the evening, working on basic literacy skills.

Thursday mornings he has another hour and a half of tutoring, in the same subject area, followed by a photography session with one other student. Maurice sees his counselor often throughout the week, and he also participates in periodic family meetings. His journal is basic—a list of his ELP hours each day with a comment as to whether they were good or bad. Maurice would like either to be a plumber or to enlist in the Army when he is old enough and can pass the entrance test.

Frank's situation is somewhat different. He is extremely immature and unable to handle any frustration or group situations. He attends evaluation sessions and has individual tutoring in basic math and reading on Monday. On Tuesday he occasionally goes on a field trip. Wednesday afternoon he works for three hours in a shop, tearing down electronic appliances from 11 to 2. Then he sees a volunteer, usually for recreational activity. Thursday mornings a tutor goes to his house and either takes him out or stays there to work on a project, such as simple art work or photography. Fridays he works another three hours. Frank has not been able to last in a foster home and is awaiting a placement that is suitable for him. His counselor goes to his home twice a week to meet with Frank and his mother. Although he has never reached full participation in the ten months he has been in the program, Frank has been retained in the program and has been able to experience some success and continuity. He has made certain advances in the socialization process and is now seen as standing a better chance of avoiding institutionalization. Frank has not been in trouble with the law since entering the program, his longest crime-free period in many years.

Job sites are required to provide on-the-job supervision and training. Vocational interests are explored as a part of the planning phase for each youth, after which an appropriate site is either drawn from those already available or is sought out by ELP staff. Since employers do not have to pay students placed with them, finding appropriate sites has not been overly difficult. Placement is based primarily on the youngster's interest, and exposure to actual job conditions in a particular field has been in itself most valuable. Many students' interest in a field wanes once they experience it, but this is not considered by staff as a failure. Instead, students are encouraged to see it as a learning experience, and then to try something else. Conversely, this sort of flexibility—allowing for experimentation—has led a number of students to take an interest in work about which they knew little or nothing at the beginning. They decide to try it because they have no idea what they really want to do. Having tried, they are able to make a more informed decision.

Students are at many different levels in their readiness for vocational training. They move through stages as they gain experience. At one end of the spectrum is the youth who knows how to work, is aware of personal vocational interests, and is motivated to put the necessary effort into learning job skills. At the other end—and this is where nearly all ELP students fall, at least in the beginning—is the student who has never really worked or accepted any responsibility, has either no idea of what he wants to or can do, or else has ideas that have no concrete basis in self-awareness. This student may want to develop skills only if they can be gained without much effort. The students at the lower level need the experience of working, preferably in jobs they enjoy, but definitely in jobs that give them something meaningful to do, and in which they can feel useful and experience some degree of competence. This type of experience can start them on the path toward the higher level, by exposing them to the fact that there is an alternative to idleness and by beginning a process of assessment and experience in narrowing vocational goals according to their individual interests. At the higher level the student needs a job where skill training is of more primary importance, and the program can be adjusted to include more hours on the job.

Field trips are planned to be enjoyable and varied. Examples include ski trips; rock climbing; tours of an auto assembly plant, an aquarium, and a science museum; horseback riding; canoeing; overnight backpacking; beach trips; team sports; movies; and a number of other activities. In addition to being recreational, these trips help build group cohesiveness and provide experiences that promote learning skills, as well as helping to develop the volitional competence that goes with such learning. When they first went skiing, for example, the students looked up the mountain and watched accomplished skiers. Nearly all wanted to know how to ski at least well enough to go way up and make it down. Two people decided to ignore the class arranged on the beginners' slope and to go right up on the chair lift. The others overcame their reluctance and self-consciousness and joined the class. Everyone learned at a different pace, but there was, in general, an appreciation for the difficulty each was going through. The pair who went directly to the top of the mountain returned to the group toward the end of the first class, covered with snow, having learned the hard way that they had to go through some training and practicing in basics before they could actually ski. By the time everyone had been on two or three ski trips they had all stuck with their instructors and practiced to the point where they could handle some of the less difficult trails from the upper part of the mountain. This experience in using volitional skills was at least as important as the actual recreational skill they acquired. Well-thought-out and well-presented activities of almost any sort can affect multiple areas of learning.

Because the ELP is so flexible and is community-based, it can work with a wide variety of students. The leveling effect that occurs in institutions where delinquents are adversely affected by those who have committed more serious crimes is for the most part avoided by having some control over the extent and the nature of contact between different students. Yet there are limitations on the type of student who can fully benefit from the program. Those who are very withdrawn and afraid of group situations can be accommodated somewhat, but by their missing group sessions and activities their potential to benefit in all goal areas is restricted.

Another area of limitation is in cognitive education. Because of the active and vocational orientation of the ELP, time spent on cognitive skills is quite limited. This presents a substantial problem, because this group generally will not tolerate heavy academic training, even though they need more. The ELP can, however, provide limited exposure to, and success in, direct cognitive learning, and aims to decrease the student's phobias toward the academic experience. Ideally, this, along with a general increase in self-confidence, can remove barriers to educational motivation, so that at a future time students can return to more intensive academic training, such as adult education courses or a program of study that prepares them for the GED test.

Traditional educational and vocational programs have not generally succeeded with delinquent youths. This is basically because they are neither comprehensive enough in scope nor sufficiently flexible or individualized to meet the unique needs of each student.

Successful programs for youthful offenders must be individualized, flexible, action-oriented, well-rounded, clearly thought out, and involve students as participants in working out their own programs. Intensive supervision is required, limits must be set, and peer pressure must be carefully scrutinized to turn it in a positive direction. To be successful, a program must be comprehensive in scope.

The Experiential Learning Program is one that has incorporated these characteristics. Educational goals of the program include development of cognitive, affective, survival or life skills in the volitional, moral, and aesthetic area. Each student's program is individualized and closely monitored. Although the program has limitations and has not been in existence long enough to accumulate hard data on its overall success, the program has managed to retain its students, and a number of individual students have undergone dramatic attitudinal and behavioral changes.

The program is continually evolving. It is a useful model of alternative education for delinquents, one that other programs working with delinquent youths might well investigate and choose to emulate. Environmentally handicapped delinquents can be educated, but only through programs that take a widely alternative route from traditional settings.

7 Foster Care: An Old-New Strategy for the Care of Youngsters in Trouble

The closing of the Massachusetts training schools forced new options to be found as a way of caring for young offenders. One of those options has been the development of foster homes. This chapter will examine the utilization of foster homes as a useful tool in the rehabilitation of youngsters in trouble. A number of case studies drawn from past experience will be used as examples. Although the events are factual, the names of the youngsters have been changed.

Why Foster Care?

For youths who must be removed from their natural homes, the foster home provides a setting that is a step beyond the natural family yet is far removed from the more traditional treatment involved in group care. The foster home simulates the natural homelike environment of the child. It provides the promise of individualized care, attention, and affection in a family atmosphere. Foster care allows the child to be placed outside the home without the destructive outcome of institutionalization. Institutionalization results in stigma and labeling; provides an opportunity for the youngster to identify with deviant attitudes, values, and behavior; and dehumanizes the incarcerated person, even in the best group facilities.

Despite the promise that foster care holds for both delinquent and nondelinquent adolescents, little use has been made of it. The reason for such limited use appears to be based on two questionable premises: (1) the aggressive, acting-out adolescent needs a strong, structured, limit-setting environment which the child's family cannot provide; and (2) adolescents are unable or unwilling to form solid object relations with parent figures—the corollary of this proposition is that the collective ego of the peer-group culture is better in the youthful struggle for independence than the family, and that the family is more likely to make the child regress.

Experience has shown these two premises to be false. It has been demonstrated that the family can provide the necessary structure and limit-setting for the acting-out teenager within a humane and individualized framework. And the foster family provides much more than simply structure and limit-setting.

The foster family can give the youngster positive experiences and simulate a normal home life. The foster home can meet the needs of the child more fully, effectively, and compassionately than any other setting outside of the child's natural home. For the troubled youngster, the foster home is usually better at meeting those needs than the natural family, for the foster family sees the child as an individual who has unique needs, wants, and desires. The child is cared for by people who have not become desensitized to the needs of the individual. And foster parents are, almost by definition, caring people who want to make a difference in the life of a young person.

The behavior of the children we are talking about (13 to 17 years old) is often of such an immature nature that it becomes clear that many of their basic needs have not been met. These young people have the emotional needs of much younger children. Their need for attention—to be center stage—is nearly insatiable. Their need for affection is enormous, yet usually the child neither knows how to ask for, nor how to accept, gestures of affection. To the child who has suffered numerous deprivations, rejections, and inconsistent attention, affection and love can be extremely anxiety-provoking. Foster parents have demonstrated the intuitive sensitivity to know that, for their child, a slap on the back can be as symbolically gratifying as a kiss or a hug. The development of basic trust, which is usually lacking in delinquent youths and is a prerequisite for the development of solid object relations, is facilitated by the caring foster family who can meet the child's need for acceptance and approval.

Firm, consistent, and reasonable limit-setting is not only necessary for the socialization of the child, but is a basic need for many youths whose lack of internal controls leaves them victims to their own unbuffered drives and impulses. Limit-setting can be accomplished in the family within a context of caring and concern. Simple rules such as curfew, being home for meals, and cleaning up after oneself, as well as more complex concepts such as respecting the privacy and autonomy of other family members, are followed when the child is made to feel a part of the family, and that he or she incurs the displeasure of family members when limits are exceeded. Families who can create an atmosphere of mutuality and equality have been especially successful with limit-setting.

Despite the fears and anxieties of placing delinquents who have histories of violence and stealing in home situations, the experience has been that delinquent activities within the home have been few. Children at this age do not usually act out against foster parents. The few reported cases involving theft from foster parents usually occurred shortly after the child was placed and before a relationship had a chance to develop. More often than not, such behavior could have been anticipated. Kevin, for example, was a 16-year-old boy from out of state who had been arrested and ordered detained for cashing a bad check. Little information about him was available, but it was known that he had a very limited court record. Based on this fact and an interview with the boy, it was concluded that he was appropriate for foster care. He was placed with a family who was utilized primarily for short-term placements because of their known inability to form solid and lasting relationships.

Kevin's quiet demeanor seduced the foster parents into a false sense of security. Consequently, they did not monitor or supervise his behavior or the people he was associating with. Kevin had a basement room and was allowed almost total freedom. The foster parents made little effort to involve him in family activities, and they were reticent about reporting Kevin's activities to the agency. So when Kevin and a friend became drunk one evening and stole several valuables from the foster home, it was understandable and predictable in view of the circumstances preceding the incident. No relationship existed between Kevin and his foster parents, and the lack of mutual attachment facilitated his impulsive stealing for a friend who needed money.

This is an exceptional case. The usual reason for terminating youths from foster homes has been personal conflict resulting from breakdowns in communication. Despite the fact that many youths continued to violate the law, they did it outside the home. The foster parents acted as advocates to promote restraints and positive behavior.

Foster Care as an Alternative to Group Care

The traditional argument favoring group placement for delinquent youths is specious in view of the evidence. In the first place, these young people typically have gotten into trouble through their peer-group membership. The group often serves to reinforce negative values, attitudes, beliefs, habits, and behaviors. Along with the ego support the youngster receives from the group can come the development of a delinquent identity and the failure to internalize socially acceptable values. Further, group care can also lead to dependence, passivity, lack of initiative, and a withdrawal from the problems and pressures of the real world. Worse, it has also been known to imbue youngsters with the attitude that institutionalization—that is, jail—is not such a bad future. So congregating youngsters in a group setting is not always effective or necessary and is more often counterproductive.

Despite their adolescent status, delinquent young people nonetheless crave and respond to object relations rather than peer-group ego support. They need individualized nurturance, and they respond much more to person-to-person influences and relationships. But, for whatever reason, society in general does not want a child they have identified as delinquent loose in the community.

Jim, for example, is a 15-year-old youth who comes from an extremely deprived and emotionally limited background. He was placed in a group-care, concept-oriented residential treatment program after becoming involved in more and more delinquent activities and school problems. This, coupled with the lack of parental supervision and control, necessitated his removal from his home. He was placed in a group-care facility.

At first Jim was extremely resistant, refusing to get involved in the group program and running home on several occasions, but gradually he began to accept the group program. He became more comfortable with the rigidly structured routine of group living. His passive-dependent style and small stature ingratiated him with the staff, and he eventually became a staff favorite and something of a "house mascot." Jim remained in this program for nearly a year and, although he was allowed to leave the facility for home visits, he did not become involved in any delinquent activity.

When Jim was referred for placement in a foster home, he was almost totally institutionalized. He was shy, withdrawn, and fearful. He spoke in monosyllables and he showed no emotion. He was unable or unwilling to make any decisions on his own. When asked what kind of work he might be interested in, he said simply that he was not ready. When asked when he would be ready to go to work, he replied, "When they tell me I'm ready." He was very fearful at the prospect of going to a foster home.

After lengthy preparation, Jim was moved to a foster home with experienced foster parents. But he refused to get involved at any level. He was almost nonverbal. He seldom went outside, and looked forward only to returning to the group home for visits.

Gradually Jim began to adjust to his environment. He started to interact with the family, and his depression began to lift. He was not as anxious or fearful. He began going out, and he also spent more time interacting with his family. Although he was making progress, after four months he was still unable to separate himself completely from the group home. His ties to the group facility were still strong, and he continued to talk about the people there and visit them.

Along with his increasing independence came an increase in his aggressiveness and delinquent activity. As Jim became more decisional and less passive, his aggression became directed more toward others and less toward himself. He was engaging in property offenses, and he was hostile to authority figures. Some authorities believed this acting out reflected the failure of the foster home. The group home immediately demanded that Jim be returned to them, citing his delinquency-free record while he was there.

Several conferences helped ease this countertransference, and served to point out that Jim's aggression was a natural part of the growth process, given his family and personal dynamics. The transition from a secure, infantilizing environment to the more demanding environment of a foster home was very difficult for Jim and the community, yet it was absolutely necessary if he was to become a responsible member of society.

Limit-Setting and Foster Care

Another basic complaint about foster care that is often cited is: "The foster home cannot provide adequate limits." This simply is not true. Foster parents have demonstrated time after time that young people accept limits and controls much more readily from people who show love and care than through groups, which are often impersonal and inflexible.

For youths in an open (unlocked) group setting, the only control one has over their behavior is either: (1) that there is some type of administrative punitive power over the young people; or (2) that the quality of the relationship between child and caretaker makes the child not want to disappoint the caretaker—"the youngster does what I want because he likes me." While the peer pressure of the group may be effective for short-term limit-setting, the group generally does not provide the youngster with the positive identifications necessary for the internalization of rules. The child conforms mainly to avoid censure and punishment.

Limit-setting in the foster home is predicated on the ability of foster parents and child to form solid object relations that can endure frustration. The foster family provides the neccessary conditions for this to occur, since they are in the unique position of being different from the child's family of origin. The child's conflicted familial relationships and misperceptions can be worked through with the foster family. The family can start fresh with the youngster and set different goals and expectations to create independence and responsibility, rather than keeping the youth regressed in infantile primary relationships. This situation generates and facilitates the establishment of object relations. The youngsters in foster homes, unlike their counterparts in group homes, do not become preoccupied with avoiding punishment, but rather move toward seeking love and affection.

An example is Mike, a 15-year-old youngster from a terribly conflicted family. His mother is a cold, angry, and demanding woman, while his father is passive. Mike's relationship with his parents was one of extreme bitterness, hurt, and disappointment. His unmet needs for love and affection left him very narcissistic and egocentric. Mike was an extremely angry boy who often regressed into violent and destructive behavior. He needed a foster family that could meet his need for attention, yet still be able to deal with his anger and set limits on his self-centered behavior. He was placed with a young couple—a warm, nurturing woman and a strong, dominating man—a configuration dynamically opposite to his natural family. There were no other children in the family with whom Mike would have to compete. He soon realized that he could not intimidate his foster father and that he had nothing to fear from his foster mother. His frustrated longings for caring, competent parents now realized, Mike developed a trusting relationship that allowed him to begin to correct his misperceptions and accept limits.

The Relationship between Foster Home and Family of Origin

Many youngsters like Mike have shown that they have either been deprived of love and caring or have been given license or improper, inadequate, and inconsistent limit-setting. The problem is that as long as the child remains in the natural home, the same set of indulgences on the part of the parent—and the same set of regressions on the part of the child—will occur.

For the child in conflict, removal from the home is often desirable; yet, for many youngsters, the prospect of severing family ties can be frightening. A unique feature of foster care is the "temporary shelter" concept. The foster home is able to serve as a temporary haven for the youth, yet it is also uniquely flexible because it enables the youngster to return to his natural family when the anxiety of separation becomes too great. Many youngsters with symbiotic family relationships are thus able to make beginnings towards autonomy while being able to return to a more regressed stage when stress becomes too great. The open door of the foster home permits the foster parents to appeal to the youngster's mature side, but it also allows the youth to return to an infantilizing environment when it becomes necessary. This feature, rather than a shortcoming of foster care, actually functions as a safety valve that allows the youngster to mature at his or her own pace. An example will illustrate how this works in practice.

Tim is a 17-year-old boy who is the eldest son still at home in a family of ten children. Although Tim had been involved in numerous minor delinquent activities, his main problem was that his level of ego functioning was that of a much younger child. He demanded constant attention and became involved in fiercely competitive relationships with latency-age children. His frustration tolerance was very low, and when he could not get his own way he would throw a temper tantrum, shouting and smashing things.

Tim's mother infantilized him. She had a need to see this boy as a baby, and Tim responded by living up (or, in this case, down) to his mother's expectations. A great deal of preparation was necessary before this symbiotic attachment could be broken enough to place Tim in a foster home. After placement, Tim and his mother stayed in constant contact by telephone, with Tim even calling his mother to say good-night to her. Intensive work with the mother eventually eliminated this telephoning.

Almost immediately after placement, however, Tim began to disappear from his foster home and show up at his real home. So that Tim's guilt would not be intensified, his going home was sanctioned and it was presented to Tim and to his mother as his need to "take a break" from his foster home. Characteristically, he would remain home for short periods and return to his foster home with the urging and coaxing of staff members and his foster parents. On some occasions he would remain home for longer periods, and both he and his mother indicated that foster care was no longer what they wanted. Invariably, though, intense conflict would develop at home as Tim struggled with dependency issues, and he would return to his foster home. It was as though Tim needed to get back to the womb for a while, and then once secure and protected, he would violently protest this infantilization and want to return to the demands of the real world. Tim's foster parents were aware of this particular need, and they accepted Tim's status as a part-time foster child.

The Placement Process

One of the most important factors influencing the course of a foster home placement is the way in which the initial stages of preparation and decision-making proceed. A youngster cannot be pushed into a placement, and must be included in the decisionmaking process whenever possible. In this way it is clear to the child that he or she is not being coerced or pressured. It is also the starting point for the establishment of the mutual trust and cooperation that must be manifested if the child's behavior is to change.

In spite of the aggressiveness displayed by troubled youngsters, most of them are very passive. Repeated failure eventually results in the perception of the self as one who fails. Such youngsters come to expect failure, and they perceive themselves as victims. They feel they are caught up in external forces which they cannot control—passive victims of fate. A young person's involvement in the placement decision is a start in the process of assuming personal responsibility for actions. One can make a tentative first step toward becoming more decisional and self-directing by having a real say in what happens in the foster home placement process.

For the child who is reluctant or unwilling to enter a foster home, the procedure obviously becomes more complicated. The youngster must be educated. The child must be convinced that care and concern for his or her well-being are involved in the foster home placement. This can be a long process involving many meetings with counselors, natural parents, prospective foster parents, and the child. In some cases several foster home placements may have to be attempted before the child comes to accept foster care.

Chris, for example, was a 15-year-old boy who did not want to leave home. His mother was overwhelmed and felt like a prisoner in her own home with her sons in control of the house and having total license. Chris would not listen to his mother, and he did whatever he wanted, whenever he wanted. He was depressed, negative, and totally unmotivated. Despite Chris's problems he rejected any attempts of help. Finally, he was presented for foster care placement.

At the initial meeting Chris sat slumped in his chair and mumbled answers to questions in monosyllables. His only spontaneous talk was to tell why he should not be in a foster home. His mother was in a psychiatric hospital at this time, so going home was out of the question. The meeting ended in a total impasse, with Chris unwilling to make any type of commitment to a foster home.

Rather than force Chris into a situation he did not want, many meetings were held with him to discuss the negative direction his life was taking and to talk about the merits and benefits of foster care. He was given the opportunity to "custom order" a foster home that would meet his specifications. His initial demands were outrageous and often funny: he wanted his foster home to have a swimming pool, horses, a game room, and a sports car. The absence of negative reactions to Chris and his outlandish requests helped convince him of the sincerity, care, and concern on the part of the people working with him. He began to trust the counselors, and after several meetings his demands became more realistic. He eventually agreed, however reluctantly, to go to a foster home.

Chris had asked for a young couple as foster parents, and he wanted his own room—preferably with a television—and with no other children in the home. He was promised these things, but was told that it would take time for his "ideal foster home" to be found. He agreed to try a foster home that did not exactly meet his specifications during the interim, and he was told that if it did not work out, another placement could be tried. Chris then began a foster home odyssey lasting four months and exhausting seven foster homes.

Chris complained about his first foster home almost immediately. He was using the deficiencies of the home (as measured by his standards) as a rationale for noninvolvement and as a ploy to try to return home. Although he did not run away, Chris demanded to be moved to a foster home more to his liking. He was accommodated; he was moved to another foster home where the cycle was invariably repeated. He was placed in four different foster homes at his request, after attempts to resolve the difficulties failed. Chris was accommodated so that he would learn that his passive-aggressiveness and complaining were outmoded, maladaptive traits that would no longer get him what he wanted. It was also done to try to meet his now reasonable demands: for example, it was observed that Chris did function better away from other teenagers, thus making his request for a childless foster home quite appropriate.

A foster home was finally found that met, and even exceeded, all of Chris's physical specifications. Since these foster parents were new and untested, however, Chris's irritating and sometimes obnoxious behavior was more than they could handle, and the situation deteriorated to the point where Chris had to leave this home also. From his experience Chris was forced to confront the fact that there is more to a relationship than the superficial standards he had sought. Chris was moved to yet another foster home.

The new foster family was exceptionally understanding and tolerant. The parents were able to deal effectively with Chris's behavior, and they established a relationship that could tolerate the frustration of limit-setting. The gains made by Chris in this foster home, coupled with individual counseling and family therapy, allowed Chris eventually to return home where, with a network of supportive after-care services, he was able to hold a job and maintain a considerably more stable family environment.

The Temporary Nature of Foster Care

The example cited above illustrates not only the necessity of the youngster's participation in the placement process, it also illustrates the temporary nature of foster care, as well. If Chris had been forced to accept one foster home, it would, in all probability, have frustrated him to the point of acting out or subverting the placement through destructive means. Instead he was given the option of moving from place to place until he found a home he liked—a procedure which is, unfortunately, often seen as negative by some referring agencies because of the administrative problems it causes. When a child must be prematurely terminated from a foster home, it is typically seen as a failure of the child. A more reasonable explanation, such as the shortcomings of the situation or a mismatch between child and foster parents, is more productive.

The foster home placement should begin by developing a contract with the youth that stresses the tentative nature of the placement and the need for the youngster and foster parents to be compatible and comfortable with each other. The placement needs to be evaluated at every step of the way. A child is never moved arbitrarily from a foster home, but only after a careful assessment is made of the strengths and weaknesses of the placement. Every effort is made to maintain a placement, yet there is no hesitation about moving a child when a situation is not working. This is facilitated by making the tentative nature of the placement explicit from the beginning. This removes the negative outcomes that the fear of failure by the foster parents or the child can have.

Occasionally a youngster will remain in contact with the foster family with whom he has terminated because of difficulties. The relationship with the child while he was in the foster home may have been confused and conflicted, but once he leaves the home the relationship alters and a friendship is able to develop. Similarly, the separation anxiety caused by termination after the successful completion of a foster home placement can be mitigated by the knowledge that the participants can remain in contact with each other just as natural families normally do after a child has grown up and moved out on his own.

It is not uncommon for a youngster to run away from a foster home. This usually occurs shortly after placement, and is a result of the child's anxiety at the threatened loss of ego support from family and peer group. Sometimes the child's running away is a response to feelings of confinement that occur simply because he or she must stay in one place. Even after the child has spent months in a foster home, the need to return home at unscheduled times may still be felt. Foster parents are made aware of this possbility and are given support to "ride out" the youngster's disappearing acts. The habitual running away of foster children occasionally results in the foster parents asking for the child's removal from the home. There are usually other issues involved in such cases, but the running serves as a focal point for the foster parents' frustration and disappointment at not having been able to reach the youth.

A youngster may be terminated from a particular foster home at the request of the foster parent or the child. Apart from the child's acting out in the home, a characteristic complaint from foster parents is that they are "not getting anything back" from the child. The young people's complaints are more varied, but usually center on the foster parents being too strict or "too square." Family meetings are held with the child and foster family to try to correct miscommunications and misperceptions that exist. Often, as mentioned earlier, the problem is simply a mismatch of the child with the foster family. If, after several meetings, the problems have not begun to be resolved, the child is usually moved to another foster home.

The move of a youngster from one foster home to another often serves as a valuable learning experience for the child. The positive things the child has done and the progress he or she has made within the home, are pointed out and emphasized by the counselors. Instead of being a failure, the child's move to another home can be a response to, and facilitation of, the growth process.

The Matching Process

It is obviously impossible to predict the course of a youngster's foster care career. Similarly, there is clearly no way to guarantee the success of a particular foster home placement. There is, however, a way in which a certain amount of confidence about the placement can be established. This is done by the individualized matching of a particular child to a particular foster family.

The youngster is assessed according to behavior, needs, habits, traits, temperament, personality type, style, likes and dislikes, and matched to a foster family having complimentary and compatible qualities. The prospective foster family is assessed along several dimensions to determine what type of youngster would do best in that home. Some of the dimensions examined in the family are: flexibility vs. authority—How well can they set limits and be confrontative?; support and nurturing vs. emphasis on self-reliance; relative ego strength of father vs. relative ego strength of mother—Is the father or the mother dominant in the home?; reflectivity vs. impulsivity—What type of role models will they be?; active vs. passive—Would a depressed child be stimulated by this home, or a hyperactive youngster be toned down? At every step of the way the prospective family is looked at with an eye to what type of child would do best with them.

Another important factor in the matching process is the size of the family and the age and sex of the children living at home. Some foster children cannot interact with people their own age, yet they do extremely well with younger children.

John, for example, developed fiercely competitive relationships with children his own age, and so did poorly with foster families with teenagers present. Paradoxically, however, he craved a family-type atmosphere and became lonely in childless homes. He was found to do exceptionally well with a foster family consisting of several younger children. He enjoyed being looked up to by these youngsters, and he took care of them with the eagerness of a big brother.

The strength of the foster father and mother is perhaps the most important single issue in the criteria for matching. Some youngsters respond well to a strong mother figure, while others may regress. Similarly, children who have difficulty perceiving limits may do well with a strict foster father; others would rebel against him.

In an earlier example it was shown that Mike profited from a foster father who could stand up to his aggressiveness and not be intimidated. Mike needed to perceive determined and up-front limit-setting from the father figure. If he had been placed in a home with a father who displayed any signs of weakness, Mike would have immediately taken advantage of him to gain control of the situation and avoid facing reality.

The cohesiveness of a foster family is another important issue to be taken into account. Some youngsters need and respond to a close family situation. The family that participates in many activities together and exudes a feeling of warmth and togetherness is the ideal situation for many children, yet other youngsters would be extremely threatened by this. For the second type of youngster, a compatible family would be one where there were no overt demands for family loyalty and participation made on the foster child. This youngster would also benefit from a room of his own where he could go to be alone when he felt the need for more distance between himself and the foster family.

While this is by no means intended to be a comprehensive examination of the issues involved in the matching process, it does serve to illustrate some of the more important considerations when matching a youngster with a foster family. The overall success of a foster-care program hinges on the matching process and on the quality of the foster parents it recruits, trains, and supervises.

Selection of Foster Parents

In screening prospective foster parents, the question is: What type of people make good foster parents? Foster parents with certain qualities have a better chance of succeeding. They need to be flexible and comfortable with limit-setting. They must be able to set limits, yet be able to talk with the child when those limits are not observed. They need to be comfortable with teenagers, their acting-out behavior, and youthful energy, exuberance, and experimentation. Foster parents who are involved with large networks of friends and relatives tend to do well. The extended family of the foster parents provides them with support for dealing with the youngster, and in many cases has been a source of additional positive relationships for the youth. Not to be overlooked as a valuable quality for a foster parent is a good sense of humor.

In selecting foster parents it has been found that there are no particular character types who are better than others. It is not uncommon for apparently maladjusted people to be good foster parents. Conversely, seemingly well-adjusted people have been known to fail miserably.

The Smiths, for example, were a middle-class couple in their late thirties who lived quite comfortably in their suburban home. They were motivated to take in a foster child out of a desire to "help a kid who hasn't had a break"—a common response given by foster parents to the question of motivation. On the surface, the Smiths appeared to be a happy, average couple.

The initial screening and training sessions revealed that Mrs. Smith could not have children. It was felt that she was probably trying to compensate for this through a foster child. To dispel any fantasies she may have had about foster children, she was cautioned about her possible unrealistic expectations of having a child fit right into her family and accept her and her husband immediately. She was told about the types of behavior exhibited by these young people and what she could expect. She said she understood the problems and gave assurance that she would not expect too much from the child. This well-meaning woman was certain that her good intentions would overcome all obstacles. Subsequently, a boy with a limited court record and a history of material deprivation was placed with the Smiths.

The placement proved to be a disaster from the beginning. Predictably, Mrs. Smith tried to mother the boy, and when he did not respond she felt him ungrateful. His poor personal hygiene and lack of self-awareness also labeled him inconsiderate in her mind. And when he failed to show up at an appointed meeting with Mrs. Smith, this was the "last straw." The Smiths requested, quite angrily, that the boy be moved—six days after he had arrived. The Smith's feelings of failure and inadequacy were projected onto the boy, and their self-righteous indignation precluded even the usual termination conference.

While in this example the "gut feelings" of staff was that the Smiths would not work out, similar situations have had different outcomes. In short, there is simply no definitive way to predict who will make good foster parents. The best test is the experience of actually having a youngster in the home, and it is here where the trial-basis nature of the placement contract becomes very important. When possible, it has been extremely useful to place a child temporarily with a prospective foster family for a weekend or a week. This is done with youngsters who may need a respite from their current living situation or who just want to get away for a short while. Observation of family-child interactions, and feedback from the child and foster parents, can be accurate indicators of the viability of the family as a foster home.

In selecting foster parents, only those with more obvious difficulties are screened out during the initial period. People from all walks of life and every social class are potentially good foster parents. Experience with working-class people, including people on welfare, has shown that they can be excellent foster parents and that they represent a valuable resource from which to draw. Divorced and single persons have often proved to be superior foster parents for youths who need an intimate, trusting, one-to-one relationship.

After the foster parent has been selected, and the appropriate match between foster family and child has been made, the real business of foster parenting begins.

The Working-through Process

The youngster entering a foster home is usually apprehensive and wary, regardless of whether this is the first foster home experience or one of many. The process of change is slow and often frought with frustration. Yet change does occur and can mean both a new beginning for the youngster and immeasurable personal satisfaction for the foster parents.

Every placement is unique and contains its own problems and rewards. There are no hard-and-fast rules or formulas that can be used to predict the course of the foster care experience. There are, however, certain generalized patterns that have appeared in numerous foster home placements. These can be recognized and conceptualized as stages the youngster and foster parent go through in the process of growth and change. The following is a generalized format describing these stages.

Stage 1. The first stage is a period of negotiation, testing, and the beginning of a contract. The youngster in this stage is usually anxious, although it may not show. This anxiety is increased by the unfamiliar surroundings and by not knowing what is expected of him. This initial stress can be eased by more clarification of the mutual expectations. This stage might best be described as the "honeymoon period," because both child and foster parents try to please each other and avoid conflict. This usually does not feel natural to either the youngster or the foster parents. Often the youngster acts angelic and the foster parents feel euphoric. So it is unrealistic at this stage not to expect some deterioration. Once conflict does occur, structured family meetings can clarify the relationship, and the foster parents can be helped to understand that when the youngster tests, he or she is really asking the question, "What is acceptable and what is not?" as well as checking whether the foster parents care.

Stage 1 can last anywhere from two weeks to two months. At times the youngster might leave and return, further testing the foster parents' patience and commitment. This is the point where foster parents sometimes become frustrated or even shocked by the child's change in behavior and decide not to continue, which is unfortunate because until this stage is negotiated successfully, it is impossible to go on to the next stages.

Stage 2. The second stage is the "feeling comfortable" period. When the foster child begins to feel at home, he acts out more often and shows his "real self." The restraints he once put on himself do not work anymore, and he begins also to ignore his agreements and contracts with the foster parents. The foster parents may also become less restrained and allow their relationship with the child to deteriorate, which creates a situation that permits more acting out on both sides. The youngster becomes more critical of the foster family, and the foster family becomes more frustrated with the acting-out child. Here, support for the foster parents is crucial, since they need to realize that the youngster's deterioration is natural and that more restraint and patience is needed. At the same time, firmness by the foster parents can help the child deal with the many issues he is raising. If the relationship survives this period, it can mark the solidification of the relationship and prepare them for the next stage.

Stage 3. The third stage is the change and growth period. During this stage, both parties make progress. As the relationship grows, the youngster begins doing things to receive approval. He shows signs of beginning to internalize some parental values. Self-control improves, and the child starts to identify and develop goals for himself; he becomes more mature and serious in his attitudes and work, and there is an honest attempt, on his part, to communicate and work through problems. Similarly, the foster parents develop feelings that though the job is hard, there can be feelings of satisfaction in the changes the youngster is making, as well as feeling "I learned a lot working with this kid."

Stage 4. As with natural families, the youngster who has learned and grown in a foster home wants to be independent. At this point two situations may develop: (1) the youngster, fearing separation and subsequent loss of security, may begin to regress and act out that anxiety; and (2) the foster parents, too, may feel disturbed by the impending loss, causing them to cling to the child, making him feel guilty, again with subsequent deterioration of the relationship.

Usually it is necessary for both sides to acknowledge the feelings of loss and the meaning this has for them. They are then able to develop a different contract that alters the relationship and allows for termination with a minimum of depression, anxiety, and guilt.

Limitations of Foster Care

Foster care is a sadly underutilized technique for dealing with delinquent young people. If it is to be properly utilized, there are some dangers and drawbacks which need to be noted.

1. Some youngsters are too destructive or disturbed to be placed in a family setting. Some cannot tolerate the closeness of a foster home and may benefit from another setting until their defenses have matured enough to allow them to enter a family situation.

2. Despite good selection criteria, it is impossible to screen out all foster parents who may prove to be poor parental figures. Inevitably some poor choices will slip through the screening process.

3. Despite a sophisticated procedure for matching a child to a foster home, it is impossible to always be right; difficult and unhealthy situations will occur.

4. The "hidden agenda" of foster parents can lead to early frustration, disappointment, and a giving up on the child. In the case of the Smith family cited earlier, for example, their hidden agenda was a longing for a child they could change, shape, and mold. They were unable to heed the warnings that the youngster could not meet their high expectations.

5. An overidentification of foster parents with the child can cause a loss of objectivity through need distortion. The following example will help to clarify this.

The McAdamses were extremely motivated foster parents who were devoted to the role of foster parents to a young girl. The problem was that the mother could not and would not accept a sexual relationship the girl was having. This relationship obfuscated their many other compatibilities and the situation finally exploded leaving bitter feelings on both sides.

6. The lack of involvement by some children leaves the foster parents feeling depleted and frustrated, and that they are "not getting anything back from the kid." This situation can also lead to an early retirement by some foster parents.

7. Referring agencies that are under pressure to place youngsters as quickly as possible tend to misuse foster care placements by not allowing the placement agency enough time for proper preparation.

Other Issues in Foster Care

Foster families should not be expected to, not try to, replace the child's family of origin. This can lead to negative outcomes such as jealousy and subversion on the part of both the natural family and the child, if there is a feeling that the child is being torn away. Rather, the role of foster parent should be that of advocate, ally, and caring authority figure.

When the goal is to return the child to his natural home, work with the natural parents is essential so that they can learn to accept the growth and change that has taken place with their child, as well as learning how to define the relationship and communicate better. It has been found that work with the natural family is often necessary immediately after placement to prevent jealous or guilt-ridden parents from undermining and subverting the placement.

Some foster parents are better at maintaining a relationship than others. For the foster families who have shown some problems in sustaining a relationship with a teenager, short-term foster placements have often provided mutually satisfying results. Routine visits by the worker to the foster home have helped to personalize the relationship between the agency and the foster parents, as well as providing them with support. These visits tend to make the foster parents more amenable to advice, suggestions, and education, as well as serving to mitigate foster parent possessiveness of the child.

Foster parents have responded well to weekly foster parent meetings, which also serve an educational and support function. Additionally, an invaluable result of these meetings has been the development of relationships between foster parents, so that a network of foster parents has been created that functions as an extended family, providing support and relief for the individual foster parent. This concept of the extended family is being carried to its logical conclusion of improving the quality of life for both children and adults by creating the concept of, and a feeling for, the caring community.

Summary

This chapter examined the utilization of foster homes as a useful tool in the rehabilitation of youngsters in trouble. Examples are given of how the foster family provides the youngster with positive experiences and stimulates a normal home life. Special problems of matching foster home and child are analyzed in detail, as are the stages of mutual accommodation.

8

Reintegration of the Young Offender into the Family and Community

What awaits the child when he or she enters the typical institutional corrections system, usually first through the detention center? What is the nature of the punishment society has decreed and the parents have underwritten?

Usually the peer group consists of children between fourteen and seventeen years of age who are awaiting trials or dispositions for auto thefts, housebreaks, assaults, or narcotics offenses. They are questioned by the police. The educational program, because of the transient population within the detention center, is haphazard at best. Unfortunately, such centers provide another kind of education for the youthful offender, who learns in detail the exploits of other inmates, their techniques for dealing with the authorities, and the names of friends to contact and enemies to avoid at the training school. The first intensive exposure to the criminal group is experienced. One may even be initiated into homosexuality. As a result of the combination of a lack of protection and collusion between parents and the courts, a young person is confirmed as a delinquent.

How, then, should one intervene to ameliorate a process that labels a child delinquent and then helps to fulfill the prophesy of that label? Should efforts be made to help the lower-class family to change by becoming more responsive to middle-class institutions? Should neighborhoods be designed so that the concept of the warm, supportive primary group is once more viable? Should the whole procedure of the juvenile courts be revised so that the latent function implied in the labeling is rendered ineffective? Should the correctional institutions be reformed so that rehabilitation becomes a workable concept? Or should the correctional institution be abolished and a program of community rehabilitation be embarked upon, a program that would enlist the aid of both the family and the community in offering protection to lower-class youths, making rehabilitation a reality?

Although all of these questions are vital to the process of bringing about a more humane treatment of young people in trouble, several are beyond the scope of this chapter. One that can be considered is: Do the correctional institutions help the child and his family? If not, is major reform a more workable alternative for creating a helping climate?

As they presently exist, the correctional institutions fail because:

1. They are symbols of punishment—"reform schools"—to which children adjudicated delinquent are sent. Here it is hoped they will be "corrected," and it is certain they will be punished.
2. They lack professional staff, and programs are frequently nonexistent; where programs do exist, they rarely offer therapeutic help for the child and the family.
3. They are perceived by the families of the institutionalized children as places of punishment.
4. Their environments present the incarcerated children with a difficult set of problems with which to deal—problems that frequently encourage recidivism. These problems include homosexuality and peer pressure to share in the antisocial tendencies of fellow inmates, the custodial staff, and the regulations of the institutions.
5. They block family involvement with the delinquent, since it is generally impossible for a poor family to travel the distance between the institution and the youth's home city.

As a result of these characteristics of the institutional setting, the child subjected to institutionalization is usually no better off than before experiencing it, and is frequently set on the road to adult criminality.

The Necessity of Reintegration

The act of closing youth correctional institutions, as was done in Massachusetts, is not enough. Unless efforts are made to reintegrate young offenders into their communities, deinstitutionalization merely means transferring a youth's problems from one place to another. Before we can consider the intervention strategies necessary to achieve such reintegration, an important question has to be answered: What part does the family play in the process of labeling and reinforcing the delinquency pattern of its children?

Family therapy and the exploration of the family as a social system have recently burgeoned into an area of prime interest in the fields of sociology and psychology. The emphasis in theory and practice, however, has been centered almost exclusively on the middle-class family. While the acting-out behavior of teenagers from such middle-class families may come to the attention of the authorities when these young people get in trouble with the law, only rarely are these adolescents labeled delinquents. On the other hand, comparable children of lower-class families do not often escape the "delinquent" label, primarily because of their parents' inability to provide them with the necessary advocacy and protection. Instead, these poorer children find themselves caught between the two competing systems of family and community. Usually it is the relationship between these two systems that determines whether such children will be labeled and confirmed as delinquents or will be able to avoid that label. The nature of the protection the family offers its teenagers in trouble will determine whether the family will be viewed as antagonistic to community expectations, as well as whether or not the child will be labeled delinquent. The lower-class family usually does not have either the training or resources to protect their youngsters when they get in trouble.

Why do children need such protection? Primarily it is needed because society has developed a highly complex bureaucratic institutional structure that is insensitive to the needs of the individual. As a result, societal systems obstruct the efforts of the individual to cope with them. The most obvious example of the destructive labeling process and the need for family advocacy for lower-class children is the school, where youngsters are consistently labeled as "underachievers," "untrainables," or "dropouts"—all words that carry negative connotations. These labels exacerbate the difficulties faced by the labeled youngsters. Furthermore, every youngster, and especially one who lives in a lower-class neighborhood in an urban ghetto, needs help and protection from the hostile environment of the community. In these disorganized neighborhoods, youngsters are subjected to violence against their persons. A child may be threatened with bodily harm, or even have to submit to rape many times over. Such a child cannot look to the neighborhood political or law-enforcement organizations for support, because they have failed before, or because the family simply does not trust these institutions. Because the civil authorities themselves frequently view such neighborhoods and their residents as run down, undesirable, and therefore unworthy of help, they are generally very removed from the families and their children's needs. The result of all these factors is that the family of the lower-class child is unable to offer protection for its youngster from either the societal institutions or neighborhood exploitation.

Destructive Collusion

R.D. Laing has suggested that collusion exists between the institution of psychiatry and the family of the schizophrenic. This collusion has the effect of removing the adolescent schizophrenic from the situation that is responsible for the youth's unacceptable behavior. The young person is labeled "mad," is institutionalized, and the family is absolved from dealing with the distorted communications in the family system that contributed to the illness. Similarly, criminologists speak of the latent function of the criminal justice system. Prisons, police, and other institutions of the system have long fulfilled latent functions of punishment and social isolation that conflict with society's manifest aim of rehabilitation.

These phenomena meet the needs not only of society at large, but also frequently of the families of the delinquent youths. In our work with delinquent young people, we have found a high number of cases in which this relationship exists between the family of the delinquent and the criminal justice system. Furthermore, since training schools or detention centers are seen by those most involved in them as punitive rather than rehabilitative measures for children, the expectation of the parents is that the institution will act as a control rather than as a rehabilitative agency.

A concrete example of this attitude can be seen in CHINS (Children in Need of Services). Most of these children are referred to the courts with a "stubborn child" complaint, frequently in situations where the mother is the only parent in the home. This parent is usually struggling with a variety of problems, such as rundown housing, inadequate food, and loneliness. She faces additional pressure from the school, which demands more socialized behavior from her child. Such a parent, feeling that legitimate authority in the home is bankrupt, turns to the courts and asks that external control be imposed on the youngster. The court, generally acting with little knowledge of the family dynamics, obliges. Thus the collusion results in committing the child to a detention center.

It is our observation, from working with youths both at the institutional level and in community-based programs, that in lower-class families the parents' desire for punishment of its young members who get in trouble is strong. The desire seems to be part of a value system that demands punishment as the consequence of external acts. (This is in contrast to certain middle-class value systems, that view punishment as a deterrent to one's intention to commit further antisocial acts.) Furthermore, lower-class parents, because of a lack of resources, often unwillingly abandon the child to the labeling process and further rejection and punishment by the criminal justice system.

The Family of the Delinquent

Minuchin et al., in their studies of families of boys at the Wiltwick School in New York, described two kinds of families of the lower-class delinquent. One is the *enmeshed family*, which they characterize as having an authoritarian structure provided largely by one of the parents, and a communication system that resembles variations of power maneuvers. The relationship of the enmeshed family to authoritarian institutions such as police, courts, truant officers, and sometimes even guidance counselors, can be viewed as an extension of the authoritarian orientation of the family. That is, the institutions are seen as tough antagonists that must be avoided, placated, or fought.

The second family structure that tends to breed delinquency is the disengaged family, characterized by the lack of a controlling and organizing adult. In these instances the single parent finds herself passive and overwhelmed, and the child, embodying as he or she does the family's characteristic styles of coping, constantly organizes adults into controlling and aggressive positions and seeks peers with whom to share the excitement of antisocial behavior. The high degree of incompetence in these families tends to push social agencies to take over to provide the control and protection the mother is unable to supply.

Conceptualizing diagnostic categories that reflect family dynamics of the delinquent is an important first step toward the development of intervention strategies with these families. The following categories were developed by the Northeastern Family Institute in collaboration with the Massachusetts Department of Youth Services. The Department reviewed 120 cases from its caseload of 1,240 for the purpose of developing need-assessment strategies for funding. Northeastern Family Institute has been working directly with the families of young people referred to it by DYS, and has revised these categories after reviewing cases where family intervention was used.

The resulting categories can provide a conceptual framework for intervention strategies. They can be used as a tool for the clinician or the case manager to assess family needs and the extent to which certain strategies may or may not work. The categories do not predict behavior; they are intended to describe family dynamics as clinicians and case workers see them and as the delinquent children themselves perceive them. Three general categories require intervention: (1) adolescent rebellion; (2) families with parental dysfunction; and (3) broken families.

Adolescent Rebellion

Families who cannot accept adolescent testing. Children in such families are otherwise adequately functioning youths who had been progressing normally until they reached adolescence. As soon as they begin to assert themselves in their need for independence and autonomy, the family responds with confusion and rejection. The youth's testing seems to trigger dormant impulses in their parents, whose own adolescent periods were either unhappy or conflictual ones. Of course the rejection on the part of the parents sends the youth into a vicious circle of reaction that may end up in delinquent behavior.

Parents who are unable to accept separation from their children. Such parents are essentially lonely people who are holding on to their children as substitutes for friends. They react with punishment and rejection as the young people attempt to build relationships outside the family. The outcome is delinquent behavior on the part of the youngsters, which serves to bring parents and youth closer together, on the one hand, while at the same time creating more possibilities for distance. Examples of this relationship are usually found between mothers and their children. Generally the mother is lonely; she develops a substitute for her loneliness through attachment to her own child. We have even seen a number of mother-daughter relationships that run in generations of dependency from grandmother to mother to daughter. Mothers in such instances perpetuate, with their own daughters, the relationship their mothers had with them, especially after the daughter becomes pregnant and gives birth to a child. The dependent daughter is not immediately able to mother her infant, and the cycle of dependency continues.

Families where one or both parents acts in a repressive manner toward the child. Usually during adolescence the child in such circumstances retaliates either by striking back at the parents or by embarrassing them with acting-out behavior. In this category is the son or daughter of a public official who, feeling abandoned or rejected by the parents, strikes back by publicly embarrassing the parents. Such children persist in their delinquent acts unless therapeutic intervention with the family is used. Another example is children whose fathers are tyrants. These children have experienced a tremendous amount of repression and hostility. When they fight back, they take out their anger on whomever is around. It is extremely difficult to work with such families because the parents themselves are generally products of parental repression, and in many ways this is the only way they are able to relate to their own children. Intervention in such families requires a great deal of structure.

Families in which the youth suffered a traumatic experience during adolescence. In these families the ability to provide support at some very difficult time was missing. As a result, the youth may turn to an adolescent peer group and involvement in delinquent activities. One example of this situation would be the loss of his father by an adolescent boy who, unable to express his grief, therefore feels angry and betrayed, and strikes back. Or the loss of her husband may affect the mother in such a way that she focuses all her grief on her adolescent son, who rebels by committing delinquent acts. Or, should a sibling die or be seriously injured, the adolescent may either overtly or subtly be blamed by the parents. His self-worth plummets; he seeks support in a delinquent peer group where negative behavior is the means of acceptance and through which the adolescent can counter parental rejection by rejecting the parents, in turn.

Family therapy is necessary in working with parents who fall into any of these categories. Our goal is to use intervention strategies to break the patterns of interaction and to help the children release themselves from destructive relationships with their parents so that they can move toward autonomy. Thus, even though family therapy is the tool, the goal is to help the youngster develop independence and enough living experience so that he or she can move toward self-reliance, away from the family and the need to retaliate against adult authorities. Extensive contact beyond family therapy sessions is used, both for the young people in helping them to move on, and for the families in helping them to cope with the everyday pressures of their lives. By taking away the need to strike out at adults, energy can be channeled toward personal growth and self-sufficiency. And the cycle can be broken rather than continued in the relationship the youth will someday have with his or her children.

Families with Parental Dysfunctions

Families with parental dysfunction consciously or unconsciously encourage their children to engage in delinquent activities. Some of these families live in neighborhoods where delinquent activities are accepted or tolerated. Others unconsciously motivate their children toward criminal activities by the enjoyment they derive from their children's delinquent acts. Such parents find vicarious satisfaction in acts against the "system" by their children.

Families who need scapegoats. Some families in which there is a tremendous amount of tension and anger may misdirect their frustration on one child, the scapegoat. When that child leaves home, the next youngster in line takes on the scapegoat role. As with the schizophrenic family, these youngsters have been required to accept a role that helps the family keep intact by focusing on a "problem child" rather than being forced to deal with parental discord and the inability of family members to relate to one another.

Parents unable to provide structure and set limits for their children. One illustration is the mother who, left with a son after the father's death or abandonment of the family, begins to live vicariously through the child. She is unable to set any limiting structure for fear of abandonment. Not only does she fail to set limits for her son, but she fights everyone else who tries, whether it be school officials, police, or the correctional institutions. Another example is the multiproblem family, in which the mother is overwhelmed by her situation and relinquishes her responsibility, letting the youngsters take charge. The father may be either physically or psychologically absent, or both. If a stepfather enters the family, he is not sure of his role. Such families benefit extremely well from the limit-setting provided in the family interviews and by clarifying family roles of parents and children.

For these families with chaotic structures and parental dysfunctions, structured family intervention is necessary. The family members need to learn how they communicate and how they affect each other. A variety of levels of intervention may be called for, including not only therapy sessions but also some sort of home-care counseling to provide support when a situation is too shaky, or to help out with everyday household management and family survival skills. One-parent families need group support in order to feel less lonely, isolated, and helpless. Group meetings with other single parents are extremely helpful.

Broken Families

In this category are included those families in which one or both parents are absent during the crucial and most critical period of the child's life. Parents in these families may be addicted to drugs, have been alcoholics for many years, have been in and out of mental hospitals for many years, and so forth. Some of these families may also have suffered death of family members, while in others a family member is seriously ill.

For such families a social agency becomes the substitute parents. Very often the children must be placed in foster homes. Intervention strategies geared to promoting substitute families are very important for these cases, despite the fact that many of the youngsters involved are self-destructive. In an adequately structured foster home or group home they can develop relationships and move toward adulthood. To facilitate this kind of development, the sense of a caring community is imperative. It is therefore extremely important for foster homes to work in clusters, providing a substitute extended family and nourishing the foster families so that they will have the energy to continue to cope with individual youngsters.

Summary

All of the categories described here shed light on the intervention strategies both possible and necessary to work with such families and their youngsters. For any intervention strategy to be effective, it is necessary first to assess the amount of structure, the amount of energy, and the amount of resources available for that family before any plan is initiated. In many cases, changing the pattern of interaction is extremely helpful, a technique that is highlighted when family meetings are held. Another useful strategy is the extended family therapy model. Such a model takes into consideration not only the immediate family, but all other family members of the extended family, as well as other community adults relevant in the life of the adolescent delinquent. By holding several extended family meetings, new resources and new energies can be found to motivate the children and create new possibilities for growth.

The Child, the Family, and the Community-Based Program

It becomes clear that the closing of institutions in Massachusetts, and the return of the youth to the home and community, is not a solution to the problems of collusion and negative labeling. It is, however, a beginning. As a second step, a new network of relationships has begun to emerge in Massachusetts, one that can serve as a model to replace punishment with protection, and collusion with collaboration. Through the development of community-based programs that offer protection to young people in trouble, which the family has been unable or unwilling to supply, further work toward reintegration into the community can be implemented. The closing of institutions has, moreover, far-reaching implications for establishing new kinds of arrangements to be negotiated between the youth, the family, and the institutions serving them. These relationships follow a general pattern.

1. The child is a participant in the decision-making process concerning rehabilitation. He or she is no longer treated as deviant, deficient, or disturbed, even if the courts have committed the youth to the Department of Youth Services.

2. The problem is no longer seen as residing in the "wayward youth." Instead, responsibility is shared among the child, the family, peers and the school—that is, between the youngster and the immediate community.

3. In order to insure protection for the child when that protection is not forthcoming from the family, DYS will act as the advocate. The intention in taking over this role is to intervene in the process of adjudication so that the child is not labeled delinquent. The Massachusetts Department of Youth Services provided for this function by placing a case worker or court officer in the juvenile courts. This person, when necessary, works out arrangements for a resource for the child outside of his or her family.

4. Residential programs, should it become necessary to remove the youngster from the home, are community-based. If possible they are located in the child's own neighborhood, and provide for individual, group, and family counseling.

5. Nonresidential programs are preferred. Wherever feasible, the youngster is maintained in the community and with his or her own family. When this is not possible, an effort is made to establish a foster home placement for the youth in his or her own neighborhood. Traditional family ser-

vice agencies are employed where appropriate as part of these arrangements to provide services to the child's family.

It is evident, however, that in many cases new, more comprehensive intervention strategies are needed. These approaches must be formulated to meet the individual needs of the adolescent and the family, and since our tools for evaluation are imperfect, they must be flexible in order to respond to the reality of each case.

Summary

It is helpful to examine the strategies called for in each of the three categories of families requiring intervention that are described above.

Adolescent rebellion calls for family therapy sessions and individual advocacy work with the youth to help break the family's destructive patterns of interaction, and to teach all involved how to separate and grow independently. It is necessary to refocus the youth's energies toward working on self-sufficiency and the development of an independent living situation. Parents must also be aided in coping with pressures and crises through the work of a home-care counselor.

Parental dysfunction requires family sessions aimed at teaching parents and children how they communicate with and affect each other. There is a need for intensive intervention beyond these sessions by counselors who can provide support in crises and who can teach practical survival skills. These counselors must also act as advocates for the family. Single-parent families, especially, need group meetings with other single parents to lessen feelings of loneliness and isolation, and to build a support system for themselves within the community.

Broken families require family substitutes for their children, most usually foster homes working in clusters. The development of the sense of a caring community of which the youth is a part is necessary in the case of troubled families.

The families that the Massachusetts Department of Youth Services deals with are almost all economically deprived, and tend therefore to be overwhelmed by pressures from all sides. The role of the nonprofessional home-care counselor is of paramount importance, since he or she can spend many hours each week in the home, responding quickly when crises arise, and helping to assure the family that help is possible.

This model of intervention permits DYS and private agencies to move away from punitive roles, through which the child is labeled delinquent and is isolated from society in a way that prepares him or her for a criminal career. While intervention by the professional family therapist is a part of the model, it is most important that assistance and support from the home-care counselor be provided as well.

9 Systems of Control and the Serious Youth Offender

Jerome G. Miller

The title of this chapter, in a sense, speaks to the paradox and indeed the dilemma which confronts those who would understand or deal effectively with the problem of violent offenses committed by juveniles. Most public concern, media comment, and, unfortunately, scientific research relate only to one or the other side of the dichotomy. More often than not, we focus on either the systems of control (training schools, new treatment modalities, ideologies of deterrence, etc.) or the description of the serious juvenile offender (new diagnostic criteria, actuarial or psychological profiles, life histories of potentially or actually dangerous juvenile offenders, etc.). In our constant search for the most effective system of control, on the one hand, and our seeking of the most valid diagnostic or labeling process for the serious juvenile offender, on the other, we may be redoing the wheel every decade or so to fit current professional ideology or public hysteria about young people, without addressing in any meaningful sense the issues which underly the dialectic. As a result, we are caught up in a dilemma of either prematurely overdefining and overpredicting violence in juvenile offenders or overpromising the capacity of our so-called systems of control (or treatment) to deliver effective results.

In this chapter I propose to examine some of the reasons for this pattern and make tentative recommendations as to how we might break out of the self-defeating, self-fulfilling cycle in which we are presently caught. In addition, I will present some personal experiences and theoretical background regarding understanding and dealing with the so-called serious juvenile offender.

The search for the "answer" in understanding the social deviant, whether he or she is "violent" or not, is hardly a new one. From the diagnostic indicators outlined in the medieval "Witches Hammer," to Lombrosian theory, to the psychoanalytic approaches of Lindner or Cleckley, to the latest round of "Aha" diagnosis of Yochelson, the futile search continues. Taking a historical perspective, however, one cannot but marvel at how closely the particular diagnoses, labels, and descriptions of behavior coincide with particular public concerns or political ideologies of the day. Denis Chapman, the British writer, has commented, for example, that Lombrosian theory of criminality coincided neatly with the prison regimens of the Victorian times. He notes, for instance, that D.L. Howard, the British criminologist, asserted that the punitive English practice in penal

institutions of the late nineteenth century found a felicitous ally in Lombrosian theory:

> The DuCane Regime (named after a British prison administrator), far from
> following public opinion was successful in directing it to some extent. Men
> and women went into prison as people. They came out as Lombrosian
> animals shorn and cropped, hollow-cheeked and frequently as a result of
> dietary deficiencies and lack of sunlight, seriously ill with tuberculosis.
> They came out mentally numbed and some of them insane; they became the
> creatures, ugly and brutish in appearance, and stupid and resentful in
> behavior, unemployable and emotionally unstable which the Victorian
> middle classes came to visualize whenever they thought of prisoners. Much
> of the prejudice against prisoners which remains today may be due to this
> conception of them not as the commonplace, rather weak people the ma-
> jority of them really are, but as a composite caricature of the distorted per-
> sonalities produced by DuCane's machine.[1]

Chapman notes that "the theories of Lombroso and others on criminal
types, and Victorian stereotype of the criminal were identical. Prison produced the criminal type, scientific theory identified him even to the pallor of
his skin and the public recognized him; the whole system was logical, water
tight, and socially functional."[2] Chapman believes that the same process exists today in a modified form. The situation is more complex since one part
of the public wishes to modify or to abolish the prison and training school
systems, while many others believe in punishment and social isolation. He
notes that in such a contemporary system, "the change in prison conditions
proceeds at a rate rapid enough to satisfy the pressures of reformers while
continuing to produce the 'abnormal', the 'psychologically motivated', the
'inner-directed delinquent' whose maladjustment is 'deep-seated' and often
'intransigent to treatment' and who, in his turn becomes the scapegoat
needed by society and the data for the latter day Lombrosos whose social
function is to provide the 'scientific' explanation required by the culture."[3]

In this context, the diagnosis relieves the strain on the social system by
diverting attention from its inadequacies and focusing attention on the individual deviant or class of deviants who, paradoxically, are largely a product of the inconsistencies inherent in the system. With this as background,
the diagnosis of the serious juvenile offender may tell us as much about the
culture, quality, and types of controls or treatment options existing in that
culture as it does about any scientific or pseudo-scientific entity or
characteristic intrinsic to the offender or class of offender. By stressing
primarily the identification and labeling of the serious offender, we may
further confuse the possibilities for understanding the greater issue involving the dynamic existing between the diagnostic process and the treatment
process (social control). The two are complementary rather than discrete.

The labeling of the offender stands opposite the systems of control which already exist and which call for "appropriate" labels. This is not to suggest that there is no need to understand violent behavior among juveniles or that we cannot do something about those juveniles who engage in such behavior, but rather to question the current one-dimensional approaches to multi-dimensional problems.

In trying to deal with the issue of the serious juvenile offender, one is immediately caught up in the insanity of the ways in which we are encouraged to form opinions on the types and extent of those offenders we refer to as "serious" or "dangerous." For example, much of the press, and particularly the press of more liberal persuasion, such as the *New York Times,* seem to be misinformed on this issue. Having read the press, one might be excused for gaining the impression that there are hundreds of thousands of violent juveniles stalking the streets with predatory intent. In these days of omen-like concern with possessed children and current (I believe irrational) panic among liberals with reference to young people, such misinformation gets a bit saddening and at other times puzzling. One hears of culture lag, but it is disconcerting to see this kind of media lag regarding the serious juvenile offender. I do not wish to minimize the extent of serious crime by juvenile offenders, but I think the facts, at least as best I can cull them from statistical information available, show that even though juvenile violence is at an unacceptable level, it has been declining in recent years. Juvenile violence in New York City, for example, peaked in 1973 and has been steadily declining ever since.

A good example would be crimes of violence on the aged. Although such crimes are a matter of very great concern, it is an odd sort of concern that comes three years after the peaking of the fact. The hysteria winds up as the problem winds down. You get a kind of inverse situation—as the events level off, or decrease, the focus on *individual cases* of violence increases. Perhaps there is something to be said about the sort of thing referred to as a "Machiavellian" theory of society. I had always associated it with Durkheim, and his view that when a society is not united around a war with an outside nation, it tends to look inward for scapegoats, generally focusing first on the poor, and then on the criminal offender. It seems these days as though it focuses on the juvenile criminal. Press reports, *not based on statistical evidence of a growing problem* but on a "case history" or "war story" approach, are usually gleaned from interviews with police, judges, or prosecutors. I think it reached its most absurd level a few months ago in the *New York Times* when the "evidence" presented in an article to show a growth in violent juvenile crime in a particular police jurisdiction was the fact that there were *fewer* arrests and *fewer* reported cases of juvenile violence in the most recent reporting period. The facts were interpreted to mean that because of a lack of police manpower on the streets, there was a lessening of reports and fewer arrests. The newspaper story emanated from interviews with several police detectives whose unit was threatened with extinction because of the current New York City fiscal crisis. The only conclusion one can draw from such a reportorial or editorial stance is that of the classic "double bind," which some say is an inducement to schizophrenia. That is, if there are statistics which show a *lessening* rate of violence among juveniles, there must be a *rising* rate of violence among juveniles. Conversely, if there are statistics which show a *rising* rate of violence among juveniles, it is indicative of a *rising* rate of violence among juveniles. This is a variation on the Zen enigma whereby the master tells the student, "If you ask me *not* to hit you with a stick, I'll hit you with it. If you ask me to hit you with this stick, I'll hit you with it." At this point the student is supposed to take the stick from the master. Unfortunately, there is no such simple pulling back from such a context within a misplaced editorial policy.

In this sort of atmosphere, therefore, it is difficult to speak calmly and rationally about the problems of the serious juvenile offender, particularly the so-called violent juvenile offender.

The term *serious juvenile offender* was recently adopted by LEAA as they developed guidelines for discretionary funding. They had begun with the term *violent juvenile offender*, but having received a study from the Ford Foundation indicating that there were not that many violent juvenile offenders, at least in juvenile correctional institutions around the country (the study came up with a figure of somewhat less than 1,000 nationally, and maybe as few as 600), LEAA did not think that there would be enough violent juveniles to warrant discretionary funding. So the definition was widened to include the "serious" juvenile offender.

This view receives some support in New York, for example. Peter Edelman, Director of the New York Division of Youth, gave a paper at a conference on the violent juvenile offender in Minnesota in which he noted that in the first 6 months of the "designated offender" law in New York, twenty-five juveniles had been sentenced under its provisions to secure facilities and about fifty had in fact been tried under the new law. If this pattern holds as the courts get used to the new law, the total number of violent juveniles in New York will be very close to the numbers projected in the so-called Cahill Report to Governor Carey on the problem of violent juveniles in New York State.[4] This report indicated that there would probably be no more than 150 violent juveniles coming into the system in any given year for a population of 18 million plus—juveniles who had been apprehended, convicted, and sentenced for those very specific violent crimes such as murder, rape, assault with a weapon, forcible sodomy, that sort of thing. A member of the study committee indicated that the real number would probably be under 100, but it was expanded to 150 in view of public perception of a much larger problem.

In addition, I think this experience is consonant with what I know personally, having headed juvenile correctional systems in a couple of major industrial states, not totally unlike New York. When I was in Massachusetts, there was always talk that what we did there was an anomaly. When addressing a group in New York, the response was that what we did regarding deinstitutionalization in Massachusetts was very interesting, but it had very little relevance to a state like New York, with its large population, New York City gang traditions, etc. Then when I went to Pennsylvania, I found that in that total state system (where, incidentally, the juvenile age goes to 18), one would be hard put to find seventy-five juveniles in the total state system under those sorts of commitments. More likely, the figure would be somewhere between forty and fifty, including juveniles sentenced to adult prisons for murder. The same would be true with reference to Massachusetts. Using those very narrow definitions of the violent offender, one would be hard put to find twenty-five or thirty such juveniles in the total state system—this in a state where virtually all the crimes mentioned would be handled by juvenile court, with sentencing in most cases to juvenile facilities. (Massachusetts has no tradition of "binding over" to adult court in large numbers.)

We often hear, therefore, that these figures are deceptive, that the offenders just have not been caught, or that the courts are treating them leniently and therefore they do not end up in our system, since they are on probation, plea bargained, etc. Once again, in no way does this perception jibe with my experience.

Courts, particularly juvenile courts, are as gossipy as the press, and are as much taken with the bizarre case as is any reporter. The average juvenile court is not about to let the violent or bizarre case slip through its fingers. Perhaps this happens in New York City, but it certainly does not happen in any jurisdiction that I have been well acquainted with in Massachusetts, Illinois, or Pennsylvania. In fact, juveniles convicted of violent crimes *do* come into the state juvenile or adult correctional system. In Massachusetts, it would be very unusual for them to go into the adult system. In Pennsylvania, murder would generally go into the adult system. But, although we would find less than seventy-five such "violent" juveniles in the state juvenile and adult correctional systems in Pennsylvania, a state with a population of 12 million, we did find over 400 juveniles *defined* by the courts as being dangerous and indeed confined to an adult prison—a regular adult prison with cellblocks, confinement to cells for 20 or more hours a day, with an average sentence of 1½ to 3 years and an average age of 16.

When we did a case-by-case breakdown on these juveniles, we found less than one in four committed on crimes against persons. Certainly the very heinous kind of crime under the so-called designated offender act would account for twenty or less—this out of a total of 400. We did find kids in an adult facility for joy-riding tractors, turning over tombstones, cruelty to animals, nonpayment of traffic fines, and a variety of other things. This view that somehow or other the juvenile courts are mollycoddling, permissive agencies has not been borne out in my experience in a couple of major states in this country. The fact that we could find only twenty or so juveniles who would fit the designated offender definition flies in the face of having ten to twenty times that number of juveniles defined as dangerous enough to need confinement to an adult prison on a long sentence.

Of course, there was nothing on the record to indicate that there were indeed that many "dangerous" juveniles. Subsequent experience in the 3 years since the closing of the prison to juveniles has borne this out. In fact, the vast majority did well in a variety of nonresidential community alternatives, while the rate of juvenile crime, and particularly juvenile violence (including Philadelphia gang violence), continues to decline dramatically. This is not to say the decline is *because* of the removal of the juveniles from prison; rather, it is merely to point out that there is no evidence that their release contributed to the higher juvenile crime and violence rate which had been predicted by those who saw the prison as necessary for "serious" or "dangerous" juveniles.

In addition, in Pennsylvania one finds hundreds of other youths confined in secure settings of one sort or another, state training schools, jails, privately run training schools, etc.—800 to 1,000 in state training schools, another 1,000 in private training schools, 3,000 annually kept (often illegally) in county jails or other secure or coercive settings. Most of these juveniles would be labeled at least tacitly as dangerous. Unfortunately, our nomenclature, legal or psychiatric, does not allow us to differentiate the violent or dangerous offender from the juvenile who is a "pain in the ass" or a "management" problem. Therefore, for want of honesty, we escalate the diagnosis to one of "violence" or potential dangerousness, even though we have no evidence of either or if the "violence" is in response to an institutional regimen and unrelated to any history of street violence.

This process of escalating the diagnosis brings me to what I view as the heart of the issue in defining the violent or serious juvenile offender. Ronald Laing, the British psychiatrist, has commented that most diagnoses are "social prescriptions." This is quite a different thing from what most of us impute to the diagnostic or labeling process. Those of us in the so-called helping professions often maintain the naive view that the diagnosis of serious juvenile offenders is a scientific exercise. At other times, when feeling less comfortable with psychiatric nomenclature or the rehabilitative ethic, we stress the legal definition of the violent offender. Having left academia and been in the administrative or political world for a few years, it is my impression that we have neglected the most crucial aspect of this process—namely, the bureaucratic and political considerations which call for certain psychiatric or legal social prescriptions. In fact, when the field of juvenile justice is distilled down to those youths in the juvenile correctional system—the apprehended, convicted, and sentenced juvenile—*diagnosis is more likely than not to be a bureaucratic response to a political problem.*

This, indeed, is the history of diagnosis as it has affected the bulk of juveniles caught up in the so-called juvenile justice system. This is the reason that most of our secure facilities for juveniles do *not* contain many dangerous or violent offenders, but rather youngsters who present management problems to the courts or the correctional system. Such juveniles reveal a bureaucratic intransigence or apathy and are thereby a political problem. The issue is not one of whether there are enough secure facilities for the dangerous juvenile offender, so much as it is that we shy away from looking at the juvenile justice system which is the definer of "violent" or "dangerous" juveniles and which must escalate the diagnosis in that direction as a means of avoiding coming to grips with its own inconsistencies.

These, therefore, are the problems at the other side of the dichotomy, in the so-called systems of control. Functional relationships exist within the helping professions' rehabilitative and treatment settings, from the most closed to the most open. Such settings reflect larger social systems and are at least partially related to social control. Therefore, when one approaches the systems of control necessary to deal with the serious juvenile offender, one again sees how culturally bound such systems are. It matters very little to the person defined as a serious or violent juvenile offender whether that definition is as the "sinner" of the seventeenth century, the "possessed" of the eighteenth century, the "moral imbecile" of the nineteenth century, the "constitutional psychopathic inferior" of the early twentieth century, the "psychopath" of the 1940s, the "sociopath" of the 1950s, the "person unresponsive to verbal conditioning" of the 1960s, or the "criminal personality" or "career criminal" of the 1970s—the treatment is basically the same, a series of variations on a familiar theme of incarceration, isolation, and exile. The systems seem to be designed to prove that we must define and treat this human being as qualitatively different from the rest of us and therefore in need of methods of control or manipulation which we would reserve only for violent strangers, never for violent friends or relatives—and that, or course, is the core of the problem. In such a system, "cure" approximates the definition given by the anthropologist, Edmund Leach. In speaking of the treatment regimens in British "approved schools," he said, "Cure is the imposition of discipline by force; it is the maintenance of the values of the existing order against threats which arise from its own internal contradictions."[5]

The diagnosis, in this context, helps relieve strain on the system by allowing attention to be focused on an individual or class of "deviants," many or most of which, paradoxically, are to a degree products of that very same system. The process repeats itself. Only the labels are changed to protect the guilty.

In all the above-mentioned labels and diagnoses, the focus is the same—we avoid coming to grips with the political and bureaucratic issues which lurk somehow below our awareness but which might enlighten the whole process. In addition, an interesting byproduct of such circular self-fulfilling exercises is that as the diagnostic or treatment system becomes more ineffective and impotent in its stated goals, the diagnosis of the individual deviant becomes more important. As this happens, the diagnosis must itself be escalated and made more extreme. Thus we redo the familiar pattern of total institutions with captive populations, whereby to the degree that an institution is ineffective or brutal, to that degree the inmates are defined themselves as brutal and inhuman. This process provides an ideal context for the bizarre "war story" approach in the press as justification for such labels as "serious juvenile offender." It also provides the ideal story for the press, whereby atypical selected individual offenders can be seen as representative of a group of new violent juveniles. Thus, we find ourselves in the current dilemma of a fantastic lack of social control innovations or treatment options on one side, with even less originality in our perception and understanding of the dangerous or violent offender on the other.

This issue is further compounded by the growth and accumulating power of the "helping professions" and the consequent bureaucracies engendered. Many of us, for example, have long bemoaned the inability of the mental health profession to provide helpful diagnostic categories or effective treatment modalities for the violent juvenile offender. However, when one sees the involvement of this profession, for example, in applying the medical model to correctional settings, one often sees more maltreatment and disregard of human rights than in many more traditional correctional institutions, penitentiaries, and jails. It has been a personal impression, for example, that medically run facilities for the criminally insane have characteristically the worse tradition of brutal and dehumanizing institutional treatment. One need not look further than the recent history of such facilities as Lima State Hospital in Ohio, Mattawan Hospital in New York, Farview Hospital in Pennsylvania, Camarillo State Hospital in California, or Bridgewater State Hospital in Massachusetts. In the last situation of "Titicut Follies" fame, one sees the issue distilled in the pleadings of a "patient" to be allowed once again to become a "prisoner," and to be returned to Walpole State Penitentiary (hardly a benign institution) since "treatment" at Bridgewater was driving him insane.

We have often maintained a naive view, taught us in some graduate schools, that the diagnosis of the serious juvenile offender is scientific and the treatment following therefrom is a consequent scientific exercise. In fact, the diagnosis is often a political problem which culminates in a bureaucratic process called treatment. This is not to suggest that there may not be a way to better understand and control violent offenders. It is simply to point out that most of the persons, structures, and systems which are ostensibly set up to do that are in fact doing something quite different; what they are doing muddies the scientific waters so much that the problem is further compounded. As a result, any scientist who steps into this arena is quickly politicized, whether he or she means to be or not. Similarly, his or her data, if drawn from this field, cannot be taken at face value because data collected from this system are often compiled, named, and outlined for purposes other than those given. As a result, "objective" labels such as "assaultive" are skewed in terms of the needs of the various juvenile justice, diagnostic, and treatment bureaucracies, and it is often impossible to know clearly what the "assaultive" behavior is or was.

It seems to me that those who prepared the so-called Cahill Report on serious juvenile offenders in New York implicitly recognized this problem. They attempted to define violent behavior in very specific behavioral terms, understanding the propensity of the juvenile justice bureaucracies to overpredict violence and to overdefine potential dangerousness. Using strict definitions of proven violence—murder, rape, forcible sodomy, assault with a weapon, etc.—they limited the potential for overpredicting or overdiagnosing violence in a particular juvenile. They thereby limited the use of psychiatric or social work jargon as the fainthearted bureaucrats' means of avoiding accountable decisions or potentially embarrassing incidents which might follow from those decisions.

As an administrator in the field looking at the issue of the serious juvenile offenders, I would date the current hysteria as beginning with the publication in the *New York Times* magazine a few years ago of an article on violent juvenile crime, which described in morbid detail the torture and sordid misuse of a couple of white middle-class youngsters at the hands of some inner-city black youths. This set the tone for a series of articles, and indeed careers were made by certain reporters in writing on this issue. Most of the articles came from interviews with police, with a strong peppering of "horror stories." It also provided ample justification for the continued high use of incarceration in this country, and indeed seemed to point to the need for more incarceration of juveniles. It justified our continued overuse of incarceration, whereby we cage more adults and juveniles than any Western or Eastern industrialized nation, with the exception of South Africa.

I did a brief survey of institutionalization in Pennsylvania, for instance, and found that if one includes homes for the aged, mental hospitals, jails, prisons, training schools, state institutions for retarded, and child welfare institutions, for a population of 12 million, there are at least 2 million who have been or are presently institutionalized—with some likelihood that the figure really approaches 3 million. This means that we are institutionalizing, at some time or other, 20 to 25 percent of the population in "total institutions." This inordinate use of institutionalization in the United States speaks to the difficulties in winding down this whole system, which seems to escalate. Whenever we have more problems, we seem to ask for more of the same, which to a degree has created the problem. The institutions exist to confirm, in ritual, the diagnosis, which in turn calls for more institutionalization, much of it disguised under professional "community-based" auspices. This is perhaps because the institution is the refuge par excellence for the edgy bureaucrat. There are few bureaucrats more edgy than juvenile court judges and staff or administrators of juvenile correctional agencies. They will generally *not* be held accountable for the youngster who is institutionalized. They will, however, be held accountable for the youngster who is not institutionalized unless he or she is lost in another system such as foster care, which itself has many of the manipulative aspects which are characteristic of total institutions.

The corrections administrator can have a youngster in a prison for 2 or 3 years sentenced on a nonviolent crime like joy-riding and after his sentence return to the streets and 6 months later assault someone, and the institution or the bureaucrats who sustain it will not be held accountable in any sense. However, if that same youngster had, even for a short time, been in a noninstitutional program where he enjoyed relatively more freedom, and the same thing occurred, the administrator would be held very accountable by the public, politicians, and fellow bureaucrats. The total institution remains a bureaucrat's asylum. And recently, it has become increasingly blessed with professionalization, which makes it an "acceptable" refuge. It is more palatable to call the "hole," "intensive care," or to name "isolation" as a "process of setting limits on acting out behavior." Terms like *sociopath* or *psychopath* seem somehow more meaningful than "bad ass," even though the treatments emanating from such labels and descriptions might be hard to distinguish one from another. A creative administrator of whatever ideology can *buy* professional support for the most brutal systems of institutionalization in any state for less than 5 percent of an average correctional or mental health budget. One can find the appropriate psychiatrist, psychologist, social worker, or chaplain to stand out front and bless the most inhumane of human treatment.

Our systems for the labeling and diagnosing serious juvenile offenders call for certain kinds of social control, and in a circular way, those very control systems constrict the potential of the diagnostic process itself. For example, in our planning for the alternative placement of 400 juveniles from an adult prison in Pennsylvania, we brought in a group of sophisticated clinicians to complete a diagnostic workup on each of the juveniles in the prison. We did not, however, simply assign them to the task of immediately interviewing the juveniles. Rather, we had training seminars in which we reeducated the clinicians to the alternative placements which existed or which could possibly be created or found for individual juveniles. These well-trained, experienced clinicians were not in any sense novices, but there was a real need to acquaint them with a new set of alternatives which they might not have otherwise considered as they made their diagnostic assessment.

So long as they thought only in terms of the existing institutional system—prisons, probation, or parole—they were constricted in their diagnostic assessments. The diagnosis was therefore likely to be escalated in the direction of seriousness or violence, since the alternatives were not known or limited—a means of "protecting" the diagnostician. Certainly, anyone who has worked for long in psychiatric settings knows well those kinds of diagnostic games—mental patients with such diagnoses as "latent schizophrenia," whereby if the patient does well, the clinician has kept the illness "latent," and if the patient fails to improve, the clinician has "accurately" predicted the breakdown. These are bureaucratic, not scientific, responses.

When we had completed the training sessions for the clinicians on alternatives, all sorts of interesting diagnoses developed, opening up new possibilities for the incarcerated inmates. When we added to this diagnostic process the sanction of an administration committed to moving juveniles out of the jail and willing to take whatever political consequences might follow, the clinicians became more secure, suggesting a series of options which they had previously not recommended or indeed considered. Diagnostic workups had been done on a large number of the incarcerated juveniles in previous years by clinicians within the correctional or juvenile court system. Those diagnostic reports suggested that the majority of the juveniles in prison needed to be there. The diagnoses appeared often to follow closely the political ideology of the courts and probation departments to which the clinicians were tied. With a new ideology and new awarenesses, we were able to move the juveniles out into a variety of settings. We did keep some small number in alternative secure settings, about forty. This was later undone by the welfare bureaucracy, which, in response to political pressure from certain judges, increased the number of secure slots to 160—*not* for serious offenders, but as a sop to punitive or faint-hearted judges. The numbers of truly violent juveniles in the 400 was probably twenty-five or less.

As the new system of alternative care becomes progressively bureaucratized in the Welfare Department in Pennsylvania, one can anticipate less and less creativity in both the diagnosis and treatment alternatives, with a consequent escalation of the diagnosis of "serious juvenile

offender'' as applied to those juveniles who present management or placement problems. There will then be a real danger of retreat to the institutional modalities, not as a "law and order" backlash, but rather as a
bureaucratic and professional wearing away of any system which holds
them accountable—and institutions do not. This has not happened in
Massachusetts yet, and although I would not be completely surprised if it
did happen, I do not think it will. If the training schools were ever to be
reopened, however, it would not be a result of rightwing backlash, but
would rather be due to the actions of professionals often associated with the
liberal community coming in and professionalizing the institutional arrangements. One of the reasons we succeeded in closing the reform schools
in Massachusetts is that there were very few professionals involved in running them or in the task of closing them. It was a much easier system to deal
with than a system, for example, such as in California, which is as brutal as
anything we had in Massachusetts, being one of the worst juvenile correctional systems in the nation, but run by people with M.S.W.'s and Ph.D.'s.

I think the problem of creating effective and lasting alternatives is further compounded by the keeper-kept relationship in juvenile corrections,
which to a large degree prevails perhaps of necessity. As Philip Zimbardo
has clearly demonstrated, there are very real problems inherent in the relationships of keeper-kept, guard-captive, problems which militate against
humane and effective care over the long haul. Perhaps even more basic than
this is the inability to introduce any amount of honest consumerism into
such a system—ultimately, the impossibility of introducing any kind of accountability. At best, such systems become paternalistic, and at worst, they
become repressive and brutal. This, of course, is the eternal dilemma of corrections as we have designed it—primarily for the poor. For the serious
juvenile offender of the upper middle classes, certainly, we have the structure of a consumerist-oriented system. It will be found in the annexes and
intensive treatment units of the expensive private hospitals of the United
States or perhaps in the back pages of the *New York Times* magazine. It
represents a consumerist-oriented shopping approach for the handling of
"difficult" youngsters who present management problems as well as in
many cases "violent" youngsters. We had an arrangement with an expensive private psychiatric hospital near Boston, for instance, for the handling
of youngsters with us on murder, particularly heinous and bizarre kinds of
murder. We found available, if we were willing to pay well, a fairly decent
locked facility wherein the clients would not be misused. I cannot say how
well they would be rehabilitated, but at least they could associate with an interesting group of other human beings without being subject to rape,
assault, and the like, which is par for the hard-core correctional setting.

In one case in which a youngster, not at the hospital for having committed a particularly heinous crime, presented the staff with a number of man-

agement problems, the staff discussed the case and decided that he needed a more structured setting, namely, an adult prison. I discussed the matter with the head of the hospital and suggested that this must be a "first" for this rather exclusive hospital, that prison would be recommended as treatment for a teenager. I took for granted that the recommendation had to do with social class of the youngster involved. When it was made clear that we would be forced to remove the other youngsters from the facility if this youngster were sent to prison, the diagnosis changed rather abruptly, and the juvenile was allowed to stay on.

Nonincarcerative options therefore become a difficult problem for bureaucratic and professional reasons unrelated to effectiveness or needs of the juvenile. It is often difficult, therefore, for people to pick up this distinction between the *need for basic change* in the system and *professionalizing* the system. The two are not synonymous. People often think that in professionalizing a system they have necessarily changed it for the better. The press is particularly prone to falling into this error. A pilot program, a model social work, teaching, or psychiatric program, and administrators are free and clear to do what they wish for or to the bulk of the clientele under their care. The basic underpinnings of a treatment or correctional system will seldom be questioned if it is run by professionals. Professionalism can in fact make matters worse vis-a-vis reform.

I do not think that it is any accident that New York State, and particularly New York City, with one of the most highly sophisticated and developed professional communities in the world in psychiatry, psychology, social work, health care, and child care, that side by side with such professionalism are some of the worst institutions for human neglect in the world—Attica, Rikers Island, Willowbrook, Pilgrim State Hospital. These are not accidents, rather they reveal a symbolic relationship. One needs the other. Regardless of the *rhetoric* of the professions—which would be condemnatory of most of the above-mentioned institutions—the *actions*, diagnostic processes, screening procedures, employment structure, and so on reinforce the survival of outmoded institutions. For to move out of such institutions would entail a different type of response to so-called social deviance by the established helping professions. Professional policies, beginning with their diagnostic processes and going all the way through their screening, recruitment, and training policies, sustain and nurture institutions. The differences between latent and manifest functions of the helping professions should be looked at more carefully in this regard. We talk about how poor the large institutional settings and the "human warehouses" are, yet most professionals would not be willing to work with the clientele presently institutionalized, and indeed, the structure of professional agencies would not allow it in most cases anyway. The major professional groups in this country—psychiatry, psychology, and social work—developed out of institutionally based consortiums. It is therefore very difficult to get *outside* the system of "care" to assess its results without immediately getting tied into institutionally biased positions. Some have tried, such as R.D. Laing, Thomas Szasz, Robert Coles, writing about Soviet psychiatry and the use of mental hospitals for incarceration of political dissidents. But few, with the exception of Szasz, have pointed to the same patterns existing in contemporary American psychiatry. In doing this, one is subjected to a certain amount of questioning, and, in a sense, one puts oneself in a position of anticipating what Robert Coles refers to as "psychological slander." Szasz was certainly subjected to this when he first began to speak up and write. I happened to be at Menninger's when Szasz's first article appeared on the myth of mental illness. I can remember sitting at a staff conference with some very eminent and nationally known psychiatrists around the table, diagnosing the "paranoia" of Tom Szasz.

The field of corrections lags even more—they have not even gotten around to discussing these issues, they are concerned with identifying the "criminal personality" and will gravitate toward those professionals who will help them in that identity quest. At the ACA conference a few months ago in Milwaukee, there was a warm reception given to Dr. Samenow who outlined for the assembled guards and administrators the fifty or sixty "errors" in thinking of the "criminal mind," with the clear implication that their charges are inherently bad and for the most part must be locked up. It was a classic meeting of small minds—the joining together of pseudo-science with pseudo-help—one reinforcing the other.

In speaking to and about the issue of the serious juvenile offender, the experience in Massachusetts, which has closed all its state-run institutions for delinquents, has immediate relevance. I grow weary of discussing the Massachusetts experience, but I feel constrained to because there are so many rumors and crazy things said about it—and it does follow you. I can remember getting off an airplane in Seattle, Washington and being met by a local reporter with a sheaf of clippings, letters, etc., asking all sorts of very specific things based on the same old material. Then, when I went to Illinois, something like 50 or 100 reports put together by a very political legislative committee in Massachusetts had been circulated to various professional groups. Although the legislative committee had no credibility in Massachusetts, it apparently did in Illinois.

I take for granted, therefore, that what we did in Massachusetts touches upon something fairly deep in the human consciousness, and therefore has some meaning. It was really an attempt to change the total context within which one considers corrections. We believed that the deinstitutionalization which we were embarked on in the early seventies did not constitute any risk to public safety. We believed the research which said that what we had been doing in the massive use of incarceration was not helping and was probably making matters worse. So we did not feel that we were taking a great deal of risk in doing some other things. Our goal was a general one—to make some of the options previously available only to middle-class youngsters available to the poor, to establish an array of programs and alternatives so that there might be a certain amount of choice, to begin to establish some account-ability to the consumer, that is, the juvenile offender himself or herself, and to do all of this in *symbolic* ways that would carry meaning for the society at large—and, in that, we succeeded. We really did not deinstitutionalize that many kids—800 to 1,000 in state institutions and detention centers. Many other states got that many inmates out of one or two mental hospitals in a year or two. But what we did reverberated. The difference was that in Massachusetts we did it *totally*. And I think we did it in ways that had an ef-fect at the deeper ends of the social-behavioral spectrum.

While still in academia, I had been very involved in reading the theories of Neil Smelser on "collective behavior." His analysis meant so much to me at the time that I thought it had meanings for behavior in general. One of the basic ways in which he approached the matter was to outline collective behavior from the most specific to the most general. He developed categories—at the most specific level he had a category of "situational facilities," then less specific, "role behavior," then "role norms," and finally, at the most general and abstract level, "values." One could place along this spectrum the disciplines of psychiatry, psychology, social psychology, sociology, and anthropology—from the most specific to the most general. What Smelser said, basically, is that the degree to which you can affect something at the role-behavioral level, for instance, you can also affect situational facilities, but you need not necessarily affect "role" or "values." Again, to the degree that you affect role, you will necessarily af-fect role behavior or situational facilities; and the degree to which you af-fect values, you affect roles and role behavior and situational facilities.

Therefore, when we made changes in the Massachusetts juvenile correc-tional system, we tried to give them as much of a value impact as possible, with the hope that they would affect the more specific areas of role and role behavior. We placed the public and political discussion in those terms, and we made our moves with that very much in mind. When we put out a regula-tion that no hair could be cut without the youngster's assent, at a time when most youngsters had long hair and those in our institutions were being given short haircuts or shaved heads, we did not do it quietly, because the mean-ing would have been lost. We did it so everyone knew our intent—the kids, the staff, everyone. We got a union dispute, and it had a revolutionary meaning, the simple matter of haircuts. We did the same with our regula-tions concerning the use of physical or corporal punishment. Again, we did it so that all the actors knew equally well what we meant. These approaches, of necessity, put the institutions in a state of disequilibrium, and that is when one is immediately accused of being a poor administrator. Unfortunately, there is no way that I know to reform these kinds of institutions in any basic way without some degree of upset. And there is no way to get out of them without a great deal of upset. I have often heard that it can be done another way, and if anyone can show me where its being done another way, I would be willing to try it. Show me any other state that has gotten out of their training schools the way we learned it in social work school, and I will be glad to do it that way. It would be a lot less trouble.

The matter of symbolic meaning was therefore an important one. The last boys training school was closed in January of 1972. The girls school was closed shortly thereafter. These schools had been the first training schools for delinquents in the world—Charles Dickens had visited them on his travels in America. It was fitting, therefore, that they should be the first to be closed.

Since January of 1972, the state of Massachusetts has not had more than sixty to eighty-five youngsters in a locked setting on any given day—that for a population of over 7 million. This would include all sentenced youngsters as well as all those awaiting trial, since our agency, the Department of Youth Services, was responsible for detention services as well as the training schools. What has been the result? Lloyd Ohlin's group at the Harvard Center for Criminal Justice is publishing some thirty articles and five books on various aspects of this deinstitutionalization experience. Their results will be open to interpretation or misinterpretation, and there is something in them for the conservatives as well as the liberals. The cohort they studied into late 1972 does not go to the present. I think this is unfortunate, particularly in view of Lamar Empey's research of long-term recidivism differences between institutionalized and community-based groups, showing community-based to be quite a bit better over the long haul. However, Ohlin's overall finding is that statewide, the recidivism is about the same—down in some regions, up in others—in the community-based programs as it was in the state training schools. However, he notes dramatic differences in recidivism in different regions of the state, and between and among different programs. In fact, certain community-based programs are dramatically more effective with kids than were the training schools, when one controls for the seriousness of the offense. In other words, I am not talking about a community-based program which takes the "easy" nonserious offenders and then does "well" with them. I am talking about controlling, as best as one can, for the seriousness of the offense and the kind of kid assigned to the program.

Ohlin does find dramatic differences, despite what Bob Martinson says about nothing working (although I'm not sure what he means anymore). In fact, Ohlin's Harvard study finds that *certain programs and combinations of support programs work very well indeed.* He finds a lot of community-based programs which do not work, are mini-institutions, and are shams. These programs, when viewed by the juveniles themselves, are seen as being as manipulative of them as any old-time institutions might have been. This was found particularly in a number of the group homes. If I were doing it again, I would not have moved so dramatically to the group-home alternative. We moved 800 kids in institutions to group homes in a 1-year period. I would rather not have relied that much on the group home. The conclusion of the Harvard study, which I hope people will attend to, is *not* that we should not have moved out of state institutions, but that we *did not move far enough*—that the so-called "radical" reform in Massachusetts was not radical enough, that we did not believe our own rhetoric enough. Those kids in certain kinds of community-based programs which have strong community linkages do very well.

Now, what are these programs? Ohlin finds that the very best programs with reference to recidivism—again, when controlling for the seriousness of the offense—are specialized foster care programs. These are very specialized programs wherein the foster parent is paid a full salary to watch after one or two youngsters. This is their job. This is by far the very best program. The second best program is the so-called community advocate program wherein people, generally college students or college-age people, are paid a minimum wage to put in anywhere from 20 to 40 hours a week with a kid in his or her leisure time. This also allows a short-term residential backup whereby most of the advocates have the authority to put the kid up in their own apartment if things are in a hassle or upset in the youngster's own home. This would generally be for a night or two. The advocacy program may also be built into other kinds of service. Advocates are assigned to group homes and other kinds of facilities. They find that the group homes across the board are not that much more effective than institutions, although certain group homes are very effective. The study has developed a measure for this, based on community linkages. The effectiveness of group homes can be correlated very closely with the number and kinds of community linkages which the programs have developed. Many "community-based" programs do not have effective community linkages.

With reference to deterrence, we were told—and many a legislative committee has focused on this issue—that even though the training school may not work for the juveniles in it, and even though it may hurt them, it at least keeps others out of trouble. I like to call this the "Pontius Pilate argument." The experience in Massachusetts, as best one can glean from available police and court statistics, is that the deterrence argument does not stand up.

Juvenile crime in Massachusetts has gone about as it has in most Eastern states since 1972. Violent crime among juveniles has declined rather dramatically, and juvenile court hearings (the docket) have declined by 15 to 20 percent in the last year. This decline reverses a trend of the past decade of climbing juvenile court dockets. To state it conservatively, there was no explosion of juvenile crime in Massachusetts as a result of the closing of the state training schools. There was no indication of an increase in crime by juveniles who knew they would not be incarcerated in a training school if they engaged in crime and were caught.

Ohlin's Harvard studies show that the greatest single predictor of later recidivism is whether or not a juvenile was kept in a locked detention center early on, say, at age 13 or 14. That is, if a youngster was kept in a locked detention early in his delinquent career, the chances of his repeating were much enhanced. The normal response to such a finding is that this should be no surprise, it merely shows how well our screening process works—people who are more likely to go on to more delinquency or to engage in serious delinquency are also more likely to be detained. However, when a large number of variables were compared on this pattern, Ohlin found that, in general, there were only two things significant with reference to whether or not a kid was likely to be detained. One was social class—there is a slight correlation here in that lower-class kids were more likely to be detained. The other variable, which was the most significant one, was *whether or not there were available beds* in the detention center on the night of the juvenile's arrest. If there were beds, he or she was detained; if there were no beds, he or she was not detained. Bill Nagel's material on use of prisons nationally says something of the same.

Another finding with reference to recidivism is that the group contributing a disproportionate share of the recidivism, which tends to make the overall rate rise, is the small number of juveniles committed to secure settings. Secure settings have not worked—not even the small ones. That is another issue that must be dealt with. However, even with those more dangerous youths who tend to be sentenced to secure settings, if one is going to have a certain level of recidivism, it might as well be as attached to a decent, caring, and humane setting as it is to the brutal bureaucracy we call a prison or training school. If we get a set level of recidivism whether we treated someone decently or indecently, I would hope that we would opt to treat him or her decently.

However, the Harvard study criticizes us by saying that we did not go far enough in our reform, not that we went too far. We relied too much on residential group care, whereas the bulk of juveniles could be well handled in foster care and advocacy programs in their own homes. I fear that we are going to see some retrenchment over the years as the new system becomes bureaucratized. For instance, the movement now toward larger single contractors, although it makes some administrative sense, will ultimately dilute and destroy the better programs. The bureaucracy will erode the reform. The single contractors will lessen the chances of juveniles "shopping," and

I have always felt that shopping and manipulation are fine old middle-class norms to be much encouraged. Our kids ought to have that choice and ability.

For example, we did not insist, at least when I was there, that if you were not making it in X group home that you had to go into the detention center. Our rule was that you should stay out of trouble and stay in touch. If you wanted to move through a dozen group homes in a year, that was fine with us. We were not there to confirm the effectiveness or build the egos of the service givers. We were there to keep crime down and to allow some ability within the system to move about and grow. When we went to do some of these things in Pennsylvania, based on Massachusetts, we found that it worked relatively well with the so-called hard-core juveniles sentenced to adult prisons. These kids were considered the most difficult in the state. They would certainly be classified with the serious offender, even though many were in fact not that dangerous. Less than one in ten would be there on the type of offense outlined under the designated offender law as we find it in New York. We did set up some small eight- to ten-bed security units for the most dangerous youngsters. These units have worked well in terms of guaranteeing security. I do not know how well they will be seen to work in terms of later recidivism. However, the youngsters are treated decently in a small setting and are less likely to be subject to the assault, rape, and assorted other aspects of a typical prison. As a result of pressure from certain judges, two fifty-bed units were set up. These have caused no end of problems, and although they are somewhat more humane than the 400-bed cellblocks, they should not have been created. To put fifty troublesome kids together in one place and expect them to get much from one another, particularly with the traditions of such settings, is a bit naive. Even six in a group home is not normal. It would be an unusual family that would have six delinquent boys, all approximately 15 years old. That would be a very difficult family.

We have found in Pennsylvania that the advocate program is a very adequate program for the majority of juveniles who would be considered serious offenders. One can surround the leisure time and activities of the youngster with enough contact to ensure less delinquency. There are dangers in such programs if in the wrong hands. One example can be seen in the so-called tracking program in Massachusetts, where the advocate has to account for his charge five times every 24 hours in a face-to-face interview. The surveillance aspect of this has been misunderstood by some, and it was distorted by Robert Martinson, who came up with his "cop a con" program, turning the whole thing into a surveillance police function. Our advocates were always privately contracted and were trained to be advocates for the youngster—to represent the youngster in the job market, school, with social agencies, etc. They were not mini-probation officers whose allegiances were clearly to the courts or correctional agencies. This distinction is clear in the minds of the clientele. David Rothman, the author of *The Discovery of the Asylum*, mentioned this danger once in conversation, noting that the institution may serve the need of keeping the repressiveness and surveillance behind the walls, and we would be in trouble if we were to get it all out into the community. This is something we must consider, particularly if one looks to plans of surveillance of offenders as proposed a few years ago by Schwitzgebel.

There has been a great deal of naivete regarding the numbers of dangerous juveniles and the extent of the problem. It is related to some of the things which we do not normally consider. In trying to understand what is going on, we rely very often on carriers of the message who are anything but objective—the bureaucracies, the people who have vested interests involved in jobs, contracts, social roles, etc. The ways in which much of the research is designed, the definitional categories set up, and the questions asked make things very dicey and difficult. James Q. Wilson makes great sense when read. But I also have another impression of a Robert Mac-Namara reading the statistics on the situation in Vietnam and fashioning a strategy from that data. For Wilson to say some of the things he says with as little experience as he has in the prison system in this country, for example, is extremely naive, at least insofar as one wishes to have a theory grounded in fact. The "new mandarins" that Chomsky referred to during the Vietnam era have now invaded corrections. Corrections is virgin territory for the intellectual. Unfortunately, a lot of people can be destroyed before the theories are shown to be false or misinformed.

It is important, therefore, that in discussing the dangerous offender, we consider who the *definers* are, and what professions and bureaucracies provide the backdrop for the defintion. We must realize that defining the "serious juvenile offender" is a subjective, nonobjective field. We must be very careful in developing any policies on these bases. Justice Brandeis is quoted as saying that we can best judge the degree of civilization in a society by looking to how that society treats its most vulnerable. We usually think in terms of the aged, the retarded, the abused child, etc. However, in a paradoxical way for those of us involved in juvenile corrections, the most vulnerable person in our society is the person who has committed the most heinous crime, has been caught, and is now with us. This is the person we can mistreat with public applause, and to political advantage. It is at that point that our own humanity and that of the society will be measured. The present concern about whether rehabilitation works or not should not lead to the conclusion that we must get back to punishment. The question as to whether rehabilitation works or not is beside the point. It is seldom asked in middle-class psychoanalytic practice. It probably works there at about the same rate it works in corrections. However, that whole process, or game, fulfills other needs for society. If nothing else, the rehabilitative process keeps us in a state of moral ambivalence. If we take that away, we must be very careful of what replaces it. I am no supporter of the rehabilitative ethic or the indeterminate sentence, but by the same token, I would not want to be identified as a supporter of kinds of repressive approaches, no matter how well motivated, which will result in even more craziness in this highly institutionalized country of ours, should we not know clearly where we are headed with a just-deserts model. Legal games may not be much more productive than psychiatric games.

In summary, therefore, it is the contention of this chapter that we cannot know or understand either the serious juvenile offender (his or her characteristics, numbers, intensity, etc.) or the systems of control (treatment, secure programs, deterrence, etc.) until we look more closely at the backdrop against which these issues and concerns are defined, developed, and implemented (that is, the juvenile justice and "helping professions" bureaucracies). To attempt to either define or treat the serious juvenile offender without due consideration for the arena in which the problem is considered is to invite further frustration and failure. I have attempted to point out some of the considerations and issues in this chapter. The solutions are, of course, more difficult, and in a sense, it is contradictory to suggest that solutions are possible in this confused system. However, directions might be plotted and for that, to paraphrase Robert Theobald, we need a compass rather than a map. This chapter has been an attempt to provide some of those bearings. As one maps the uncharted territory, there are a few suggestions which might be helpful in keeping our directions straight.

As we seek an understanding of the serious offender and the systems of control which we set up to deal with him or her, we must stress the following—although in the present juvenile justice system context, some of the suggestions might appear absurd. Perhaps it is time to send in the clowns, and perhaps, they might help us keep our bearings. The following must take place:

1. Accountability to the client (in this case, the invalidated, captive "serious" juvenile offender) must be stressed. He or she remains the best judge of the effectiveness and appropriateness of our diagnosis and treatment.
2. The diagnosticians must be changed constantly and must be from outside the juvenile justice system.
3. Research on the problem of serious juvenile crime must focus on the political and bureaucratic characteristics of the juvenile justice system while attempting to understand the serious offenders.
4. There must be constant movement of clientele and staff to new roles between, among, and within diagnostic and treatment settings. The

movement must be vertical as well as lateral, to the degree to which program consistency and public safety allow.

5. We must build systems whereby there is constant pressure to limit, proscribe, and deescalate the diagnosis of serious or violent offenders as a means of counteracting the natural bureaucratic process of overusing and overdefining dangerousness as a rationale for social control.

6. We must increase the possibility of choice of treatment, even for those clearly violent and dangerous juveniles who are caught up in the juvenile correctional system. For example, if they have to be in a locked and secure setting, they might be given some choice as to which facility they feel best meets their needs, given a state voucher, and allowed to "shop" a bit. They also might be allowed to leave an unsatisfactory locked unit for another locked unit, and to take the state's money with them.

Notes

1. D.L. Howard, *The English Prisons* (London: Methuen, 1960).

2. Denis Chapman, *Sociology and the Stereotype of the Criminal* (London: Tavistock, 1968), p. 237.

3. Ibid.

4. Governor's Panel on Juvenile Violence, "Report to the Governor from Kevin M. Cahill, M.D., Special Assistant to the Governor on Health Affairs," panel report, Albany, N.Y., 1976.

5. Edmund Leach, *A Runaway World,* BBC Reith Lectures, 1967 (New York: Oxford Univ. Press, 1968).

Part III
Staff Training and
Program Monitoring

Introduction to Part III

Planning, training and evaluation are each optimized when they proceed hand-in-hand. Just as there is a process in the evolution of an effective training program with continuous feedback from the participants, so it is true of evaluation. Too often evaluation is regarded as a static phenomenon. Typically, a researcher selects one or another instrument to tap the independent and dependent variables, and then the costly procedure in gathering data with the aid of these instruments precludes further dynamic development of the evaluation process itself.

Too frequently the researcher and evaluators of a project begin their work with the naive assumption that a new program is clear about its goals and its methods. This is far from the truth for the development of the community-based programs on the scale projected and carried forward after deinstitutionalization in Massachusetts. It became clear both to the evaluators and the trainers that they were in for a gradual refinement of their concepts and procedures, and that this would take a considerable period of time to perfect to the point where they would be consonant with rigorous scientific research. And this is necessarily so. Training and research can never proceed in a one-sided fashion with the so-called superior knowledge of the researcher and trainer setting the stage for evaluation and training before it has been thoroughly tested. Just the opposite is true.

A dynamic program of evaluation and training must proceed on a test-by-test, step-by-step basis. When the new programs were projected for youths in trouble in Massachusetts, a whole new tradition had to evolve. It seemed best to proceed by experimenting with a wide gamut of programs. Release from the rigidity of walled institutions meant that practitioners could now evolve over a longer period of time a variety of settings, people, and programs, interacting with the community and youths with different kinds of strengths and weaknesses. It made sense to go slowly and give each of the programs time to find itself. It made sense to "fail" in the beginning and learn from these mistakes. And it also made sense to become sharper and more skillful in working with youngsters in diverse communities that accepted the youngsters to quite varying degrees.

And so it was with training as well. We started with an overall scheme of what some of the basic competency skills that the staff could apparently be trained to master, and then examined how the use of these skills impacted upon the youngsters.

In both evaluation (perhaps a better term is monitoring) and training, the strategy was to evolve a much more explicit paradigm of what the independent variables consisted of. That is, the first stage in evaluation is to find out what the programs consist of that have been established to help the youngsters. We had first to evolve a strategy of training before we could assess the impact of the training upon the staff and the youths.

This gradual process of defining treatment components potentially yields a much larger payoff in the eventual attainment of effective outcomes of accountability, both on the results of the program they impact in an overall way on the youngsters and the specific effects of training upon staff. It must be clearly understood that this is merely the first phase of a long-range program of evaluation and training.

There is another important consideration in the discussion of evaluation of any programs dealing with youths that are by and large economically deprived and have suffered together with their families from a variety of social, economic, and cultural oppressions and injustices. Social workers, counselors, and other professionals and paraprofessionals that work with the "casualties" of our society are constantly in a bind. They have to believe in their work in order to be effective. And there is no question that they have *some* impact on their charges. At the same time, we have to become more clear than we ever have in our history that the work we do with our clients can have an impact; but unless there is a significant change in the economic and social conditions of our society, many of these "casualties" will continue to suffer and continue to "fail."

We are making a plea for humility. The problems and difficulties that these youngsters have are only in part (and what part that is we could debate endlessly) due to personal deficiencies. A substantially larger part of their difficulties stems from the deficiencies of a market economy. Today we are questioning more than we ever have in our history the capacity of free enterprise to provide justice and opportunity for all its citizens. In a period when there is a continuous unemployment rate of 7 percent, or nearly seven million people, when teenage unemployment is double adult unemployment, and when minority youth unemployment is triple that of white youths, it is obvious that as much of the cause of these youths' failures lie in an inadequate social-economic system. If that is the case, then an evaluation process must take into account this kind of variance and be much more specific and wary about what constitutes "success" of one or another rehabilitative program.

Perhaps an effective evaluation procedure should test the capacity and abilities of the social workers and other personnel working in these programs to challenge society so that it can provide more meaningful opportunities for these youngsters. It is as important, if not more important, than "fixing-up" these youths so that they might be more skilled and more motivated to adapt to an adequate society.

It is in this context that we believe it will be most useful to look at the ensuing chapters on monitoring-evaluation of the programs in Massachusetts, and the initial projection of a scheme for staff training and development.

10 Training and Development of Staff for the Community-Based System

The professional child-care worker thinks and acts deliberately (as well as spontaneously) in accordance with sound mental health principles in encounters with children, their parents, and fellow staff. Three sectors—knowledge, that is, the ability to discriminate significant differences in encounters; the specific skills of how to reinforce psychosocial health; and the talent of enabling individuals and the community to internalize a humanitarian culture—must flow together for maximum normative impact.[1]

A different kind of relationship between child-care workers and their charges is needed today. There are enormous strains, both in child rearing as well as in new kinds of responsibilities in building team cooperation and maintaining high morale. It is no longer sufficient to speak about having "good human relations," because that is far too ambiguous and vague without specifying the skills necessary to integrate developmental needs with basic human concerns and relationships.

The necessary human relations skills of the effective worker can be detailed in practical conceptual terms.[2]

Cognitive and Relational Skills in Working with Individuals and the Group

As human beings, whether or not in a supervisory role, each of us looks out into the world and finds acceptable or unacceptable what others do and say. Some people's behaviors are more acceptable to us than others. But each of us has this shifting line between what we find acceptable and we consider unacceptable.

Figure 10-1 presents this idea graphically. The line in the middle is from the point of view of the worker, his "window"—the way in which he looks at behavior as acceptable or unacceptable. The first idea within this window is "no-problems" behavior. Here, children under the worker's supervision behave at an acceptable standard. This no-problem arena is divided into *follow through* and the extent to which the child takes *initiatives*.

The important point to stress here is that it is crucial for a worker to be able to identify what each child is doing well, and to give proper recognition and reinforcement to that behavior. By giving recognition to what an in-

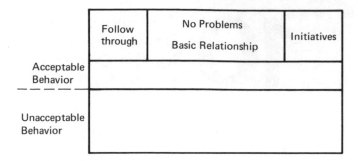

Figure 10-1. Acceptable and Unacceptable Behavior from the Worker's Point of View.

dividual or a group is doing well, we build up a positive reputation for that individual or group. If good performances are taken for granted, we may end up giving recognition and attention to individuals and groups when they are in trouble or are doing something wrong. In this way, problem children and problem units can inadvertently be rewarded. We should go in the opposite direction. No longer should we take for granted that people are doing well; behavior of individuals and groups that is above standard level should be recognized and reinforced. Then we can go on from there to upgrade other areas of functioning as well.

This takes skill both in searching out what is done well and giving the reinforcement in such a way that the individual not only continues to do well, but gains a reputation for consistently high performance in that particular area. The worker must be keenly aware of the powerful incentives that lie in giving recognition and reinforcement to performances that are above normal and not merely take them for granted. But such recognition should not either overpraise or criticize in a sardonic or sarcastic manner. Appropriate recognition should be given by telling an individual, group, or team precisely what it is they are doing well, asking what their feeling is about that, and what the consequences are for people who perform well in one or another area. This is a very necessary skill that child-care staff should develop first of all.

Figure 10-2 adds another segment to the child-care worker's "window." Here we are dealing with an area of supervision that is primarily concerned with the child who is running into some difficulty or problem. A child is neglected by peers, does poorly on a school test, is angry about not having some particular thing, and so on. From the worker's viewpoint these recurring difficulties, whether or not of the child's own making, are in an important sense *acceptable*. We all have difficulties. We all have problems. It is how the young person works at those problems that spells the important dif-

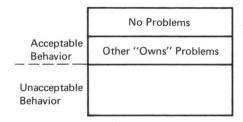

Figure 10-2. Acceptable Behavior from the Worker's Point of View.

ference between the effective and the ineffective child-care worker or human being in general.

It is critical for the worker to separate out those problems that are the children's alone from those that are also his own problems. The worker must be clear that it is natural for his charges to have problems, and to have feelings about those problems. Coping with problems can help one find a better way to live. A worker's response to the children's problems demands the skill of being congruent with his charges, being able to listen to their feelings, and to understand their difficulties and their solutions. The ability to implement a plan and follow through with it should be cultivated. The worker's skill in being able to "listen with the third ear" should therefore be maximized.

It is through this kind of process that the worker fulfills another important function, namely that of influencing the child's peers and creating a culture in which children assume more and more responsibility and intitiative in resolving their own problems. This comes about through the children observing the worker's interaction with an individual child or a subgroup. But this cannot be done if the worker does not separate out his own problems from those of his charges. Knowing that distinction, the children can be permitted to grow to the point where they are able to resolve their own difficulties.

The child's unacceptable behavior from the worker's point of view is treated in figure 10-3. For example, if a child constantly messes up his room or the living room, or does not do a share of home chores, this behavior also becomes the worker's problem. When the problem becomes the worker's, he must have certain kinds of confronting skills in order to influence his charges maximally. The child's behavior needs to be influenced without putting him down, and without destroying the worker-child relationship.

Confrontation consists of two major components: (1) the worker must be able to express his feeling in specific terms that correctly describe what the child is doing that is unacceptable, and why this is so. The worker can say, "Your clean-up has been below our standards, and I am very upset

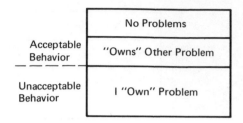

Figure 10-3. Problematic Situations from the Worker's Point of View.

about it. This could make our home messier and messier." This is a very straightforward, assertive remark. However, in order for confrontation to be most effective, the worker, after making such an assertive statement, can maximize his influence in changing the child's behavior by listening very carefully and letting the child respond with his own perceptions and feelings on the same issue. This process is shown in figure 10-4.

Confrontation at first inevitably raises people's defensive walls. When confronted, people automatically begin to rationalize and to justify their behavior. If, after a confrontation, the worker can invite the child who has been confronted to come back at him, the emotional barometer will go

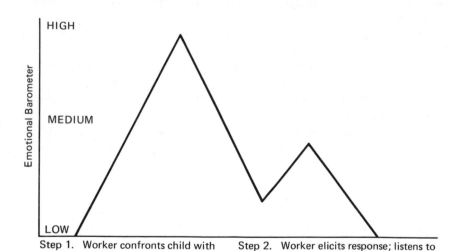

Step 1. Worker confronts child with the child's unacceptable behavior; child's feelings peak; thinking is clouded. Inevitably, the child becomes defensive.

Step 2. Worker elicits response; listens to child's comeback; is congruent with child's feelings. Child's feelings subside; thinking becomes clearer. A workable compromise is more feasible.

Figure 10-4. The Child's Emotional Reaction to the Worker's Two-Step Confrontation.

down and the child will be able to get involved in a different course of action. The two basic skills needed here are confrontation and congruent or responsive listening. The worker straighforwardly confronts the children, but does so in such a way that he can engage in a pointed but fruitful discussion about what has to be done. A specific plan to correct the problem can then be worked out, but before solutions evolve, the worker patiently listens with the "third ear."

Few organizations fail to bemoan the lack of communication within and between levels of staff, workers, and children. Under pressure each person tends to dictate what he wants and tends not to get significant feedback from the person to whom he is addressing his message. Communication can be improved in a very specific way through a method called "acknowledgement theory."[3] It is a very old but simple and dynamic idea. Instead of discounting or ignoring or criticizing what someone says to you, *first* tell yourself that what he says has some core of validity to it. When anyone is telling someone something—however distorted it is—if that person listens carefully some measure of truth will be found in it. The listener may not want to believe it, or may significantly disagree with it, but there usually is a 95 percent chance that there is validity to it. Being able to tell the other person that you heard what he said can be enormously reinforcing to him, and can improve the dialog between two people so that they can move toward a solution—or a workable compromise—to the objective or problem that they can work on *jointly.*

In our training programs we encourage this process of acknowledging what the other person says. This means the ability to sharpen your listening skill so that you can hear the possible validity within what the other person is saying. Acknowledgment means that while you do not necessarily agree with the person, you can accurately tell that person what he told you, and suspend your judgment with the idea that you will look into it more carefully or think about it more dynamically and see whether or not what he is saying may have some measure of significance or some element of truth.

After you have acknowledged what the other person has said in such a way that he knows that you accurately heard what he said, then you can add whatever you would like, possibly clearing up some distortions. But taking that first step, letting the other person know that he said something that might be important, can go a long way toward improving relationships and teamwork among associates at every level.

So in various meetings and discussions we model and teach acknowlegment theory and process. Instead of jumping to one's defense, instead of putting the other person down, instead of ignoring or evading what the other person has said, be able to reflect and tell him accurately what he has said without necessarily agreeing to it. This clears the air and enables the participants to go on to some really creative problem-solving. By including the other person's ideas and thoughts, his commitment and involvement are increased.

The last important conceptualization and skill that the worker has to master is how to deal with direct conflict with the young people in his charge. This is illustrated in Figure 10-5.

In this area there is a definite needs conflict between supervisor and subordinate. Life does not come in chunks of black and white; most of life is made up of grays. Rarely is one side completely right and the other side completely wrong. Often we can distinguish a conflict of needs. For example, suppose that the worker requires a youngster to be in the house by a designated time. The youngster's peers are pushing him to stay out later, which he wants to do. This is a conflict of needs in which the worker is concerned about the youngster's safety; the child, perhaps pushing adulthood, wants more freedom, not to be "a baby" all his life.

There is a learning process here. Worker and child appear to have priorities that are at odds. Rather than getting into a win/lose situation where the worker demands that the curfew order be carried out unequivocally—which theoretically he can do, given his authority over the child—there are other ways. By asserting his authority the worker can get obedience in the short run, but he also generates so much resentment that the child can become rebellious and retaliate in other ways, such as by becoming a "guerilla" fighter. So the win/lose situation, in which the worker has it completely his way, should be avoided because it will ultimately result in the youngster, through delaying tactics and procrastination, finding ways to rebel against all attempts at socialization.

Consider instead a win/win strategy of problem-solving, where the worker and the child together try to define the main issue, generate some solutions, devise a practical program, and then implement and follow through on it. The three methods are shown graphically in Figure 10-6. Table 10-1 summarizes worker-child interaction in the ownership problem.

This table assumes a number of important distinctions. First, we un-

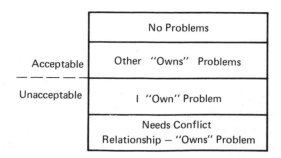

Figure 10-5. Orientation toward Problem Situations from the Worker's Point of View.

necessarily put roadblocks between ourselves and the children. We often solve problems for them when it is unnecessary, or put them down; we do a lot of labeling and stereotyping; we probe, question, and analyze; we praise falsely. In contrast, table 10-1 carefully distinguishes different responses to different kinds of issues and problems that arise in the daily operation of resident living.

This approach represents a set of explicit values, a coherent philosophy of residential life. It is a belief that we care enough about children to listen to them and their points of view, but we also do not abdicate parenting responsibilities in that we will confront others' behavior when it is unacceptable—not up to our home and community standards. We have to learn how to do both: (1) listen to the children and motivate them to do better what they are doing well; and (2) confront them in an honest and direct way when we have differences, and back that up with further listening in order to work constantly at win/win strategies as a daily practice of life in our community residences.

Their program can best be implemented by teaching these skills first to the top team of administrators and then, moving down into each of the residences, focusing primarily on the workers and their charges. A new way of looking at the parenting function of the worker is introduced. It creates a philosophy of being able to confront when necessary, but also one of listening carefully to what our children and our associates are telling us, and being able to react to different kinds of problems and situations in an appropriate manner so that we do not confuse issues. Then it will be possible to develop the specific skills for resolving problems and problem areas in ways that will raise all our behaviors to a higher, more effective level of functioning.

Conceptualizing a Dynamic Use of the Group Culture

The main impetus to creating a positive resident culture lies in the health-growing encounters just described. These encounters precipitate a group culture that in turn reinforces positive human relationships. It is important

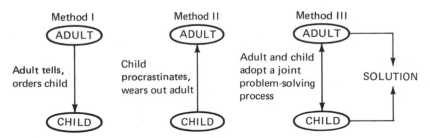

Figure 10-6. Needs-Conflict Problem Solving Methods.

Table 10-1
Skills and Value-Assumptions in Acceptable and Unacceptable Problem Situations

	Problem Distinction	Skill	Value-Assumptions
Acceptable	No problems	(a) Not taken for granted. (b) Appropriate recognition and reinforcement	1. Self and other acceptable.
	Other "owns" problems	(a) Avoid putdowns. (b) Congruent relating (active listening).	2. Faith in being able to influence others and be influenced by others.
Unacceptable	I "own" problem	(a) Assertive statement, with shift into (b) congruent responsiveness.	3. People grow by maximizing the opportunities for them to help themselves.
	Needs-conflict relationship	Joint problem-solving.	

for workers to recognize this and constantly build the resident culture as well as individual worker-child relationships along the lines of the discipline described.

We do not yet fully comprehend the meaning of group power. It is illustrated in the context of this chapter in figure 10-7. It is a well-known maxim that the whole cannot be comprehended by adding up its components. This is true because when something is put together it achieves a new entity. But what is less understood is that when a cohesive culture in a group has been established, it has an enormous impact upon the individual members. In groups, the motivated individual member internalizes the whole culture to some extent, and in becoming a part of the individual, the group influences further in a dynamic way his continuous interaction with other members, and thus reinforces the group culture.

This is the way a culture is developed: it grows, elaborates, regresses, advances, takes up challenges, continues to strengthen the bonds among its members, and so on. It is only through this continuous build-up of the internal bonds of the members that a culture is created that can influence its individual members. In figure 10-7 this is illustrated by the diversity of various arrows to and from the members in the group. Not all members are influenced by or influence others in equal fashion, but there is a cogent growing identity of individuals with the group.

Choice of the group facilitator, or leader, is critical. Too little leadership can lead to diffusion and anarchy; too strong leadership can lead to dominance to the degree that the group feels imposed on and believes that it is the leader who is running the whole show. In this situation the children see themselves as there only to carry out the leader's errands.

The professional group leader is as concerned with the successful resolution of problems and the development of new ideas as he is with strengthen-

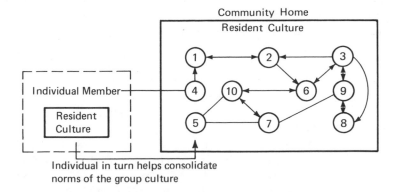

Figure 10-7. The Individual as a Component of Resident Culture and Resident Culture as a "Component" of the Individual Member

ing the group culture itself. This distinguishes the professional from the worker who "shoots from the hip." The "shooting-from-the-hip" leader is primarily concerned with getting the job done. He wants problems solved and quick results. And this is important and necessary.

The essential ingredient that the professional adds is that he also wants to build up the culture and the individuals *in the process*. For example, it is not sufficient for the professional worker simply to tell his charges what to do. He should help them figure things out, which often they do not know how to do. If there is some lack of knowledge or understanding, it should be brought out into the open so that next time the residents can carry out the process more on their own and under their own initiative.

Thus the group facilitator is critical in the development of the resident group and the group culture. Insofar as the leader can begin to understand the principle of how individuals can be influenced through the build-up of the group culture, and see how it influences and becomes part of individuals, the next important step is to determine what kinds of norms are helpful to build into the group culture. The essence of that culture is learning how to give and take in such a way that individual and group needs are balanced.

The key to understanding this chronic gap between the leader's expectations and subordinates' actual behavior lies in the inability to use the concept of culture in a dynamic way. A culture can never be created by fiat. Nor does it evolve by people telling other people what to do. A culture evolves through the contributions of its members and through a feeling of being a living part of it. Thus, if each member contributes to the milieu in which the group members are actively giving and taking with one another to the point where they feel that the culture is theirs and the group belongs to them, then the norms that evolve through their interaction will be internalized in their personal system of knowledge, values, feelings, and behavior.

But this cannot be done through any kind of mechanical manipulation. A group and its culture constitute a growing, living, breathing entity that emerges through the caring and constructive contributions of the members. It is important to think through what kinds of norms we want to foster in these groups, for they will become part of the repertoire of behavior of the individual members. The following norms are important in creating a constructive group resident culture.

1. *Interdependence.* This is a crucial norm of the group culture, and includes people taking responsibility for each other. This means following through on commitments. It is a concern for the functioning of the home, not just individual concerns. It is an understanding that if someone is in trouble, others can fill in, and they in turn can expect help from their colleagues when they are in difficulty.

2. *Engagement.* A community home fosters the norm of individuals being willing to come to the group with their problem without fear of being "shot down" or thought less for it. Engagement means the ability of people to give and take with one another and to use each other in terms of building oneself and building one's home. It means that difficulties in the home or community belong to everybody, and the way to solve them is by directly confronting them through trust so we can work together to resolve them.

3. *The use of the group.* Individualism is vey important, but vastly overplayed in our society. We are taught to be independent, aggressive, initiatory, thrusting, bold. What we are not so good at is learning how to depend upon one another to build constantly our sense of being in this together and moving together as a group. One does not negate the other; but we have a long way to go toward efficiently and effectively using the group as a force to advance everyone's interests and concerns.

4. *Learning from one another.* In the highest sense the group is a vehicle to get better understanding of their own blind spots or weaknesses and improve themselves. No person is without some deficiencies which, if improved upon, could make him a much more dynamic human being. Some individuals are not good on follow-through; others are so interested in getting the task done that they wipe out individuals in the process; others are not aggressive enough; still others are too aggressive. A group offers an opportunity for individuals to share with one another, in a constructive and caring way, how—if they so choose—they can continue to expand their skills and self-knowledge.

The power of the group and its culture is going to make the crucial difference in developing successful community group homes. A good deal of pressure is building up both from the outside community and from inside the homes. The main way to turn these challenges into constructive resolutions is to develop to a much finer degree our ability to work and live together.

In the community home, as in all resident living, it is not long before workers and children take one another for granted. It is assumed that they will somehow find the stimulation to continue to develop and expand both as workers and as human beings. This does not necessarily flow from the work alone. Rather, this kind of constant challenge, stimulation, and growth must come out of the human interaction in the home. We have to work harder at creating resident cultures and groups to which individual members can contribute, and in the process achieve a growing feeling of identity by influencing and being influenced by the evolving dynamic cultural system. Only with this kind of vision can we continue to grow on all levels—the individual, the group, and the entire residential community.

Notes

1. The key article which set out this point of view thirty years ago was written by Kurt Lewin, "Conduct, Knowledge and Acceptance of New Values," in Gertrude Weiss Lewin, ed., *Resolving Social Conflicts* (New York: Harper, 1948), pp. 56-68.

2. The framework in which the first section of this chapter is cast is the parent effectiveness training (P.E.T.) model developed by Thomas Gordon. See Thomas Gordon, *P.E.T.: Parent Effectiveness Training* (New York: New American Library, 1975).

3. For a somewhat similar approach, see Manuel J. Smith, *When I Say No, I Feel Guilty: How to Cope—Using the Skills of Systematic Assertive Therapy* (New York: Dial Press, 1975).

11 Monitoring and Evaluating Purchase-of-Care Providers: The Massachusetts Model

Paula Cardeleen

The problem of developing satisfactory criteria for organizational perform-ance is a very difficult one. It is clear that some conceptual clarification is needed, because so many different kinds of "outcomes" can be selected. Organizational effectiveness has become a treacherous chimera, connoting some kind of good gestalt of organizational performance.

This chapter proposes a rather open-system approach and supplies a rough measure of assessment of key elements that go into a model of a human organization that is taking care of young people in trouble. One overlooked aspect of the large institutions that deal with troubled youths is that they represent in a restricted sense a kind of monopoly from the societal point of view. The political effectiveness of the monopoly is generally viewed as an additional cost in the lack of competition to challenge the efficiency of such a monopoly.

It is highly probable that gains in organizational effectiveness can come about through improved competition among different agencies. This can result in a considerable gain for society, if there can be continued refine-ment of the assessment of such agencies' outcomes according to clear and specific criteria. Thus gains in the overall organizational effectiveness of the agencies dealing with youth could come about through gains in their political decentralization. Here is an example where a challenge to an in-stitutional "monopoly" can be a gain for society as a whole.

Organizational effectiveness has generally been defined as the max-imization of return to the organization by all means. This includes not only technical means which have to do with efficiency, but also political means to increase effectiveness without adding costs to increase efficiency. The authors have argued here that there could be increased effectiveness by an increase in the competition among different agencies that have different ap-proaches to rehabilitation of troubled youths, provided we can refine our evaluation process. This is precisely what the Massachusetts Department of Youth Services is now attempting, and what follows is a preliminary description of the content and process of its assessment effort.

Historical Perspective

Since the closing of the Bridgewater institution for juveniles in December 1970, DYS has been moving toward a system of community-based programs capable of providing more humane treatment for youth in its care. Following the closing of Bridgewater, one by one the state-run training schools were closed. Shortly after this process of deinstitutionalization began, DYS recognized the critical nature of, and need for, evaluation in an agency that was now based primarily on a purchase-of-services system.

DYS was no longer in the position of providing direct services to its clients; rather, it had become a conduit and had to become a monitor and evaluator of those services provided by the private agencies. However, private agencies were as new at the business of serving youth as DYS was at administering these services. Administration and programmatic problems were evident early on. It did not make sense for DYS to pour funds and youths into unknown and possibly unstable programs. Many new community-based programs, on the other hand, had the desire but frequently not the knowledge to run humane and effective programs.

Efforts to meet both DYS's administrative needs for monitoring and the programs' needs for assistance culminated in the development in September 1972 of the evaluation unit. Without a well-developed evaluation and monitoring unit DYS could not fulfill its task of ensuring that their youths were being provided with quality services.

The Function of the Evaluation Unit

In deciding what course the new evaluation unit would take, DYS staff were concerned that major emphasis would be placed on determining program effectiveness or outcome (such as using recidivism rates as measures of "success"). Most traditional evaluation processes focus solely on input and output systems as they relate to and affect clients. It was decided that what was needed were not necessarily measurements of recidivism or specific outcome achievement, though these were recognized as important, but a focus on the here and now—an in-depth analysis of what was happening in a program daily, not the effect it would have on its youth two or three years later.

The function of evaluation within DYS became that of monitoring, evaluating, and providing technical assistance. The specific type of evaluations being conducted can be described as diagnostic; that is, the evaluation unit focuses on areas and issues in a program, describes that process, identifies problems and informational needs, and develops data about the problem area or other important areas.

The transition from institutions to community-based programs was fraught with many difficulties. The changeover occurred rapidly without a great deal of planning or program development. Vendors received contracts before they or DYS had defined the purpose and goals of the individual program. No explicit criteria existed for funding, nor were there criteria by which DYS could regulate the services to be provided.

Many new programs, after struggling to get off the ground, were plagued with untrained staff, community resistance, confusion over purpose, and constant problems with state payment and support. Many of these exploded or just fell apart.

Often these programs originated with a strong belief that providing youths with care and friendship in a noncoercive environment would be enough to ensure quality programs. However, as both they and the department were soon to learn, without careful planning and program development, these factors alone could not ensure a successful or smoothly functioning program.

So the first year of the evaluation unit's existence was devoted primarily to putting out these "fires". Evaluation teams went from program to program, helping vendors to understand and deal with the crises that were disrupting their programs, often providing recommendations and technical assistance, sometimes recommending that programs be closed.

After that first year, perhaps through natural attrition, programs seemed to settle down. There was no longer the need for a strictly firefighting, crisis-oriented evaluation unit. The evaluation unit and the programs began to settle into a process whereby ongoing evaluation, monitoring, and technical assistance were feasible. DYS was still operating without explicit criteria or policies by which it could regulate services and by which programs could know what was expected of them. Many youths in such programs, although not being abused, were not receiving services such as education, counseling, and so on. However, the evaluation unit had developed guidelines by which it could evaluate and provide technical assistance to new programs. It took many months, but eventually there evolved recognition—both within the unit and within the private sector providing services—that there was a set of critical factors that appeared to determine the functioning of a program.

For example, it became clear to the evaluation unit staff that every program must as an initial task define for itself its treatment objectives. It was learned that programs must provide training to staff, especially in the area of behavior management. Without such training, it became apparent that old-line staff reverted to punitive measures of discipline; or, as might be expected, young and inexperienced staff people who approached behavior management without the ability to set limits soon became frustrated and responded to the ensuing chaos with inconsistent bouts of rigidity and intolerance. In reviewing programs the evaluation unit became aware of the critical necessity for community linkage in programs. Programs operating in isolation with no tie-in to the youths, parents, and community generally did not fare well. It was found that specific attention must be paid to communication systems with programs, such as record-keeping, scheduling, meetings, and the like. The evaluation unit began to identify a number of factors that, when coalesced in a total system, appeared to produce a well-functioning, humane program prototype.

The Evaluation Process

From the start of the unit's existence there was a deep-seated belief on the part of the staff that relevant and meaningful program review could only be accomplished if the evaluators were willing to experience the program in the way the youths and the staff in the program were exposed to it, rather than as a group of professionals viewing the system from afar. As a result of this belief, the evaluation process has developed into a system in which a team of evaluators (generally four) go into a program and spend anywhere from sixty to two hundred hours on site, depending on the size and complexity of the program.

The evaluation format includes both qualitative and quantitative information-gathering. The process begins with the team reviewing the program's contract and proposal in an effort to ascertain what the program's purpose and objectives are and what services it has contracted to provide. Unfortunately, the contracting system was developed—and remains—as a mechanism solely to ensure that programs receive payment, not, as it should be, a mechanism by which a program explicitly defines the services to be provided. The contract and proposal does provide the evaluation team with some basic facts, including the kind of program (group home, nonresidential, detention), the number of youth to be served, and the rate of payment. Armed with this basic information, the evaluation team has its initial meeting with the program director, who has been previously notified of the impending evaluation.

The meeting with the program director is a key element in the evaluation process. Not only is essential information about the program gathered, it can also set the tone for the rest of the evaluation.

The team goes to great lengths during this interview to clarify the process and function of the evaluation. They explain that the team will be spending many hours, including evenings and weekends, at the facility, and further request that they have access to all facets of the program that impinge upon the youths' life in the program. This accessibility, they explain, must include the presence of individual team members at staff meetings, house meetings, therapy groups, educational classes, and so on.

Frequently the program director is anxious and tense during the evaluation. He may have recently undergone other such evaluations or licensing studies, or view the team as an extension of some DYS administrators with whom he has had negative experiences. The team is trained in the importance of allowing the director adequate time to voice his concerns and vent his feelings.

After the team has explained who they are and what their purpose is, and the program director has questioned them and expressed his opinions, the team asks him to explain in detail what his program provides. With the information provided by the director the team leaves the program and meets to discuss what they have heard and decide what course of action they will pursue with the evaluation. Certain sections of the program are assigned to each individual team member, and a schedule is set for on-site time. From the information gained from the program director they conclude what meetings and what activities must be covered. They return to the program the following day to begin their information-gathering, interviewing, and observation.

The evaluation team coordinator assists each team member in deciding what will be the most efficient utilization of time within the program. For instance, the member assigned to evaluate the clinical component of the program must be certain to make an appointment to interview the clinical staff, while the member responsible for interviewing line staff will learn more if he spends time informally on the floor and talks with the line staff when it is most convenient for them (such as when the residents are in bed, or when they are engaged in other activities).

Although the team works as a cohesive group to gain a comprehensive picture of the program, it has responsibility for different programmatic components. This task differentiation appears to be a useful model, for: (1) it is less disruptive to the program—only one team member is present at any one program activity or meeting; (2) it provides a system of checks and balances by which team members can check information; and (3) it serves to increase interobserver reliability.

The team proceeds with its on-site involvement, attempting to gather the necessary data, conduct confidential interviews with all staff and clients, and observe the day-to-day functioning of the program. Throughout its time in the program the team meets every day away from the program to keep each other up to date and share information.

Feedback and Agency Realignment

Perhaps one of the most important functions any evaluation unit can provide is specific and generic feedback. The DYS evaluation unit provides direct and specific feedback to each program about the strengths and weaknesses of each program component and an overall analysis of the quality of the system in the program. To each region, the evaluation unit provides information on the quality and kind of services each program provides, which allows them to make budgetary and placement decisions, and provides specific client flow-chart data so that they can see, in a comprehensive and clear-cut manner, what kind of youths the program is dealing with and what has happened to them while in the program and after they have left.

To the central DYS administrators the evaluation unit is able to provide feedback and recommendations on individual programs. Additionally, and perhaps equally important, it is able to provide an overview of where the system is going: in general, what is working; what trends are developing; and what needs exist. Although when the large institutions were closed DYS took a philosophical stand against the notion of "intrapsychic supremacy" and the medical model, for instance, through the process of evaluation it was discovered that 85 percent of all programs serving DYS youths are still operating on that medical model; that is, they are still diagnosing and "treating" the individual as if the individual's problems—independent of the social realities and opportunities that define the limits of his or her existence—are primarily psychological.

Although a major thrust of deinstitutionalization was to provide community-based services, the evaluation unit has found that up to 50 percent of the DYS population may at any given time be placed in programs very far from their homes.

In reviewing over 150 programs, the evaluation unit has found that though the DYS philosophy, at least as it was articulated throughout the period of deinstitutionalization, dictated that intervention and rehabilitation should be focused on the child's home and family and not oriented toward isolating the child from society, in most cases these rehabilitation goals become custodial goals of maintaining peace and quiet within the program and insuring the individual's adjustment to that system and microcosm. All of these trends are fed back to the administrators and major decisionmakers within DYS, and armed with this information they can choose to ignore it, readjust the future course of the agency, or, as has happened often, become angry at or disbelieve the evaluation unit.

The process of providing feedback is often fraught with severe difficulties for the evaluation unit. The experience has been likened to that of the messenger who bore bad news: his head was cut off. The overall impact of the information provided by the evaluation unit appears to depend greatly on the degree of discomfort it causes. Specifically, positive feedback is welcomed and such data responded to, while negative feedback, or information that creates agency problems, is ignored or suppressed.

Following each evaluation an elaborate process of feedback occurs. The vendor receives a copy of the evaluation report two days prior to the formally scheduled feedback meeting. Prior to this time, they have received no feedback whatsoever. While visiting a program the team strives not to give feedback, though it is often sought. To give feedback while still visiting the program would disrupt and change the natural dynamic the team is attempting to observe.

The feedback meeting is held in order to discuss the facts and the analysis presented in the report and, in general, to sit back and reflect on the process and outcome of the evaluation. The team members and key program staff go through—often line by line—the evaluation document. If any factual discrepancies or errors exist, the vendor points them out, and they are changed in the document accordingly. The vendor has the option of writing a rebuttal or addenda which, if received within two weeks following the feedback session, will be attached to the evaluation report. Since all reports are public documents, most vendors take this opportunity to affix their response to the evaluation report.

As one might expect, the experience of the evaluation unit has been in general that programs receiving fair to good evaluations respond favorably to the process and view it as helpful, while those that receive negative evaluations are angry and view the process as adversarial. Out of about 150 evaluations, 15 vendors were angry and have sought to discredit the evaluations.

From the DYS central administration also, negative or threatening feedback is unfortunately viewed with anger and distrust. Although given the role of critic of the system, the evaluation unit inevitably meets problems when it exercises that function. Throughout the period of deinstitutionalization DYS was its own loudest critic. Jerome Miller sought to expose the cruelties and inhumanities of that system. By 1973, however, DYS was caught up in a severe political backlash and sought to calm the storm by ignoring or suppressing negative information about the new system. Evaluation reports that showed that some programs were still involved in inhumane treatment, or even beginning to neglect the youths in their care, made DYS officials nervous. Apparently they were afraid that such information would give angry community groups and legislators the armament needed to destroy the new system. Also, the purchase-of-service system became a vendor's market. DYS needed the services provided by private agencies even if they were bad. Inevitably, the evaluation unit, when providing critical feedback on a program, was met with the response, "We have no alternatives. What can we do with these kids?"

There had been a major and significant change in DYS thinking; while Miller believed that providing no treatment was better than providing bad treatment, the aftermath of deinstitutionalization brought a belief that any treatment was better than none. The evaluation unit became enmeshed in a struggle of trying to get administrators to implement its recommendations.

Frequently that struggle was lost; occasionally, after long months of debate and pressure, action was taken. Some bad programs were closed, and some good program prototypes were replicated. Some vital information about the system—for instance, the fact that security as provided by heavy locks, handcuffs, and isolation inevitably leads to higher levels of acting-out behavior and higher rates of recidivism—was recognized.

One major lesson the evaluation unit has learned. Feedback given in the absence of department standards and overall philosophy is frequently a futile process. There must be a context into which the feedback fits; otherwise, the evaluation unit operates in a vacuum and is subject to recurring difficulties. What the department believes in and desires for its youths must be explicitly laid out. Without such basic support and structure, it is inevitable that any evaluation effort will be met with suspicion and antagonism from the parties who feel threatened by the process.

Issues

We have identified several issues that the DYS evaluation unit has faced from its inception. There are additional ones that are important factors in the process of evaluation.

The focus of program review, as stated, involves primary emphasis on the day-to-day life in the program rather than major concern with outcome variables like recidivism, although it is recognized that such measurements of impact or effectiveness are important. Programs serving DYS youth vary immensely in the way they view youths in their care and the strategies they employ to "help." The evaluation unit has had on several occasions the opportunity to review programs which, according to the unit's values and guidelines, were utilizing treatment mechanisms that were dehumanizing and appeared to constitute cruel and unusual punishment. The problem, of course, comes when a number of different people attempt to define what is dehumanizing and abusive. The team has often observed situations that all agreed were somewhat extreme, but which program personnel and DYS administrators justified on the grounds that such mechanisms are effective and therapeutically justifiable for "these kinds of kids."

Often these programs have elaborately articulated therapeutic philosophies on which they base their approach to young offenders. They employ psychiatrists whose credentials lend credibility to their system. And they "hold onto" kids. From the system's perspective they are effective because their residents do not escape.

One would think that in the twentieth century, especially in the new Massachusetts system, no child would be subjected to beatings or forced physical confrontation with other youths, forced to eat off the floor, be tied to beds, handcuffed and leg-cuffed for days, held incommunicado, or sub-jected to extreme psychological abuse in the form of ridicule, labeling, and ego destruction from staff and other residents. Yet it happens and it is justified therapeutically because it "works." At least temporarily such pro-grams remove the youth and do not allow escape. We are still fighting the same issues that were raised in the institutions, but now the labels have changed. Punishment is now therapy, guards are called counselors, isola-tion is called "time-out" or the "quiet room." A whole new Pandora's box of child abuse has developed.

Though there are many committed and caring individuals working to en-sure that humane and quality treatment is provided, they are faced—as is the evaluation unit—with the real issues of political pressures and supply and demand. It is the truth when DYS officials tell the evaluation unit that the political pressure is such that certain kids must be kept "on ice"—that is, must not show up in court again or they will be bound over to adult court. It is also true when they say, "Yes, the program is bad, but we have nowhere else to put these kids."

The evaluation unit has, in an effort to deal with some of these issues, developed various processes and approaches. It is understood that no magical answers exist, but there must be a constant and combined effort to initiate and maintain good programs. This understanding has caused the unit to employ a system of technical assistance. Feedback and recommenda-tions to programs are essential. No program will automatically function op-timally. It must be given assistance.

There must also be the recognition that the new purchase-of-service system will be subject to pitfalls. Simply dismantling the old repressive in-stitutional system does not ensure that the new sytem will be humane and growth-producing. Recognition of this fact has led to a system of ongoing monitoring so that there can be a continual outside review.

In attempting to deal with internal and external political pressures, the evaluation unit has developed a community-based approach to evaluation. Judges and probation staff, community volunteers, program providers, central and regional DYS staff, teachers and other professional community people have been asked to participate in evaluations. This community-based approach has had some drawbacks, but over all it has had the effect of opening up the new system so that those people who represent the com-munity and the law can view the new system for themselves. In the year and a half this approach has been used, individuals have been outraged by the liberalism of the new system, but still more have found a degree of empathy and understanding or because of the experience, have become advocates for the youths and for a more humane system of treatment. The political pressure that the unit has not been able to eradicate has originated from powerful private agencies that, through their own direct pressure or through a powerful parent agency or political friends, have been able to undermine the evaluation effort. Interestingly, of all the programs whose closing was recommended by the evaluation unit, only small and relatively powerless programs were closed; programs that had a secure financial and political base were not closed.

In this context of political pressure, deinstitutionalization backlash, and an overall agency fear of controversy, it is clear why it is and has been so difficult to maintain an honest and thorough evaluation effort.

Programmatic Variables

In reviewing programs over the past four years, the evaluation unit has come to recognize that a relatively large number of variables affect the functioning of any program. This array of variables when coalesced to form a program seems to contribute to a conceptually sound, humane, organizationally functional, fiscally viable, and—most important—more effective program that can meet the needs of youths.

In an attempt to look conceptually at the systems that operate in programs serving youths, the evaluation unit has developed a schema that concentrates on eleven program components. These components when analyzed individually and as part of a comprehensive purchase-of-service system, appear to affect significantly the program's functioning:

1. Facility
2. Administration and staff
3. Intake
4. Program (daily services provided)
5. Clinical
6. Controls
7. DYS residents
8. Records
9. Termination
10. Relationship to community
11. Relationship to DYS

In analyzing these components, the methodology involves extensive interviewing of staff and youth (in confidence, utilizing questionnaires), hours of observation (perhaps taking time samples), and data collection (review of records and logs).

Facility. In looking at each component the evaluation unit focuses on a number of variables. For instance, in evaluating the facility, the team focuses on measurable aspects, such as size, ventilation, suitability for the youth being served, as well as variables that must be viewed somewhat more subjectively, such as the overall atmosphere of the facility, whether it is conducive to staff-client, client-client interaction, whether it is stigmatizing, and so forth.

Administration and staff. In reviewing this component the team questions critical variables, such as communication, administrative support, training and supervision, explicitly and implicitly defined role responsibilities, interaction of staff and youth, the presence or absence of dichotomy between professional and paraprofessional staff, staff input into decisionmaking. All these variables appear to play a role in ensuring genuinely effective services.

Clinical. The salient characteristics of the clinical component include the assumptions that the clinicians (counselors) make about the youngsters, whether they view them as inherently sick, bad, in need of personality restructure, or as victims. The team attempts to find out how the youths' emotional needs are met: are they seen regularly by their counselor or do only those who are most aggressive and appealing receive counseling? Is the clinical component geared toward fostering dependency or independence? Do coercion and punishment play any part in the therapeutic approach? What staff and/or youths are being utilized as change agents in the youths' life? Does the clinical component fit every individual in a slot with a convenient label? Can the staff deal with the youths' individual problems and needs? Are the youths involved in the "treatment plan"? Are measurable long- and short-term goals made? Can the efficacy and validity of treatment techniques and procedures be measured? The list of key ingredients that operate on this component's effectiveness is fairly long and complex. Furthermore, these variables are intricately linked to variables identified in the second and sixth components.

The clinical component is perhaps the most difficult to evaluate. Often the issues and procedures involved in treatment are intangible and difficult to grasp. The review and analysis of such clinical systems are always subject to criticism from one therapeutic school or another. One major and recurring difficulty the evaluation unit has faced in analyzing the clinical component involves accessibility and confidentiality. Many programs utilize therapy groups (primal, sensitivity, confrontation) as a major therapeutic technique. The evaluation unit feels that it is critical for DYS to review these groups as part of its evaluative process.

Arguments abound on both sides of the issue: evaluators feel they have the skill, right, and obligation to observe groups that DYS youth are subject to; program personnel often feel, on the other hand, that such review of the therapeutic process is potentially damaging to the group and to the clients as well as being an invasion of privacy. To date this issue has not been resolved, although the evaluation unit has held firm in its approach to reviewing the groups. The most vociferous reaction against this scrutiny has come from "concept" programs, which run, generally, very confrontive groups. Representatives from these programs state that the evaluator observing the group would disrupt the process or would have to become a participant in the group; others maintain that evaluators would not understand the very sensitive and sophisticated procedures and thus would come away with a distorted perception of the process. When faced with such resistance, the unit has agreed to view a videotape of the therapy group, taped during the evaluation by program personnel.

Dilemmas in Evaluation

In Massachusetts, as in many other states, there is a fairly clear line of distinction between dependent and delinquent youths. Youths from both groups are served by different state agencies and, ostensibly because they have different needs, receive different services. However, for the most part programs serving dependent or neglected youth are also serving DYS youth. There has been during the past four years a fair amount of difficulty over the issue of a private program serving youths from a variety of state agencies. The evaluation effort suffers particularly in the case of multiservice programs. While one agency (such as DYS) has certain expectations and guidelines by which it expects programs to operate, another agency (such as Welfare) has others. The inherent difficulty in such a situation comes to bear when one agency finds a program serving its youths to be inappropriate and perhaps even destructive, while the other agency finds that the same program is quite acceptable.

Attempts to deal with this dilemma have taken many forms over the past few years. There have been task forces and joint committees and efforts to establish joint evaluation teams. To date, however, the problem still remains. A variety of state agencies is placing youths in the same programs, but noting great discrepancies in their views of the program. This situation becomes serious when, as was the case several times in the past few years, one agency feels the program is so bad that it must be closed, while the other agency feels the service is good, or at least adequate, and is needed. A consistent and uniform mechanism for standards and review processes among state agencies utilizing the same facility is needed.

A related issue seriously affects programs. They are evaluated by numerous different groups and agencies several times a year, with the groups using different criteria and process. The private vendors in

Massachusetts have begun to organize themselves on this issue, for they feel—justifiably so—that it is unfair to subject a program to myriad evaluations throughout the year.

Another major dilemma faced by the evaluation unit has to do with the role of evaluation itself, within the agency. The unit makes recommendations; it does not make policy. The inherent difficulty stems from the fact that though the unit's concerns will be heard, no real power exists to assure that the research findings will be acted on. Although an evaluation may conclude that without a rate increase and the addition of two staff members a particular program will disintegrate, the evaluation unit has no direct access to or means of facilitating the mechanism for getting the program more money. Vendors are frequently pleased to see that at last an agency representative has recognized the difficulties and struggles in which they are enmeshed. Too often they are sorely disappointed when they realize that the evaluation unit does not have the power or capacity to provide what both groups know is necessary for the program's functioning.

This role dilemma regarding power and access of the evaluation group is directly related to the issue of locus. Should the evaluation process itself be contracted out to a private vendor? The question has no easy answer. Most time and discussion with DYS and other state agencies have centered on deciding what is the best approach to the issue. Various suggestions and alternatives have been explored. The option of selecting staff from several state agencies, all of whom use the same programs, who would work together as an interagency state team reporting directly to the state's attorney general, was explored.

Every option, however, is fraught with difficulties. The experience in Massachusetts has demonstrated several key factors in this dilemma of locus of evaluation. Placing it in the agency is sensible, for it gives the evaluators direct access to information and to those administrators who establish policy. By living in the real world of an agency the evaluation group does not exist in some sterile, idealistic microcosm. On the negative side, however, it is clear that keeping the evaluation effort honest is more difficult when it is located within the agency it is expected to evaluate, and whose staff work and administrators they are expected to assess objectively. Internal scrutiny is perhaps by far the most difficult to accept. Conflicts, distrust, and alienation emanate quite easily from this situation.

However, being located within the agency does appear, overall, to increase the likelihood that the evaluation process will be better informed, more sensitive to the agencies' and the programs' real needs and problems in the larger context of the juvenile justice system. Studies conducted by outside evaluators are often seen by the program and agency as too theoretical or too superficial. The process that has developed in Massachusetts seems to have solidly entrenched itself in identifying and dealing with the real factors that affect juveniles, programs, and DYS.

Part IV
The Significance of the
Massachusetts Experience

Introduction to Part IV

There is a basic theoretical distinction about organizational settings. The energy that goes directly into fulfilling its mission and the energy used in maintaining the system have to be carefully distinguished. When an organization turns its means into a self-serving end, then the flow of energy necessary to hold the people in the system and persuade them to carry out their activities as members of the system become paramount. Every organization needs both—attention to fulfilling its goal and paying some attention to the internal needs of the organization, including workers' and clients' motivation and their relationships.

In the corrections field, the gap between organizational maintenance and productivity (that is, rehabilitation of offenders) can grow increasingly wider. This can evoke a split standard that rationalizes institutional deficiencies by stressing the difficulties and dangers of the job and the need to protect the community. The administrative response can be to use this "means" standard to play a political game with the community.

In time this results in institutions becoming custodial warehouses that give the appearance of treatment and provide substantive social justification for it. Administrators divide their audiences and speak out of both sides of their mouths. When speaking to the public or the media, they defend their system by saying, "It's as good as can be expected, given the adverse conditions" (for which they, of course, are not to blame). But to their colleagues and professional circles, administrators will readily admit that the system is destructive and largely custodial. Other penologists frankly admit to "spreading the disease."

The issue quickly becomes polarized; will the administrator play the game the society and legislatures are asking, or will the administrator open up the issue by creating various avenues for dialog, discussion, public information, education, and reform?

Conventional wisdom has held for many years that the best approach for bureaucrats to take is to avoid conflicts and smooth over polarized attitudes among legislators and pressure groups within the organization and the community. Alternatives to institutionalization have been denounced as unduly dangerous to the community. The system—and the bureaucrats' jobs—have remained secure as a result.

Polarization provides the administrator with an opportunity to rally reform support. An attack against reform by reactionary forces can generate even more enthusiasm and support for reform, because polarization forces the ambivalent into taking a position.

Part IV is divided into two chapters that analytically probe this institutional change process. Chapter 12 reviews cultural, political, and ideological forces in society that set the pattern for total institutional structures. Total institutions were constructed from the same basic blueprint. These blueprints consist of the rules and regulations governing corrections, as well as the explicit and implicit norms rationalizing and justifying the system. It is ideologically made manifest in bricks and mortar. Chapter 12 also delves into the significance of the Massachusetts experience in correctional reform for altering the societal blueprint of total institutions.

Chapter 13 takes a closer look at correctional reform on a microsystem level. Here we untangle the complex of relationships between corrections and the Commonwealth of Massachusetts to uncover the motive for change. The central thesis of this chapter is as follows: ultimately, the radical outcome was achieved through the steady and consistent subordination of structure to institutional mission, to the point where an outmoded organizational form had to give way to new, partially tested, organizational forms.

12 Radical Reform of Youth Corrections: Cultural, Political, and Theoretical Considerations

Two key clusters of values were instrumental in overcoming opposition to deinstitutionalization in Massachusetts. The moral position was that these institutions did not help youngsters but indeed consolidated deviant careers among them. As Florence Nightingale is reputed to have said, "Whatever a hospital does, it should not spread the disease."

The second important value cluster concerns the pragmatic functionality of radical change. Here we question whether a humanistic corrections system is functional. Total institutions like those in corrections tend to imbue themselves with a symbolic legitimacy over and above that of reality. This surplus moral authority has become more and more eroded and is more frequently attacked by all kinds of reformers. When the organizational leadership attacks its own principles, it gives support to an alternative system. What then is exposed is that the providers have become self-serving and are ritualistically going through the motions of providing rehabilitation to young offenders.

Once organizational loyalty is punctured by its leader's turning upon the institutional setting, there are few values left to keep people loyal. There is no longer the top official supporting the raison d'etre of the organization. It leaves the institution wide open to criticism from all quarters.

Jerome Miller, as director of the Massachusetts Department of Youth Services, was careful not to become too dependent on his staff. Here he tried to subvert the general principle of reciprocity—"You scratch my back and I'll scratch yours"—so common in the bureaucratic scheme. By maintaining a solitary position in the system, he was able to offset the quid pro quo mentality that can, and had, become so prevalent in this type of total institution. Miller simply did not play the game of winning over the staff by insisting on loyalty to the system. Instead he struck out against his own institution and, by implication, the people who ran it.

It is clear that all the subsystems within an organization are not equally potent in their influence on the total system. The primary system in a total institution exerts a far greater influence than the other associates, staff, and workers. This primary system becomes crucial when the institution is being dismantled and restructured.

The most powerful argument used over and over by Miller was the high recidivism rate and the assertion that there was very little rehabilitation go-ing on in the institutional setting. The expense of these institutions is borne in major part by the community, through public subsidies. But penal in-stitutions are less constrained by the immediate influence of the marketplace, so the community is somewhat lenient with them. They are not, after all, designed as economic organizations that are supposed to make a profit.

As Miller zeroed in more and more on the incompetence of these institu-tions to do the rehabilitation job, more support for his position on deinstitutionalization was generated in a variety of groups and communities throughout Massachusetts. What Miller did was to heighten the conflict between the competing demands made upon the institutions—they were supposed to rehabilitate their charges and return them as "safe" people to the communities—and use these cross-pressures to expose the contradic-tions. Miller asserted that neither end was being served—that is, no rehabilitation meant, in the long run, that the community was less and less safe. Eventually, enough people were made aware that there could be no community security without rehabilitation; that one feeds into and rein-forces the other; that one could not be gained at the cost of the other; and that ultimately they would have to get both to have either one.

Structural versus Psychological Interpretations of Institutional Functioning

The vision of Miller included the ability to look at institutions not only as they were and as they had been, but also as they might be. His awareness of the possibility for change and winning converts within and outside DYS made it possible for deliberate transformations of a social institution to take place. There are other options besides putting up with institutions and justi-fying them. Institutions are not inevitable or eternal, and one task of the practitioner and social scientist is to discover the means to change them—fundamentally, if need be.

The Massachusetts experience shows that the training school as an ideal is no longer valid. Correctional administrators and workers have reopened the question of new social arrangements and the capacity of practitioners to control and direct the institutions and conditions that affect their lives, rather than the other way around.

What was placed squarely on the agenda in Massachusetts was an ex-planation of a social phenomenon in terms of the *structure of institutions* rather than the attitudes and behaviors of individuals. If we take for granted existing institutions, such as the corrections system, then we will focus on procedures within it or on the failure of individuals to adjust to it.

We will not search for structural alternatives. Supporters of the prevailing system continue to ask questions about social reforms necessary to reduce the recidivism rate and maximize rehabilitation. How can we resocialize youngsters so that they can be motivated to participate in institutional life, and then expect them to function in a noninstitutional setting in society? Critics of institutions begin by asking whether the cause of recidivism is to be found in the very system of "rehabilitation."

The willingness to initiate a conflict redefined the entire problem as a struggle between competing interest groups. It was a struggle between those who were dissatisfied with the prevailing system, realizing that it could not be reformed except by demolishing it, versus those who had powerful self-interests in maintaining it or were convinced of the necessity of punishment.

This conflict occurred within a larger theoretical framework. One view saw the young offender's problems as lying within the scope of his or her individual life space and personal relationships with family, friends, and so on. That is, the problem was seen as one of dealing with each individual offender within the institutional setting. The other approach, the one adopted in Massachusetts, identified the problems that these youngsters were experiencing as a collective phenomenon and as a reflection of the institutional arrangements set up by the state to relieve the problem.[1]

Much of the problem with the first view stems from an overemphasis on psychology, which views youths' troubles and contradictions as the sum of individual problems, which forces us to solve them on a strictly individual basis. Some youngsters, no doubt, need to be treated within a secure setting, although we still do not know who benefits and who does not. But the consistently high rate of recidivism made it clear that for many, the problem lay precisely in the social structure of the institutional setting itself.

It is also an object lesson of how humanistic disciplines can in one context be a powerful source of personal growth and liberation, and in another become potent instruments of repression. This occurs when they hold to an overemphasis on individual troubles without realizing that a good portion of the cause may indeed lie within the entire system of relationships. In Massachusetts the basic questions began to center on the social structure itself rather than on individual behavior within it and after release.

Once the fallacy of psychology is laid to rest, it soon is overtaken by the *amelioration orientation*, which sees institutional maladjustments as curable by administrative action. One simply must attack the imbalance of goals and means. In this context the administrator accepts the structure of his or her organization and treats all problems as errors in administration, which can be rectified without altering the basic framework of the organization. This approach has been most clearly characterized by Mannheim as the bureaucratic administrative response to social dysfunctioning and to social problems: the attempt to hide all problems of politics under the cover of administration can be explained by the fact that the sphere of activity of the official exists only within the limits of laws already formulated. Hence the genesis or the development of law falls outside the scope of his activity. As a result of his socially limited horizon, the functionary fails to see that behind every law that has been made there lie the socially fashioned interests and the *Weltanschauungen* of a specific social group. He takes it for granted that the specific order prescribed by the concrete law is equivalent to order in general. He does not understand that every rationalized order is only one of many forms in which socially conflicting irrational forces are reconciled.[2]

The Institutional Leader as Mediator and Missionary

One way of conceptualizing the role of an institutional leader in promoting change is to analyze what kinds of functions, qualities, roles and character one allocates to oneself. The leader who is attempting radical change regards himself as a missionary, in contrast to the mediator who maintains the status quo by keeping all the vested interests tolerably satisfied. The missionary rapidly reaches a point where he or she believes that the present organization can no longer fulfill its mission, and becomes increasingly incapable of compromise. Deviation from a new organization objective is then regarded as a sellout. These kinds of leaders are typical in social movements that are in the process of becoming established social organizations. A unique characteristic of Jerome Miller is his ability to transfer his role of leader of institutional change into that of social movement leader.

Mediator-institutional leaders have learned how to manipulate skillfully different organizational frameworks and both internal and external publics. They are politicians less enamored with utopian ideals than with the practical realities of survival and keeping all its auxiliary parties in line and viable.

It is important to point out that Miller, in contrast to his rhetoric, was not enamored with change for change's sake. There was a definite philosophical and motivational orientation underlying deinstitutionalization. He had an articulate ideological orientation that was essentially anti-system. He saw that once an organization becomes encrusted with an habitual pattern of doing things, it begins to lose its usefulness.

The Role of Public Definitions in Institutional Change

One critical issue raised by the closing down of institutions in Massachusetts centered on the way in which social problems and the institutions created to resolve them are popularly defined. A problem becomes a public problem when a certain critical mass of people in society becomes aware of it. Once this happens, the next difficulty lies in making clear which groups in the population define the problem in which way, and how to decide, among the conflicting ideas, what is problematic and what is not.

A naive person would suggest immediately that the remedy for institutionalization and all the evils it brings in its train is simply to do away with the institutions. But for decades this solution was rejected because it would interfere with the vested interests that became institutionalized themselves as a result of the institutions, and fed off them. In this case the taken-for-granted framework is the principle of "lock 'em up and throw away the key" security for the community. The social problem became the cure. People did not want to "cure the cure" because they were unwilling to alter the basic conditions, conditions in which the inmates simply received further training in deviant activity. Thus the definition of a solution to a social problem, in this case the cure that was to remedy the problem of troubled youths, became a political issue involving opposing ideologies of conflicting groups.

Miller constantly and consistently probed the basic assumptions of institutionalization. Most social problems, like that of institutionalization, are written about by professionals in the context of tacitly accepting the basic structure of the institutions. They restrict their treatment of problems to maladjustments within that structure rather than examining possibilities of demolishing the structure itself.

Another conventional idea that is reinforced by professionals is the idea that social change must be gradual to be realistic, and also that change is better when guided by experts. This whole approach was turned on its head when their expert, Commissioner Miller, unmasked the institutions for what they were—brutalizing penal colonies that fostered antisocial behavior on the part of the young people it was supposed to be socializing through rehabilitation.

Miller cracked the "gentlemen's agreement." He saw the *institution* as the problem. Heretofore, most critics had seen institutions as simply having "organizational problems." The focus was not on the effect of the institution itself, but on the problems of maladjustment within its apparatus.

It took the very top leaders of the institutional complex to zero in on the discrepancy between idealized standards and the actual conditions of life in the institutions. The basic dilemma corrections evolved into was that the institutions persisted not to serve people but for people to serve the institutions. They became more and more vulnerable to the discrepancy between rhetoric and reality as they became more and more accountable to the community at large. Where an institution is found to contradict its rhetoric or basic mission, people come to believe that the institution ought to be changed or abolished. But that is not usually what happens. Generally, vested interests can convince the public that the institutions are basic necessities for community safety, and that "rehabilitation" is taking place. Unfortunately, both for the community and the inmates, this perpetuates society's problem by encouraging deviant behavior. This is confirmed by recidivism statistics.

The Politics of Change

The argument about the value of large institutions in the professional and nonprofessional communities reflects genuine conflicts. But "correctness" of position is quickly reduced to a practical issue of power and political persuasion. The clashes of perspectives, however, also reflect normative theories, values, and ideologies. These orientations become important when they are promoted and sustained by vested power groups. Concepts of deviance and social problems are not only discussed in the context of some objective social standard of rehabilitation and a secure society, but must also be linked to vested interests and political motives. We are too well aware today of how these definitions and judgments placed on human action and not the action itself depend on varying power groups.

The practical social scientist must find out not only what perspectives are being employed, by whom, to what extent, and where they are operating in our society, but how they are linked to interests that feed off institutionalized structures.

In Massachusetts there was no single movement on either side for or against the youth correctional institutions in the state. Conflicting positions were taken across congeries of groups, professional and lay, within the legislature, within the different parties, among religious groups, and so on. These different tendencies and factions within and between these groups and associations gradually polarized, but there was plenty of disagreement on each side.

The essentially fragile nature of social systems becomes apparent in periods of rapid change. How imperfectly a system was made and how it passed its usefulness is made more vivid by change. It is astonishing how institutions rise so quickly and go on for years and years full of contradictions and grossly inadequate in relation to their mission. One also learns how social systems are steered and propped up by group self-interests. The attitudes, perceptions, beliefs, motivations, and expectations of human beings operate at different levels, but underlying the altruistic and professional rhetoric lies self-survival.

One is reminded that social systems can have a tremendous range in structural arrangements for achieving the same objective, and also that any given system acquires new and different functions during its life history. Too frequently the energy of large institutions is funneled into devices of control. This control becomes more and more potent as less and less rehabilitation is accomplished.

The betrayal of his system by an organizational leader throws a mighty wrench into the belief systems of people both within and outside an institution. An organizational leader epitomizes the system's values, and the identification with such leaders is a strong integrative force within the institution. When the leader denounces that institution, it lets loose the then-powerful centripetal forces that have the potential for congealing into a force for bringing about radical structural change.

It is at this point that the reformers of all kinds in a progressive state like Massachusetts begin to impact upon the organization by demanding internal change. In most formal organizations there arise, therefore, structures specifically concerned with sensing relative changes in the outside world and translating the meaning of those changes for organizational self-preservation. The leader of an organization—particularly an organization like corrections, which is so vulnerable to public opinion—must anticipate and neutralize potential attacks.

However, when the director denounces the system, everyone is thrown into disarray. Moreover, when this is done in the name of a higher justice and fair play, the medicine becomes too powerful to dilute. It was this combination of enormous authority given to the institutional superintendent and his lofty claims to justice that transcended his own instinct for institutional preservation and personal self-interest. This is what congealed the forces for radical change and broke the backs of those forces that wanted to preserve the status quo.

Another indication of the power of the commissioner of a system to spark reform is related to differences of beliefs held by staff about the value of institutions. In no institution is it possible for every member to hold the same ideal and value about its work. Deinstitutionalization in Massachusetts began with one man, Jerome Miller, who actually believed that all the DYS institutions should be closed down, and, further, that he was going to do it. That belief stood against the great majority of institutional personnel, who believed institutions were not only worthwhile and impregnable, but necessary. This again points to the authority given the director of institutions, and it is nowhere more vividly illustrated than in the power that this one man had to set loose the forces and create the momentum to bring about this radical restructuring of correctional institutions.

Ouside the institutions a great number of individuals and groups also favored deinstitutionalization. However, these groups grossly underestimated the amount of public support each of them would receive for closing down the institutions. This is the classical phenomenon of pluralistic ignorance. Here again, Miller, the inside, unquestioned top authority in position and knowledge, was in a most advantageous position to knit together the forces for change and confuse the opposition.

The Release of New Energy in Program Innovations

The restructuring of the youth corrections institutions into community-based agencies had a profound effect upon rehabilitation policies. The momentum set by Miller in deinstitutionalizing the system released an abundance of energy that flowed into new and creative providers, programs, and services.

An important function of policymaking is to make generalizations about which organizational behavior shall be, which implies that there will be significant changes in the organizational structure.[3] Policymaking flows from organizational change and consolidates it. Policymaking is an aspect of systematic leadership that involves fundamental changes in organizational structure.

Deinstitutionalization created a vacuum within which policymaking was reinvigorated at the level of the formulation of new substantive goals, objectives, and methods in the rehabilitation of young offenders. Now that the institutional basis of custodialism was removed, energy could be used more directly and unambiguously to rehabilitate the youngsters in conjunction with all available community resources.

Policymaking within this vacuum implied the formulation of new procedures and devices for achieving goals and new methods of evaluating performance. Here progress was slow, although sustained and continuous, because the system did not have the historical experience of working from a community base. This new opportunity meant that precedents had to be created de novo.

Decentralization also meant that policymaking would now be in the province of smaller subsystems—the agencies from which the corrections department purchased service. So policymaking is not only the product of deliberate consideration of long-run problems, but is created emergently through day-to-day decisions on an ad hoc basis. Administrators rather than designated policy makers make de facto policy.

Thus energy not only flowed into new providers, services, and programs, but generated new policies about modalities for working with youngsters in trouble. The criteria that emerged were not based on an overall systemic perspective of the organization, but rather were produced by the cumulative process of decentralized administrative decisions in almost a hundred different agencies that had become involved with troubled youth.

The new system bridges the gap of an apparent but false distinction between policymaking and adminstration. Policymaking does not necessarily include deliberate attempts at decisionmaking by specialized groups assigned such a function within a total system. Policy does not flow out of pronouncements by one or another departmental head far removed from the action, but flows from the decisions of people in administrative and front-line positions.

The Changing Role of DYS

Another way of viewing reform in Massachusetts is to see it from the perspective of broadening goals and widening the previous narrow self-interest of organizational maintenance. The tendency toward expediency is also diluted as new organizations strive to put their objectives into practice and to create organizational forms that best fulfill them.

Radical change imparts to people a fresh feeling about the principles upon which the agency is based, and during the honeymoon permits a more distinctive character to emerge. The public at large gives an organization undergoing such radical change a period of grace to adjust internally and to establish a novel character with distinctive contributions and capabilities vis-à-vis society.

However, an agency will not be given too long a period of time to make its goals effective without various community pressures beginning to make themselves felt. Once the honeymoon is over, the organization again is faced with the risk of becoming ineffective as it tries to adapt to the various public elements.

But even an organization undergoing radical change must survive. This initially becomes the paramount goal for agency policymakers. Rededication to new goals, of a new mission by radical restructuring, imparts to an agency a new credibility. When people begin to realize that the organization is willing to undergo massive internal changes, there is a new empathy with the organization in its efforts to reestablish the priority of its substantive goals rather than the more narrow self-interest of maintenance survival. It gains further credibility by emphasizing a singleness of purpose, which in the case of radical reform of institutions takes on the mission of rehabilitation an community protection by original placement within the community, not within isolated and outmoded institutional "schools of deviance."

The correctional system in Massachusetts did not change its objectives of rehabilitation and community protection. But its willingness to restructure itself radically committed it to a more open, community strategy, which gradually increased the freedom of its youngsters and its teams of staff members in the community. Its decentralization, and the handing over of authority to autonomous agencies, was a recommitment to its original objectives.

One important function DYS assumes in the centralization and purchase of care is planning new directions. Perhaps this is the most important function of all—a central planning, coordinating, and evaluating system, now not responsible for day-to-day functioning but for monitoring processes and outcomes.

It assumes a crucial decisionmaking place within the network of agencies that purchase care when it decides which programs can be reinforced, which ones replaced, which agencies improved, and programs for innovation wherever there are serious gaps within the total system of care. It would indeed be a missed opportunity if the department did not now assume this central planning function. It would be diminishing its own importance if all it became was a fireman for extinguishing problems as they arose within the system. Now the department is in the position to develop its planning function systematically.

This planning by the central administration at DYS can be implemented through projecting new alternative community-based treatment programs in anticipation of changes within the environment and through gathering information about the ongoing evolution of its hundred-odd agencies. It now can replace guesswork with more precise information of both environmental trends and the strengths and weaknesses of its agencies.

Another central function is the development of procedures in the agencies. Policies concerning general procedures profoundly affect planning potential. The department is in a good position to rapidly increase certain types of services that are proving themselves. This kind of action leads right into planning; the failure to plan efficiently postpones and accumulates problems that will intensify and multiply over time. Now that they can make plans based on reliable information, there is less possibility of ignoring critically emerging problems within its realm of operation. The same is true of surplus services when their necessity declines.

Because of the basic need for these new agencies to survive, policymaking and administration become fused at the local level and statewide. The new agency network is in constant flux, with the sharpening and clarifying of agency purposes, excluding irrelevant and nonproductive activities, adding and integrating new objectives, shifting priorities among objectives, and even reviewing the basic mission of the agency.

Thus the decentralized network of services develops a logic of its own, adapting to the department on the one hand and to a variety of forces in the community that impinge upon its functioning on the other. Persistent imbalance exists, and the external difficulties—both from the department and the community—are constantly precipitating new organizational objectives and policies.

Notes

1. For a further application of this general approach, see Urie Bronfenbrenner, "Toward an Experimental Ecology of Human Development," *American Psychologist* 32 (1977): 513-31.

2. Karl Mannheim, *Ideology and Utopia* (New York: Harcourt, Brace & World, 1936), p. 118.

3. Daniel Katz and Robert L. Kahn, *The Social Psychology of Organizations* (New York: Wiley, 1967), p. 259.

13 Notes toward a Theory of the Change Process in Corrections

Most experimental and practical attempts to produce change in organizations have been directed at segmental components of the system and not at the organization itself. Few attempts are made to change its basic structural characteristics, but rather to modify individual roles or procedures. Any attempt to generate change in the subsystems making up a total institution is extraordinarily difficult. Systemic change can come about from pressures from without or revolution from within.

There have been very few attempts by social scientists to manipulate organizational variables in order to understand radical restructuring in an organization. This is so mainly because of the practical difficulties in introducing organizational change or swaying leaders who are already planning a change to carry it out with experimental controls and measurements. Self-interest at all levels of an organization has prevented both externally- and internally-financed researchers from recognizing *organizational* variables as determinants of a social-change process.

We are not speaking here of some kind of demonstration project sponsored by the National Institute of Mental Health. We do not change organizations basically by occasional demonstrations of new therapeutic models or by participatory democratic involvement of inmates in fixed institutional structures. These demonstrations do very little to influence the ongoing forces that are structurally fixed in the system, and the legitimate authority is little affected without a direct attack upon the *fixed* structure. Total organizational change is regarded universally as almost impossible to bring about because it means impacting on so many powerfully interlocking vested interests.

The role of leadership in organizational life occupies an ambiguous status among theorists. Summarizing a great deal of work in the field, we can argue that leadership is relatively less important when jobs and procedures are so specified and routine that within very broad limits differences among individuals in carrying out policies become irrelevant. Leadership in this static organizational arrangement is minimal. This is not to say that some leaders even within a static organizational system cannot develop some kind of innovative elaboration or revision of ongoing procedures and practices.

However, we argue that leadership becomes crucial, basic, and systemic when it leads to *structural organizational change.* Perhaps we go too far in the "great men" school of history, which views whole epochs as essentially the biographies of great leaders writ large upon society. But cultural and social determinists see history and, derivatively, institutions in terms of social patterns relatively uninfluenced by the intervention of leaders.

Our analysis of the radical restructuring of youth corrections in Massachusetts has led us to emphasize the dynamic role of leadership, particularly that of Jerome Miller, in bringing about this nationally pace-setting reform.

Systemic Perspective, Charisma, and Institutional Leadership

When we view leadership as giving direction that goes beyond monitoring routine performances in an organization, we begin to realize the potential of system change when the critical opportunity presents itself. We adopt the central concept of organizational leadership presented by Katz and Kahn: "We consider the essence of organizational leadership to be the influential increment over and above mechanical compliance with the routine directives of the organization."[1] The initiation and implementation of structural change are the most challenging tasks of all to top institutional leaders.

Katz and Kahn have pointed out that the major cognitive requirement for system change of an organizational structure is: (1) a systemic perspective; and (2) a major affective requirement, which is called charisma.

Mastery of the systemic perspective entails a keen understanding of the interrelationship between the organization and the pertinent external environment in which it functions. As we have noted, Miller was a master at manipulating key organizations that impinged upon the correctional system: government agencies, lobbies, professional associations, legislators, and the public media in general. His ability to appraise and penetrate the demands and opportunities posed to DYS by its critical environments was great.

In a change process the sensitivity to public demands requires internally imposed requirements that the organization must meet in order to maintain and sustain a changed system. It demands a perspective that is quick to see changes in the environment and to follow the action as the change process picks up momentum and is supported or attacked by various external groups.

The director of DYS was not the sole source of this external perspective. He depended heavily on others within the organization to back up and sustain him. *But the basic requirement for radical structural change of a system demands an accurate external perspective,* because such a change impinges quite directly upon a variety of powerful outside groups. Thus the importance of such a perspective increases with the degree of radical surgery performed upon the organization.

The test of a competent internal perspective is the ability to appraise the reactions of diverse internal elements that have a different power base from the external groups. This differential power must be accurately assessed.

The Subordination of Structure to Institutional Mission

The truest measure of an institutional leader's grasp of a system perspective is the ability to subordinate the value of the structure that has evolved in the organization when it no longer serves its goals and mission. The corrections field is notorious for the conversion of means to an end in itself. Institutions survive and persist as much to fulfill all kinds of external and subsidiary goals—such as jobs for people who have themselves become institutionalized (sometimes as much as the inmates themselves)—as to serve the original purpose for which the goals were created.

The effective change agent does not get trapped by an unswerving loyalty to structure and its defense. The acid test of such leadership is to change the structure when it no longer serves to fulfill organizational goals. This is what we mean by the subordination of structure to the original mission for which it was created, and to imagine the possibility for changing that structure or indeed doing away with it when it no longer essentially fulfills its mission.[2]

The subordination of structure means that the effective leader frees himself from the requirement of regarding the existing structure as untouchable. He can propose and, indeed, struggle to reform that structure in order to achieve the organizational mission rather than be used by the structure and thereby compromise or indeed subvert organizational goals.

Advocating subordination of structure to organizational mission, in the concrete way in which Miller did it, was at the level of high genius. Truly effective leaders have the ability to subordinate structure when the reality requirements are clear and when the possibility of gaining the necessary support, both external and internal, to bring about such change is created through proper strategy.

The indispensable, uneven concordance of the subordination of structure to the goals of the organization in a sytemic perspective that does not confuse the two—but rather sees structure as following function—is crucial in bringing about radical restructuring of an organization. The juvenile corrections systems in the other forty-nine states are so entrenched that drastic action would be be required to change those structures and subordinate them to the original mission of the organization. Their leadership groups tend to reinforce the structure of the organization as they have basically inherited it, hence subordinating and diluting its mission in favor of strengthening its structure.

Subordination of structure varies, of course, with the echelon of leadership, and cannot be accomplished without the direction of the leader at the apex of the organization. Needless to say, basic organizational change is difficult indeed where there is little deliberate development of the organization itself and little consciously planning modification of its accumulating structure. All kinds of vested interests maintain the organizational structure and promote its maintenance as an end in itself. Its mission becomes only rhetoric, and very rarely an agenda item that is realistically considered for basic change.

The Transitional Stages of Deinstitutionalization

The top unit in the organization, which has the power and controls, the rewards and the sanctions, and which can mobilize support for its policy, must also generate the charisma needed during the difficult transition period. Whenever an organization, an institution, or indeed a society undergoes a critical period, the times are ripe for the production of charisma. Bold and dramatic acts of leadership tend to create the charismatic image.

It is difficult to assess the extent to which various groups in Massachusetts were able to put their trust in Jerome Miller to manage DYS and to do the things that he was supposed to do. We have examined in detail how Miller was able to take the offensive so that it was difficult for his critics to bombard him with objective feedback and evaluation. This very human and very valuable person was able to build an aura of power and to create the impression that he could accomplish the impossible. His constant attention to his mission and subordination of structure to the original goals of his organization were projected at a level that people could identify with, and he was its chief advocate. Thus an emotional tie was created through the media between various groups in Massachusetts and the leader that even surpassed in some respects the emotional tie between the rank and file within the system and the upper echelons and top leader.

Few others, if anyone else at all, within DYS were in a position or had the requisite background to originate, promote, and sustain this major institutional change. They were caught by their past, justified ad nauseam, and by their present, and therefore could not risk a new future. And since Miller always had his trunk half-packed, he was willing to risk going all the way. Yet, despite these risks, there was something else Miller was able to evoke in people both within and without the institution that led to emotional identification with him. The leader must be like his followers in some ways so that a common bond can be forged. The basis of that common bond was a reasonable and compassionate belief in setting things straight again. A common recognition evolved that it is insane to build and sustain a structure that contradicts, works against, and foils the very mission for which it was created.

As a charismatic leader, not only was Miller able to provide a common emotional bond between himself and his followers, but in addition he rose above the people in his organization as well as various groups outside the institutions by exhibiting a quality that permitted them to participate vicariously in that quality. That quality was the courage to put into practice his fundamental convictions.

The Institutional Leader as Double Agent

Administrators who want to deinstitutionalize their systems have a vital role as double agents. They have to expose the sytem for which they are responsible and air the false issues in public: "cleanliness," "staff qualifications," "security," "recidivism," and so on. The ambivalent find it more awkward to hide behind these false issues.

Many people are sympathetic to this approach. They are afraid to take any initiative without strong leadership and pressure for change. Polarization can win over ambivalent sectors that favor reform, though they also worry about security and are afraid to set loose incorrigible youngsters into the community.

An administrator engaged in correctional reform must take into consideration the diverse ways in which different groups react to radical reforms. One has to assess early where one's support is coming from and where the opposition is now, as well as where potential support and opposition lie. The Massachusetts experience provides insight into these different categories of reaction to radical reform:

The old guard. These people usually espouse a law-and-order philosophy. They do not believe in reform and they do not hide their dissatisfaction with the new morality of permissive behavior, lack of discipline, and the like, which they feel accompany reform. Despite their vocal opposition, they are largely uninformed about the real situation since they are so rigidly opposed to change and, given the reform-minded environment of Massachusetts, are usually isolated. Oftentimes they provide a good vehicle for consolidating the reform efforts. Their intentions and philosophies are usually exposed and serve as a stimulus to the other groups.

The ambivalent reactors. These include groups of liberals, who generally believe in reform. Their support wanes quickly because they tend to shy away from confrontation and polarization. At best they tend to agree with the reform and that it will not create disorganization or chaos; however, they often give only lip service to reform. They can be constantly pressured through intellectual arguments. They have to be made aware that they share the responsibility for keeping the system institutionalized.

The fuzzy-headed liberals. This group will embrace reform with full commitment. They tend to be young, inexperienced, naive, and idealistic. Though their support is unequivocal, they present many problems because of their lack of experience. At various stages in the process of radical change, it may not be to the administrator's advantage to be overly identified with them or represented by them, since they may lose support among establishment forces.

The opportunists. This group is comprised of people who go along with a leader as long as he succeeds, but abandons him as soon as his power fades or is challenged. They can be a good source of support if they feel they are following a star on the rise. However, they cannot be overly trusted because they often do not really believe in a cause per se but only in being identified with a winner.

The radical realists. These people become a solid support for change. First of all, the group is committed to change and realizes that to continue institutionalization the way it is perpetuates a fraud upon everyone. They see clearly the double standard. However, they are also realistic about the difficulties in overcoming stereotyped myths and challenging vested interests, and they appreciate the dialectics of developmental change. They do not wither away when the going gets rough, but at the same time they are willing to retreat in order to go forward again as soon as possible.

Maximizing Organizational Effectiveness through Political Means

Organizational effectiveness can be defined as maximizing the attainment of objectives by all means that are necessary, especially subordinating structure to the ends of the system. Maximizing technical and organizational know-how and full utilization of the resources the organization possesses is defined as *efficiency*. For too long, organizations in corrections have proclaimed their *efficiency*. For too long, organizations in corrections have proclaimed their efficiency at the cost of attaining their true mission.

In order to subvert this conversion of means into ends, through which a variety of vested interests is fed, there has to be a new alignment between the system and the political environment in which it must function, as well as a confrontation of those vested parties within the institution. Thus one critical way of maximizing the attainment of an organizational mission is by political means.

Radical change implies not only individual motivational changes or alteration of policies, but also structural changes in the organization and in its relationship to the environment. The radical reform in Massachusetts can never rest on its laurels. Our society is held together today by a morality that no longer has a common moral code. The older, traditional morality is changing. Societal integration is suffering. The authoritarian training characteristics of our society both within and without institutions wane and wax in a troubled economy.

Nevertheless, the democratic egalitarian ethic is also alive and vigorous and has expanded beyond political equality to embrace social justice, equality of opportunity, access to education, employment, and what is now called the quality of life. Although there has been a passing of traditional morality, this has been replaced by a practical morality, an ethics from below replacing an ethics from above.[3]

It is in this context that deinstitutionalization has received its most important impetus. The old institutional system does not work, and moreover it is very expensive. Thus we see an infusion of support for new attempts at rehabilitation within the community not only because it is better for youngsters and in the long run safer for the community, but also because it is less expensive.

Deinstitutionalization is also part of a movement toward decentralization and dispersal of decisionmaking down to levels of action. This decentralization is accompanied by a shift in the source of authority from upper-echelon levels far removed from daily supervision to direct worker-client interaction. Expanded line responsibilities for a variety of tasks in small community-group settings can ensure greater psychological involvement and caring among individuals in the organization.

Notes

1. Daniel Katz and Robert L. Kahn, *The Social Psychology of Organizations*, (New York: Wiley, 1967), p. 302.
2. Ibid.
3. Ibid., p. 469.

Bibliography

Alper, Benedict S. *Prisons Inside-Out*. Cambridge, Mass.: Ballinger, 1977.

Ares, Charles E.; Rankin, Anne; and Sturz, Herbert. "The Manhattan Bail Project." In *The Sociology of Punishment and Correction*, edited by Norman Johnson, Leonard Savitz, and Marvin E. Wolfgang, pp. 146-163. 2nd ed. New York: Wiley, 1970.

Bakal, Yitzhak, ed. *Closing Correctional Institutions: New Strategies for Youth Services*. Lexington, Mass.: Lexington Books, D.C. Heath and Company, 1973.

Bavelas, Alex. "Leadership, Man and Function." In *Current Perspectives in Social Psychology*, edited by Edwin P. Hollander and Raymond G. Hunt. London: Oxford University Press, 1971.

Bazelton, Judge David L. *Beyond Control of the Juvenile Court*. Washington, D.C.: Youth Development and Delinquency Prevention Administration, Department of Health, Education and Welfare, 1971.

Becker, Howard S. *Outsiders: Studies in the Sociology of Deviants*. New York: Free Press, 1963.

Benne, Kenneth D., and Birnbaum, Max. "The Principles of Changing." In *The Planning of Change*, edited by Warren G. Bennis, Kenneth D. Benne, and Robert Chin. 2nd ed. New York: Holt, Rinehart and Winston, 1969.

Bennis, Warren G. *Changing Organizations*. New York: McGraw-Hill, 1966.

_____; Beene, Kenneth D.; and Chin, Robert, eds. *The Planning of Change*. 2nd ed. New York: Holt, Rinehart and Winston, 1969.

Brager, George A. "Advocacy and Political Behavior." *Social Work* 13 (April 1968):8-13.

Brennan, Tim; Blanchard, Fletcher; Huizinga, David; and Elliot, Delbert. *The Social Psychology of Runaway Youth*. Lexington, Mass.: Lexington Books, D.C. Heath and Company, 1977.

California Department of Youth Corrections, and California Youth Authority. *See* Palmer, Theodore B.; and Warren, Marguerite Q.

Chapman, Dennis. *Sociology and the Stereotype of the Criminal*. London: Tavistock, 1968.

"Children in Custody." Advance Report on the Juvenile Detention and Correctional Facility Census of 1974. U.S. Department of Justice, Law Enforcement Assistance Administration, National Criminal Justice Information and Statistics Service.

"Children in Custody." Advance Report on the Juvenile Detention and Correctional Facility Census of 1975. U.S. Department of Justice, Law Enforcement Assistance Administration, National Criminal Justice information and Statistics Service.

"The Closing Down of Institutions and New Strategies in Youth Services." Proceedings of a conference held at Boston College, June 26-28, 1972.

Coates, Robert B.; and Miller, Alden D. "Evaluating Large-Scale Social Service Systems in Changing Environments." Unpublished report, Center for Criminal Justice, Harvard Law School, 1972.

————. "Neutralization of Community Resistance to Group Homes." In *Closing Correctional Institutions: New Strategies for Youth Services*, edited by Yitzhak Bakal, pp. 67-84. Lexington, Mass.: Lexington Books, D.C. Heath and Company, 1973.

————. "Youth Reactions to Programs in the Massachusetts DYS Institutions, 1970-72." Unpublished report, Center for Criminal Justice, Harvard Law School, 1972.

————, and Ohlin, Lloyd E. "A Strategic Innovation in the Process of Deinstitutionalization: The University of Massachusetts Conference." In *Closing Correctional Institutions: New Strategies for Youth Services*, edited by Yitzhak Bakal, pp. 127-48. Lexington, Mass.: Lexington Books, D.C. Heath and Company, 1973.

Cohen, Albert K. *Delinquent Boys*. New York: Free Press, 1955.

Cressey, Donald R., ed. *The Prison*. New York: Holt, Rinehart and Winston, 1961.

"Diagnostic Review of Financial Systems and Procedures." Prepared for the Massachusetts Department of Youth Services by Peat, Marwick, Mitchell and Livingston, 1971.

Doleschal, Eugene. *The Female Offender*. Washington, D.C.: National Institute for Mental Health, Center for Studies in Crime and Delinquency, 1971.

Dye, Larry L. "Juvenile Junkyards: A Descriptive Case Study of the Organization and Philosophy of the County Training Schools in Massachusetts." Ed.D. dissertation, University of Massachusetts, 1972.

————. "The University's Role in Public Service to the Department of Youth Services." In *Closing Correctional Institutions: New Strategies for Youth Services*, edited by Yitzhak Bakal, pp. 117-26. Lexington, Mass.: Lexington Books, D.C. Heath and Company, 1973.

Elliot, Delbert; and Voss, Harwin L. *Delinquency and Dropout*. Lexington, Mass.: Lexington Books, D.C. Heath and Company, 1971.

Empey, Lamar. "The Group Home and the Local School System." In proceedings of a conference, "The Closing Down of Institutions and New Strategies in Youth Services," Boston College, June 26-28, 1972.

————; Lubeck, Steven, G.; and LaPorte, Ronald. *Explaining Delinquency*. Lexington, Mass.: Lexington Books, D.C. Heath and Company, 1971.

Erikson, Erik, H. *Insight and Responsibility*. New York: Norton, 1964.

"Evaluation Report: Overlook Cottage in Lyman School for Boys." Internal document, Massachusetts Department of Youth Services, 1971.

"Evaluation Report: John Augustus Hall, Oakdale." Internal document, Massachusetts Department of Youth Services, 1971.

Feld, Barry C. "Variations of Inmate Subcultures in Juvenile Correctional Institutions." Unpublished report, Center for Criminal Justice, Harvard Law School, 1972.

Feld, Barry C. "Subcultures of Selected Boys' Cottages in Massachusetts Department of Youth Services Institutions in 1971." Unpublished report, Center for Criminal Justice, Harvard Law School, 1972.

Fleisher, B. *The Economics of Delinquency*. New York: Quadrangle, 1966.

Gibbons, Don C. *Society, Crime and Criminal Career*. Englewood Cliffs, N.J.: Prentice-Hall, 1968.

Gleuk, Eleanor and Sheldon. *Family Environment and Delinquency*. Boston: Houghton Mifflin, 1962.

Gold, Martin. *Status Forces in Delinquent Boys*. Ann Arbor: University of Michigan Press, 1963.

Goldman, Nathan. "The Differential Selection of Juvenile Offenders for Court Appearance." In *Crime and the Legal Process*, edited by William J. Chambliss, pp. 264-90. New York: McGraw-Hill, 1969.

Harvard Law School. Center for Criminal Justice. "Progress Report on the DYS Study." Unpublished report, 1971. (For further reports by the Center, *see* Coates, Robert; and Feld, Barry C.)

Harvard Law School. Center for Criminal Justice. "Report for 1973 of the Center for Criminal Justice on the DYS Study." Unpublished report, 1973.

Hess, R.D.; and Goldblatt, Ira. "The Status of Adolescents in American Society: A Problem in Social Identity." *Child Development* 28 (1957):459-68.

HEW. *See* U.S. Department of Health, Education and Welfare.

Horlick, Reuben S. "Inmate Perception of Obstacles to Readjustment in the Community." *Proceedings of the American Correctional Association* (1961).

James, Howard. *Children in Trouble*. New York: David McKay, 1969.

Johnson, Norman; Savitz, Leonard; and Wolfgang, Marvin E., eds. *The Sociology of Punishment and Correction*. 2nd ed. New York: Wiley, 1970.

Jones, Maxwell. *Beyond the Therapeutic Community: Social Learning and Social Psychiatry*. New Haven: Yale University Press, 1968.

Jones, Maxwell. *Social Psychiatry; A Study of Therapeutic Communities*. London: Tavistock, 1968.

Konopka, Gisela. *The Adolescent Girl in Conflict*. Englewood Cliffs, N.J.: Prentice-Hall, 1966.

Lewin, Kurt. "Frontiers of Group Dynamics." *Human Relations* 1 (June 1947):5-41.

Laing, R.D. *The Politics of the Family*. New York: Random House, 1969.

Light, Patricia K. *Let the Children Speak*. Lexington, Mass.: Lexington Books, D.C. Heath and Company, 1975.

Lipsitz, Joan. *Growing Up Forgotten*. Lexington, Mass.: Lexington Books, D.C. Heath and Company, 1977.

McCleery, Richard. "Communication Patterns as Bases of Systems of Authority and Power." In *Theoretical Studies in Social Organization of the Prison*. New York: Social Science Research Council, 1960.

McKay, Henry. *Report on the Criminal Careers of Male Delinquents in Chicago*. Chicago: University of Chicago Press, 1938.

Martin, John M. "The Creation of a New Network of Services for Troublesome Youth." In *Closing Correctional Institutions: New Strategies for Youth Services*, edited by Yitzhak Bakal, pp. 9-12. Lexington, Mass.: Lexington Books, D.C. Heath and Company, 1973.

Massachusetts Committee on Children and Youth. *Report and Recommendations*. Boston: CCY, 1967.

Massachusetts, Commonwealth of. Advisory Committee to the Department of Youth Services. *Annual Report*, Boston, 1971.

_____. Department of Youth Services. *Annual Report*, 1971-72.

_____. Department of Youth Services. "Delinquency Trends in Massachusetts, Fiscal Years 1954-1968." Boston: DYS, 1969.

_____. Department of Youth Services. *DYS Courier* (various issues, 1971-1972).

_____. Department of Youth Services. "Institutional Treatment: Rehabilitation Program Report, Title 4A." Internal document, 1971.

_____. Department of Youth Services. "Perspective on History and Strategy for Phasing Out State Juvenile Institutions." Internal document, n.d.

_____. Department of Youth Services. *The Issue of Security in a Community-Based System of Juvenile Correction*. November 1977.

_____. Department of Youth Services. Planning Unit. "Background Information on the Department of Youth Services." Internal document, 1970.

_____. Department of Youth Services. Planning Unit. "Department of Youth Services Comprehensive Plan: 1972-1976." Boston: DYS, 1972.

_____. Department of Youth Services. Planning Unit. "Preliminary Statement of Philosophy, Goals and Major Program Objectives for the Department of Youth Services: Framework for a Purchase-of-Service Approach to Accelerated Deinstitutionalization." Boston: DYS, 1971.

_____. Department of Youth Services. Planning Unit. *Programs and Policies of the Department of Youth Services*. Boston: DYS, 1972.

————. House. *Report of the Special House Committee to Investigate and Study the Number, Causes and Prevention of Runaways from the Industrial School for Boys at Shirley.* House . . . No. 6152, August 1970.

————. Senate. "Report of the Special Committee of the Senate on Investigation and Study of the Division of Youth Services." Senate . . . No. 1310, June 1967.

————. State Council on Juvenile Behavior. *Second Annual Statistical Report.* Boston: SCJB, 1972.

Mead, George H. "The Psychology of Punitive Justice." *American Journal of Sociology* 23 (1918):577.

Miller, Jerome G. "Corrections: Reform or Retrenchment?" Unpublished paper, Massachusetts Department of Youth Services, 1972.

————. "The Dilemma of the Post-Gault Juvenile Court." *Family Law Quarterly* 3 (September 1969):229-39.

————. "The Latent Social Function of Psychiatric Diagnosis." *International Journal of Offender Therapy* 14 (1969):148-56.

————. "The Politics of Change: Correctional Reform." In *Closing Correctional Institutions: New Strategies for Youth Services,* edited by Yitzhak Bakal, pp. 3-8. Lexington, Mass.: Lexington Books, D.C. Heath and Company, 1973.

————. "Professional Dilemmas in Corrections." *Seminars in Psychology* 3 (August 1971):357-62.

————. "Report to the Governor and General Court, for the Period November 1969 to November 1970." Boston: Department of Youth Services, 1970.

————. "Research and Theory in Middle-Class Delinquency." *British Journal of Criminology* (January 1970):33-51.

————. "Social Work and Therapies of Control." *British Journal of Criminology* (January 1970):33-51.

————. "Troubled Youth in a Troubled Society." Unpublished paper, Massachusetts Department of Youth Services, n.d.

National Committee on Crime and Delinquency. *Standards and Guides for Detention of Children and Youth.* New York: NCCD, 1961.

————. Committee on Mental Health Services Inside and Outside the Family Court in the City of New York. *Juvenile Justice Confounded: Pretensions and Realities of Treatment Services.* New York: NCCD, 1972.

Nye, Ivan F. *Family Relationships and Delinquent Behavior.* New York: Wiley, 1958.

Ohlin, Lloyd E. "Conflicting Interests in Correctional Objectives." In *Theoretical Studies in Social Organizations of the Prison.* New York: Social Science Research Council, 1960.

_____. "Reform of Correctional Services for Youth: A Research Proposal." Unpublished paper, Center for Criminal Justice, Harvard Law School, 1970.

Palmer, Theodore B. "California's Treatment Program for Delinquent Adolescents." *Journal of Research in Crime and Delinquency* 8 (1971):72-94.

Platt, Anthony. "The Rise of the Child-Saving Movement." *The Annals of the American Academy of Policy and Social Science* 381 (January 1969):21-38.

Polsky, Howard. *Cottage Six: The Social System of Delinquent Boys in Residential Treatment*. New York: Russell Sage Foundation, 1962.

Powers, Edwin. *The Basic Structure of the Administration of Criminal Justice in Massachusetts*. Boston: Massachusetts Correctional Association, 1968. (*See also* annual supplements.)

Rutherford, Andrew. "The Dissolution of the Training Schools in Massachusetts." The Academy for Contemporary Problems, 1974.

Sarri, Rosemary C. "Juvenile Delinquency and School Psychology: Issues and Opportunities." Paper completed in conjunction with the National Assessment of Juvenile Corrections. Presented at the American Psychological Association Convention, Chicago, 1975.

Schucter, Arnold. "Draft Policy Paper Re: Reorganization of Children's Services." Internal document, Massachusetts Department of Youth Services, 1972.

Segal, Brian. "Politicalization of Deviance." *Social Work* 17 (July 1972).

Shaw, Clifford, R. *The Natural History of a Delinquent Career*. Chicago: University of Chicago Press, 1931.

_____; and McKay, Henry D. "Are Broken Homes a Causative Factor in Juvenile Delinquency?" *Social Forces* 10 (1963):514-24.

Slocum, Walter, and Stone, Carroll. "Family Culture Patterns and Delinquent-Type Behavior." *Marriage and Family Living* 25 (1963):202-08.

Sofer, Cyril. *Organizations in Theory and Practice*. New York: Basic Books, 1972.

Spergle, Irving A. *Community Problem-Solving: The Delinquency Example*. Chicago: University of Chicago Press, 1969.

Sternberg, David. "Synanon House." In *The Sociology of Punishment and Correction*, edited by Norman Johnston, Leonard Savitz, and Marvin E. Wolfgang, pp. 617-26. 2nd ed. New York: Wiley, 1970.

Street, David; Vinter, Robert D.; and Perrow, Charles B. *Organization for Treatment: A Comparative Study for Delinquents*. New York: Free Press, 1966.

Thacher, Alexandra. "Report on Watchusetts—Worcester Cottage and the Elms Cottage." Internal document, Massachusetts Department of Youth Services, 1971.

————. "Report on Group Homes." Internal document, Massachusetts Department of Youth Services, 1971.

Thacher, Frederick. "Effecting Changes in a Training School for Girls." In *Closing Correctional Institutions: New Strategies for Youth Services*, edited by Yitzhak Bakal, pp. 87-106. Lexington, Mass.: Lexington Books, D.C. Heath Company, 1973.

Toby, Jackson, "The Differential Impact of Family Disorganization." *American Sociological Review* 22 (1957):505-12.

U.S. Department of Health, Education and Welfare. Children's Bureau. *A Study of the Division of Youth Services and Youth Service Board.* Washington, D.C.: HEW, 1966.

————. National Center for Social Statistics. "Statistics on Public Institutions for Delinquent Children." Washington, D.C.: Government Printing Office, 1970.

————. Office of Juvenile Delinquency and Development. *The Handling of Juveniles from Offense to Disposition.* Washington, D.C.: Government Printing Office, 1970.

————. Youth Development and Delinquency Prevention Administration. *Delinquency Prevention Through Youth Development.* Washington, D.C.: Government Printing Office, 1971.

U.S. Department of Health, Education and Welfare. Youth Development and Delinquency Administration. *State Responsibility for Juvenile Detention Care.* Washington, D.C.: Government Printing Office, 1967.

U.S. President's Commission on Law Enforcement and Administration of Justice. *The Challenge of Crime in a Free Society.* Washington, D.C.: Government Printing Office, 1967.

————. Task Force on Juvenile Delinquency. *Juvenile Delinquency and Youth Crime.* Washington, D.C.: Government Printing Office, 1967.

Vodopivec, Katja. *Maladjusted Youth.* Lexington, Mass.: Lexington Books, D.C. Heath and Company, 1974.

Vorrath, Harry H. "Positive Peer Culture: Content, Structure and Process." Red Wing, Minnesota: Minnesota State Training School for Boys, 1968. (Mimeographed.)

Wald, Patricia M. "Poverty and Criminal Justice." In *The Sociology of Crime and Punishment*, edited by Norman Johnston, Leonard Savitz, and Marvin E. Wolfgang, pp. 271-96. 2nd ed. New York: Wiley, 1970.

Ward, David A. "Evaluations of Correctional Treatment: Implication of Negative Findings." In *Law Enforcement Science and Technology*, edited by S.A. Yerskey. New York: Thompson, 1967.

Warren, Marguerite Q. "The Community Treatment Project: History and Perspectives. *Law Enforcement Science and Technology* 1 (1967):191-200.

_____; and Theodore B. Palmer. *Community Treatment Projects and Evaluation of Community Treatment for Delinquents*. Los Angeles: California Youth Authority, 1965.

Willman, Herb. "Memo to Assistant Commissioners Bakal, Leavy, Jeffers, and Madaus, Re: Forestry Camp Extension." Internal document, Massachusetts Department of Youth Services, August 12, 1971.

Wolfgang, Marvin; Figlio, Robert; and Sellin, Thorsten. *Delinquency in a Birth Cohort*. Chicago: University of Chicago Press, 1972.

Wooden, Kenneth. *Weeping in the Playtime of Others*. McGraw-Hill, 1976.

Wootton, Barbara. *Social Science and Social Pathology*. New York: Humanities Press, 1972.

Zald, Mayer N., ed. *Organization for Treatment: A Comparative Study for Delinquents*. New York: Wiley, 1965.

_____. "Power Balance and Staff Conflict in Correctional Institutions." *Administrative Science Quarterly* 6 (January 1962):22-29.

Index

About the Authors

Yitzhak Bakal has devoted many years of work and study to the field of juvenile corrections, both in Israel and the United States. He served as assistant commissioner in charge of institutions during the period of deinstitutionalization in Massachusetts from 1970 to 1973. He also edited the book *Closing Correctional Institutions*, published by Lexington Books. Presently, he is the director of the Northeastern Family Institute (N.F.I.), which he founded as a nonprofit organization engaged in developing community-based programs in Massachusetts for delinquent youth.

Howard W. Polsky is professor of social science and research at the Columbia University School of Social Work. He is the author of *Cottage Six: The Social System of Delinquent Boys in Residential Treatment*, and has written and edited numerous books and articles on the subject of residential treatment. He is a licensed psychologist and consultant to organizations and communities.